Simply Effective Group Cognitive Behaviour Therapy

Group Cognitive Behaviour Therapy (GCBT) and guided self-help widen the availability of evidence-based treatment for common mental health disorders. This volume provides GCBT protocols for common disorders as well as session-by-session teaching materials and self-help survival manuals covering:

- Depression
- Panic disorder and agoraphobia
- Post-traumatic stress disorder
- Social phobia
- Obsessive compulsive disorder
- Generalised anxiety disorder

The specifics of selecting and engaging clients in GCBT are first addressed and general group therapeutic skills are detailed. Transcripts of sessions show how group processes can be utilised to enhance outcome. *Simply Effective Group Cognitive Behaviour Therapy* adds to the armamentarium of tools for low intensity intervention and complements the high intensity individual approach of the companion volume *Simply Effective Cognitive Behaviour Therapy*. It will prove essential reading for all professionals using CBT with groups.

Michael J. Scott is a practising Consultant Psychologist working in Liverpool and author of seven books on CBT. He taught CBT for 15 years at the University of Manchester and was External Examiner for the MSc in Cognitive and Behavioural Psychotherapies at the University of Chester and currently holds this post at Sheffield Hallam University.

Simply Effective Group Cognitive Behaviour Therapy

A Practitioner's Guide

Michael J. Scott

Routledge
Taylor & Francis Group

LONDON AND NEW YORK

First published 2011
by Routledge
27 Church Road, Hove, East Sussex BN3 2FA

Simultaneously published in the USA and Canada
by Routledge
711 Third Avenue, New York NY 10017

Routledge is an imprint of the Taylor & Francis Group, an Informa business

© 2011 Michael J. Scott

British Library Cataloguing in Publication Data
A catalogue record for this book is available from the British Library

Library of Congress Cataloging in Publication Data
Scott, Michael J., 1948-
Simply effective group cognitive behaviour therapy : a practitioner's guide /
Michael J. Scott.
    p. ; cm.
  Includes bibliographical references and index.
  ISBN 978-0-415-57341-2 (hbk) – ISBN 978-0-415-57342-9 (pbk.) –
ISBN 978-0-203-80819-1 (ebk) 1. Cognitive therapy. 2. Group
psychotherapy. I. Title.
  [DNLM: 1. Cognitive Therapy–methods. 2. Anxiety Disorders–
psychology. 3. Anxiety Disorders–therapy. 4. Psychotherapy, Group. WM
425.5.C6]

  RC489.C63S366 2011
  616.89'1425–dc22

                                                          2011002327

ISBN: 978-0-415-57341-2 (hbk)
ISBN: 978-0-415-57342-9 (pbk)
ISBN: 978-0-203-80819-1 (ebk)

Typeset in Times by Garfield Morgan, Swansea, West Glamorgan
Printed and bound in Great Britain by TJ International Ltd, Padstow,
Cornwall
Paperback cover design by Aubergine Creative Design

Contents

Chapter 1

Group cognitive behaviour therapy

Cognitive behaviour therapy (CBT) is distinguishable from its psychotherapy forebears by its educational emphasis. However, for the most part CBT clients have undergone an individual rather a group intervention. The reasons for this are probably multifarious: a lack of training opportunities in group CBT (GCBT) interventions, the logistics of running a group, the unpopularity of group interventions amongst clients and a feeling of many therapists of being particularly exposed in a group.

Unfortunately therapists using individual CBT (ICBT) treat the tip of the iceberg of clients with psychological problems; in England only 10% of sufferers from depression or anxiety disorders receive a talking therapy (*Adult Psychiatric Morbidity in England, 2007* 2009). This has led to a demand to widen access by utilising innovative modes of service delivery such as GCBT, bibliotherapy and computer-assisted therapy (IAPT 2008). The educational nature of CBT makes it particularly suitable for dissemination in group format. There are four key features of CBT that lend themselves to an educational group format:

1   *Therapy begins with an elaborated well-planned rationale.* This feature encourages the client to believe that by changing their thoughts and behaviour they can affect how they feel. There is a cognitive model of each disorder; for example, in panic disorder catastrophic cognitions about unusual but not abnormal bodily sensations (e.g. 'my heart racing means I am having a heart attack') are held to play a pivotal role in the maintenance of the disorder. The model of a disorder can be presented just as well to a group as to an individual, with examples of the model (case formulation) used that are pertinent to all group members. Thus various examples of catastrophic cognitions would be offered, 'I am going to faint and there will be nobody there for me', 'I am going to choke to death', etc. Therapy is then described as challenging these beliefs both cognitively and by actions.

2   *Therapy provides training in skills that the client can utilise to feel more effective in handling daily life.* A group session is probably more easily

construed as a training session than is an individual session and lessens the possibility of dependence. The focus is on giving clients strategies to try out before the next session that may make a difference. In individual sessions a client can easily feel a failure if they do not do the homework task perfectly. However, in a group it soon becomes apparent that mastery is an inappropriate standard and the group norm is one of gradually learning to cope better: 'two steps forward and one back'; further difficulties are reframed as learning opportunities.

3 *Therapy emphasises the independent use of skills by the client outside the therapy context.* The knowledge that other group members are also being asked to engage in similar activities outside of a therapy session is likely to enhance compliance. It is not simply that group pressure is enhancing compliance but because the activity has been sold to other group members it has credibility. For example, if in a depression group members are asked to plan an activity to offset their anticipated low spot in the week, the endorsement of the rationale by others enhances motivation.

4 *Therapy should encourage clients to attribute improvement in mood to their own skilfulness rather than to the therapist's endeavours.* In GCBT the therapist is more likely to be construed as a teacher rather than a therapist, more like a 'driving instructor', important initially, but with a knowledge that it is essentially independent practice that makes a difference.

In the understandable rush to give psychological help to all in need, there is an ever present danger of a sacrifice of quality on the altar of quantity. Fortunately, with regard to GCBT the evidence is that GCBT is as efficacious as individual CBT for depression and probably most anxiety disorders. Further, the goal of this volume is to assure the reader that there is a simplicity (and fun) in GCBT and that it can be conducted effectively in routine practice. This chapter begins with a review of the evidence supporting the efficacy of GCBT for depression and anxiety disorders and then looks at whether there is evidence that GCBT is effective in routine practice. It is suggested that ICBT and GCBT are not mutually exclusive and can be judiciously combined to address the needs of real world clients with more than one disorder. Finally, the strengths and limitations of heterogeneous groups are discussed.

Individual versus group CBT

One of the key axioms of Beck's cognitive theory of psychological disorders (Alford and Beck 1997) is cognitive content specificity, i.e. that the different disorders have a different cognitive content necessitating a different approach with each. For example, the sufferer from depression might regard themselves as worthless, the future hopeless, whilst the sufferer from anxiety by contrast might see themselves as vulnerable and the future uncertain. As a consequence of cognitive content specificity, different protocols were developed and evaluated for different disorders. This development was made possible by Beck's earlier work on improving the reliability of psychiatric diagnosis (Beck *et al.* 1962), so that in discussing, say, a person with depression there was clear agreement as to what this label meant. Beck *et al.* (1962) noted the poor reliability of routine unstructured psychiatric assessments (32–54%) in terms of diagnosis, making research impossible, and paved the way for structured interviews with much higher levels of reliability. For the most part it is disorder-specific CBT treatments that have been evaluated and the focus below is on studies of depression and the anxiety disorders.

Depression

A review of ten studies of the relative efficacy of ICBT and GCBT for depression by Tucker and Oei (2007) concluded that GCBT for depression is more cost-effective than ICBT. However, five of the studies showed the superiority of ICBT over GCBT and five showed the equivalence of the two modalities.

Social phobia

In a comparison of GCBT for social phobia with a waiting list control condition, Hope *et al.* (1995) found that the former was superior, with treatment gains being largely maintained in the year afterwards (Salaberria and Echeburua 1998). More recently Stangier *et al.* (2003) compared GCBT and ICBT delivered over 15 weekly sessions and found the latter superior, with 50% of clients in individual CBT no longer meeting criteria for social phobia at the end of treatment compared with 13.6% in the group condition. However, only the first seven sessions of the Stangier *et al.* (2003) programme included training in shifting attentional focus to external cues, stopping safety behaviours, video feedback to correct distorted self-imagery, behavioural experiments and cognitive restructuring. The majority of the second half of treatment was devoted to cognitive work on schemas rather than behavioural experiments. It may be that had the latter half of the Stangier *et al.* (2003) programme been more behavioural, capitalising in the group modality on group norms about 'daring' to engage in social situations, the differences between ICBT and GCBT would have been less and both interventions more powerful. However, at present it is difficult to come to any firm conclusions about the relative effectiveness of GCBT and ICBT for social phobia. Marom *et al.* (2009) found that whilst the presence of coexisting depression did not affect the immediate outcome of GCBT for social phobia, those who had depression suffered an exacerbation of symptoms post-treatment, suggesting that people with depression and social phobia may need additional interventions to maintain gains.

Panic disorder and agoraphobia

Roberge and colleagues (2008) in a comparison of GCBT and standard CBT in the treatment of panic disorder and agoraphobia found that GCBT incurred lower treatment costs and had a superior cost-effectiveness ratio. (Whilst, as in most outcome studies for any disorder, clients with a severe comorbid disorder were excluded from the study, in the Roberge *et al.* (2008) study 30% of those treated met criteria for another anxiety disorder and 8% criteria for depression). If clients are given a free choice between ICBT and GCBT following initial assessment, the overwhelming majority (95% in Sharp *et al.*'s [2004] study of panic disorder clients) will opt for individual therapy.

Post-traumatic stress disorder (PTSD)

GCBT can produce results comparable to ICBT. Beck *et al.* (2009) assigned individuals with PTSD following a serious motor vehicle accident to either GCBT or a minimum contact comparison group. Of treatment completers, 88.3% did not meet criteria for PTSD at the end of treatment compared to 31.3% of the minimal contact condition; further treatment gains were maintained at 3-month follow-up. However, earlier efforts by Taylor *et al.* (2001) to transport individual treatment into a group setting without modification were much less successful with only 38% of clients no longer meeting criteria for PTSD after treatment. In their translation of an individual programme into a group format Beck and Coffey (2005) addressed issues such as group cohesion and the possibility of a re-traumatisation of clients by hearing the stories of other group members about their accidents.

Engaging clients in GCBT is a particular challenge and Thompson *et al.* (2009) found that just over half of the people invited to consider attending a PTSD group chose not to do so. Further, there is evidence that the severity of PTSD symptoms varies by type of trauma – sexual assault, road traffic accidents, sudden death of a loved one – and the pattern of PTSD symptoms also varies (Kelley *et al.* 2009) suggesting that PTSD treatment groups should not be totally heterogeneous.

Generalised anxiety disorder (GAD)

In a comparison of GCBT for generalised anxiety disorder with a waiting list control condition, Dugas *et al.* (2003) found that the active condition was superior and the results similar to those in ICBT treatments reported in the literature. However, Dugas *et al.* (2003) add a cautionary note in that 5 of the 48 participants in GCBT dropped out compared to none out of 26 in an earlier study of ICBT for GAD. But Dugas *et al.* (2003) also pointed out that many participants reported that the group therapy format was particularly useful because it helped them to feel less isolated and better understood and it gave them the opportunity to learn from others in the group.

Obsessive compulsive disorder (OCD)

GCBT is an effective treatment for OCD but often, it seems, less so than ICBT. In a comparison of ICBT and GCBT for OCD conducted by Cabedo *et al.* (2010), though GCBT was effective in decreasing OCD severity, with 41% classified as recovered post-treatment, this was less than the 69% recovered in ICBT. At 12-month follow-up the figure for GCBT was 32% compared with 63% in ICBT. The results of Whittal *et al.* (2008) were slightly more promising for GCBT, in that recovery status or relapse rates were equivalent for ICBT and GCBT, but the psychometric test results for OCD and depression favoured ICBT. (Further, within the Whittal *et al.* [2008] study a comparison with exposure and response prevention was made and the cognitive therapy was better tolerated and resulted in less dropout. Interestingly in the GCBT programme, one session was held in the presence of a family member or friend. Overall about 50% of OCD sufferers recovered with cognitive therapy.) However, in a study by Jaurrieta *et al.* (2008), GCBT and ICBT appeared equally effective at 6- and 12-month follow-up and there was no difference in the dropout rate.

In a study of GCBT for obsessive compulsive disorder (O'Connor *et al.* 2005) 38% of clients refused treatment in a group format. Reasons for the refusal included anxiety about sharing problems with others, social anxiety, lack of personal attention and fears of acquiring new obsessions from others in the group.

Delivering effective GCBT

Whilst the above review of GCBT interventions for depression and the anxiety disorders makes clear the potency of this intervention modality, it also indicates that it is not a simple matter to translate proven individual protocols into an appropriate group format or to engage clients in GCBT. It is suggested in this volume that group intervention needs supplementing with individual sessions, some of which would be concurrent with the group sessions but some sessions may precede the group if motivation for the group is an issue. Further, if the group programme is ineffective clients should be offered an individual programme. The motivational sessions can be used to address fears about attending a group. For example, a client with obsessive compulsive disorder who is besieged by repugnant thoughts/ images of a sexual or harmful nature may be very fearful about any possibility of disclosing such material in a group. Such concerns would be a focus in individual sessions and if the client's fears were allayed, they may then opt into a GCBT programme. The particulars of how to address such concerns are detailed in Chapter 2. In routine practice clients should not be 'assigned' to GCBT but invited to engage when fears are assuaged; if they are not ready, individual treatment should continue. Attention to clients' motivations with regard to GCBT could increase the uptake of the latter and reduce defaulting from a group programme.

The individual sessions can also be used to address other comorbid anxiety disorders/depression or associated marital problems. Individual sessions do not necessarily have to take place face to face and when conducted over the telephone typically take about 20 minutes (Clark *et al.* 2009); in the Clark *et al.* study (2009), about a quarter of sessions were face to face. Telephone consultations take place at a prearranged time and the therapist follows up the call if the client is not available. The comorbid disorders are addressed using a combination of at least one face-to-face individual session and CBT guided self-help (CBTgsh) – brief telephone/ e-mail contact based on the disorder-specific manuals (Appendices H–M), self-help books and blank self-help forms.

Group members can affect each other for both good and ill and good group therapeutic skills are required of the therapist to maximise the former and reduce the latter. Thus the therapist not only has to have competence in treating the specific disorder at an individual level but also has to develop group work skills; this latter is addressed in Chapter 3. The succeeding chapters describe ten-session group programmes for depression and each of the anxiety disorders.

Transdiagnostic groups

There is an added convenience in running a transdiagnostic group that covers depression and the anxiety disorders (Free 2007) but they appear suboptimal. Hagen *et al.* (2005) examined the efficacy of GCBT in a mixed group of patients with depression and anxiety disorders. Whilst the authors concluded that the programme seemed to have a favourable effect both in the short and long term they added that specific treatments for specific disorders seemed to be more effective than their GCBT programme for depression and the anxiety disorders. These results are echoed by Oei and Boschen (2009), who examined the effectiveness of GCBT in a in a client population, 17.3% of whom were suffering from depression, 30.2% panic disorder, 14% generalised anxiety disorder and 8.4% post-traumatic stress disorder. Only 43% of individuals showed reliable change and 17% were 'recovered' from their anxiety symptoms. Oei and Boschen (2009) concluded that their mixed group treatment was less effective than a disorder-specific treatment but was comparable to the individual CBT treatments (Westbrook and Kirk 2005) that are common in routine practice without fidelity to a disorder-specific protocol. However, GCBT appears effective in groups of limited heterogeneity. For example, Norton *et al.* (2008) examined the effects of GCBT in a sample for which the primary diagnosis was an anxiety disorder; for 50% of the sample the primary diagnosis was social anxiety disorder and for 35% the primary diagnosis was panic disorder but no client had PTSD and only one OCD, thus although the intervention was effective caution has to be exercised in terming it 'transdiagnostic'. It may be that in a group largely composed of clients with panic disorder and social phobia, there is such a commonality in the need to confront feared situations that neither population feels significantly different to the other.

The viability of evidence-based treatment in routine practice

There is a concern that the results of studies conducted in research centres, i.e. of efficacy studies, may not generalise to routine clinical practice. Necessarily in efficacy studies the focus is on clients with relatively 'pure' conditions. Further, the therapists in research centres have higher levels of training and supervision than those found amongst therapists in routine practice. It is therefore important to determine how well CBT for depression and the anxiety disorders holds up in actual clinical practice. Fortunately there are now effectiveness studies that indicate that the protocols from research centres can be applied to routine practice with little if any loss of power with regard to depression and the anxiety disorders.

In a study conducted in inner city Liverpool, an area of high deprivation, Scott and Stradling (1990) compared the effectiveness of ICBT and GCBT for depression with a waiting list control condition. The active conditions were equally effective and the results comparable to those in efficacy studies of ICBT. In line with Shaw and Hollon's (1979) recommendation, Scott and Stradling (1990) provided supplementary individual sessions; however, the former recommended up to six whereas the latter provided only three such sessions. Scott and Stradling (1990) concluded that the GCBT modality resulted in a 25–50% cost saving. Bright *et al.* (1999) also examined the effectiveness of GCBT for depression and found that therapist adherence to the manual-based treatment was associated with greater improvement in clinician-rated depressive symptoms. Observers rated four general objectives associated with cognitive therapy: set and/or followed an agenda, presented information as an educator, discussed automatic thoughts and/or cognitive distortions and reviewed and/or assigned homework. A high score indicated greater compliance with the protocol, which was predictive of a better outcome. Further, acquired skills in cognitive restructuring were associated with greater improvement. The dropout rate for GCBT was 35% and the number of dropouts was significantly correlated with group size. Interestingly this study included a mutual support group comparison condition which did as well as the GCBT. The mutual support group had a number of specific goals, including interpersonal insight, the acquisition of disclosure skills and the sharing of feedback and advice. This suggests that there can be mechanisms of therapeutic change in a group that are not necessarily specific to CBT and consideration of group process may also be of importance. The subjects in the Bright *et al.* (1999) study were media recruited and had mean initial Beck Depression Scores of 23 compared to 28 in the Scott and Stradling (1990) study, suggesting a less troubled population. Further, in the Bright *et al.* (1999) study clients were not offered any individual sessions, it is possible that this may have increased attrition.

In the 56 anxiety disorder effectiveness studies reviewed by Stewart and Chambless (2009), large effect sizes were found for panic disorder, post-traumatic stress disorder, generalised anxiety disorder and obsessive compulsive disorder and a medium effect for social anxiety disorder. Overall, CBT in routine settings had an improvement of 78% versus 22% for control groups, with large pre-test–post-test effect. Stewart and Chambless (2009) also found that effect sizes decreased significantly when therapists were not asked to follow a manual and when there was little or no monitoring to make sure the treatment was followed. Stewart and Chambless (2009) assessed the clinical representativeness of the studies they reviewed on a nine-point scale, where points were awarded for clinically representative setting (e.g. outpatient mental health clinic), clinically representative referral (e.g. from GP), clinically representative therapists (e.g. clinicians for whom service is a substantial part of job), clinically representative structure (e.g. treatment with a structure used in clinical practice), clinically representative monitoring (e.g. no formal adherence checks), no pretherapy training (e.g. therapists did not receive special training immediately before study in specific techniques to be used), no randomisation (e.g. clients were not part of a trial), clinically representative patients (e.g. no exclusionary criteria aside from psychosis, suicidality, organic brain disease or substance dependence) and medications allowed. Whilst the study showed that the more representative a study was the smaller the impact of CBT, the magnitude of the relationship was quite small.

Most of the effectiveness studies considered by Stewart and Chambless (2009) related to individual CBT and though they included GCBT effectiveness studies they did not perform a separate analysis for this modality, most probably because there are too few GCBT effectiveness studies at present. In the same year, Oei and Boschen (2009) published a study of the effectiveness of a GCBT programme for clients with a variety of anxiety disorders. Oei and Boschen (2009) concluded that whilst their study demonstrated that treatment was effective in reducing anxiety symptoms to an extent comparable with other effectiveness studies, only 43% of individuals showed reliable change and 17% 'recovered'. Further, Oei and Boschen (2009) claimed that their results were comparable to those found in an effectiveness study of individual CBT conducted by Westbrook and Kirk (2005). The effect sizes in both the Oei and Boschen (2009) and Westbrook and Kirk (2005) studies were less than in efficacy studies conducted in research centres. There are a number of possibilities for this; in the Oei and Boschen (2009) study it could be that having a variety of anxiety disorder clients in the same group resulted in a less than optimal dose of treatment for each disorder. The suboptimal performance in both studies could have arisen because neither used a treatment manual and there was no monitoring to check adherence to a protocol. Alternatively the poorer performance could have arisen because of differences between the population/therapists in the research centres and routine practice; the different explanations are not mutually exclusive. Though the precise reason for the lower effect sizes in these two studies remains unclear, it seems sensible to use a manualised approach with adherence checks and where possible not to have a mixed group of anxiety disorders.

Comorbidity

The presence of additional disorders (comorbidity) can affect outcome. To some extent this can be prevented by excluding those who are psychotic, substance dependent or suicidal, but comorbidity is the rule rather than the exception. Zimmerman et al. (2008) found that 50–75% of clients receiving a diagnosis of PTSD, GAD, OCD, depression, social phobia and panic disorder (with or without agoraphobia) met criteria for at least one additional diagnosis. In a study of clients with either panic disorder or generalised anxiety disorder receiving different forms of CBT, van Balkom et al. (2008) found the additional presence of depression led to less improvement. Further, there was a lower remission rate for those comorbid with depression than for those comorbid with another anxiety disorder or those with no comorbidity, i.e. it is not just comorbidity per se that makes a difference but the type of comorbidity. However, some caution is necessary in generalising from these results about the significance of a comorbid anxiety disorder in that in the van Balkom et al. (2008) study, of those comorbid with another anxiety disorder only two clients (4%) had PTSD and three clients (5%) had obsessive compulsive disorder.

Evidence-based treatment protocols can be blended together (Scott 2009) for the effective treatment of principal and comorbid disorders. However, in combining evidence-based protocols for disorders the therapist runs the risk of providing a sub-therapeutic dose of any one protocol. A combination of a therapeutic dose for one disorder and a sub-therapeutic dose for another will yield an unsatisfactory outcome and may lead to a result that is worse than if just one disorder were targeted. When it is necessary to utilise more than one protocol, say A and B, it is inappropriate to decide in advance on the appropriate number of sessions for each, as there are likely to be some common elements in treatment foci, e.g. low mood and treatment method such as thought record (i.e. transdiagnostic features); rather, doses of each should be slowly titrated until there is a significant change in the combination of disorders, see Figure 1.1, as assessed by a structured interview. (Thus any one client may need more or fewer sessions than the standard ten session programmes outlined in Scott [2009].) During the titration the therapist must remain aware of the different properties of A and B. Just as the end point of mixing two colours together is a particular colour, so too the end point treating principal and comorbid disorders is a change in the diagnostic status of each of the conditions with which the client presents.

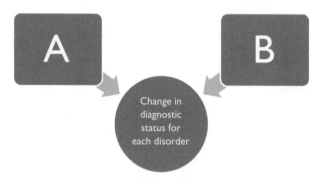

Figure 1.1 Blending protocols.

Each protocol is guided by a Sat Nav (see Appendix A) which summarises treatment targets and treatment strategies. At any point in time during treatment the therapist must be aware of which Sat Nav they are using for what. Each Sat Nav draws upon the variety of available evidence-based CBT protocols for that disorder. In this volume the protocols are presented in such a way as to minimise confusion between the different theoretical inputs into a Sat Nav.

Candidates for GCBT can be allocated to a group either on the basis of their principal diagnosis (the main disorder the person wants treating) or in terms of the disorder which produces the greatest functional impairment. The author knows of no empirical reason to prefer one method of selection over the other and in practice there are often two disorders worthy of focus. The author offers the rules of thumb in Table 1.1.

In support of the allocation rules in Table 1.1, a study by Teng *et al.* (2008) of clients with both PTSD and panic disorder found that whilst a

Table 1.1 Allocation to group on basis of diagnoses

Depression	Depression trumps social phobia and generalised anxiety disorder except if the depression is mild. However, PTSD, panic disorder and OCD trump depression unless the latter is severe.
Social phobia	Social phobia can be the prime focus if depression is mild or not present. However, if other anxiety disorders are present they should be the prime focus with the possible exception of GAD.
PTSD	PTSD should be the prime focus unless depression is severe and trumps the other disorders except if panic disorder or OCD are severe.
Panic disorder and agoraphobia	Panic disorder trumps social phobia and GAD but not PTSD or OCD or depression when the latter is severe.
Generalised anxiety disorder	GAD trumps only mild depression.
OCD	OCD trumps the other disorders except for severe depression, severe PTSD and severe panic disorder.

CBT programme focused on the latter disorder resulted in substantial reduction of panic frequency, severity and distress, there was no reduction in PTSD symptoms. The intent of Table 1.1 is to construct a group whose needs can be comprehensively met by a group focus on the principal disorder, graded exposure to feared situations, and typically up to three individual sessions for 'personal' issues/extra focus on comorbid disorders, but the number of individual sessions should be determined by those that are necessary to resolve the comorbid disorder/s.

Though a client may be assigned to a group on the basis of their principal disorder using Table 1.1, group sessions need not necessarily have an exclusive focus on just one disorder. For example, social anxiety disorder can lead to depression and if depression is an issue for the majority of the social phobia group (bearing in mind that given Table 1.1 it would have to be mild) then it would be legitimate to integrate the materials from the depression protocol. (The pathway from social anxiety disorder to depression is discussed in the Chapter 7 [Jack 1999].) The key principle is that the groups be as homogeneous as possible so that disorder-specific interventions can be dovetailed. But there should be a clear mechanism of how one disorder relates to another, otherwise if a multiplicity of disorders is addressed in the group each is likely to receive an inadequate dose. For example, many clients with PTSD have substance abuse/alcohol problems. There is evidence that the addictive behaviours can be construed as an attempt at self-medication, indeed that improvement in PTSD symptoms leads to improvements in addictive behaviours rather than vice versa (calling into question the conventional wisdom that clients need to be alcohol/drug free before commencing PTSD treatment). Thus it is perfectly possible to run a group for clients dually diagnosed as suffering from PTSD and substance abuse (Najavits 2002) and produce significant results for both conditions (Hien *et al.* 2010), though interestingly homogeneity has been engineered by confining such groups to women.

Craske *et al.* (2007) have looked at two different ways of addressing comorbidity in GCBT in clients with panic disorder. All clients were given in addition six individual sessions; for one half of the sample these sessions were used to reinforce teaching in the group session and for the other half these sessions were utilised to address the most severe comorbid condition. Addressing the most severe comorbid condition resulted in a poorer outcome both for that condition and for the panic disorder. But it could be argued that six sessions of treatment for whatever was the most severe comorbid disorder is not an evidence-based treatment for any disorder and it is therefore unsurprising that it conferred no additional benefit; arguably an evidence-based protocol is needed for the comorbid disorder. It may also be that addressing the full range of comorbid conditions, (clients in the Craske *et al.* [2007] had on average 2.4 comorbid conditions), rather than just the most severe, would have produced a better outcome as clients do wish for treatment of the full range of conditions from which they suffer (Zimmerman and Mattia 2000). A further possible explanation of the results of the Craske *et al.* (2007) study is that those who received individual sessions to reinforce teaching in the group session were in effect receiving a form of motivational interviewing with regard to the group material, increasing homework compliance and expectancy for anxiety control, as there is some evidence that motivational interviewing improves outcome in GCBT (Westra and Dozois 2006). At present the jury is out on the best way of addressing comorbidity in GCBT. The approach adopted in this volume is to include both motivational interviewing and evidence-based treatment protocols for each comorbid disorder in the supplementary individual sessions. Whilst the best way of handling comorbidity is a matter of debate, there is agreement that reliable diagnosis is an important issue (van Balkom *et al.* 2008).

Reliable diagnosis

Historically, diagnosis has been very important in CBT, determining which evidence-based protocol is to be used with which client. This approach is an outgrowth of Beck's cognitive-content specificity theory (Alford and Beck 1997) that the disorders are distinguished by their differing cognitive content. Beck *et al.* (1962) paved the way for reliable diagnosis by noting the poor levels of agreement (32–54%) that arise from traditional open-ended interviews and suggesting that if clinicians were to have a common language about what constitutes a particular disorder, e.g. depression, then there had to be a consensus on what range of symptoms were considered pertinent (information variance) and on the threshold needed to determine whether a symptom was present at a clinically significant level (criterion variance). As a consequence of these considerations structured interviews were developed that minimised information and criterion variance, resulting in reliabilities of 80–90% (e.g. the SCID, First *et al.* [1997a, 1997b]). Further, without a structured interview assessors are likely to stop at the first disorder/problem identified (Zimmerman *et al.* 2008).

DSM-IV-TR (American Psychiatric Association 2000, p. xxxii) has echoed Beck's strictures by stating that proper use of its diagnostic criteria means directly accessing the information in the criteria set and requiring that a question/s be asked about each symptom that comprises a disorder; for a symptom to be regarded as present it must significantly impair functioning. As an aid to diagnosis, in Appendix A, the author has provided a CBT Pocketbook with interview questions about each of the DSM symptoms that cover depression and the anxiety disorders.

Assessment and treatment pathways for GCBT

Potential clients for GCBT can be assessed and treated using the decision tree in Figure 1.2.

Screening clients

The first step in assessing referred clients is to screen them for the whole range of disorders from which they might be suffering and not just depression and the anxiety disorders. This can be accomplished using the 7 Minute Mental Health Screen/Audit – Revised (Appendix B) or the self-report counterpart the First Step Questionnaire – Revised (Appendix C). Using the Interview or Questionnaire, key questions are asked about each disorder followed by a question that asks clients whether this is something with which they would like help (the screening questions for panic disorder, for example, are shown in Table 1.2).

The screening questions for depression have been found to correctly identify 79% of those who are depressed (i.e. the sensitivity is 0.79) and correctly identify 94% of those who are not depressed (i.e. the specificity is 0.94). Importantly, including the question 'Is this something with which you would like help' greatly reduced the number of false positives (Arroll *et al.* 2005). This question has therefore been added to the screening for the other disorders. The screening symptom questions for post-traumatic stress disorder (Prins *et al.* 2004), obsessive compulsive disorder (Fineberg *et al.* 2003) and substance abuse (Ewing 1984) have also been subjected to empirical investigation and found to be reliable. Further, the screening questions for generalised anxiety disorder (GAD) symptoms cover the same content area as the two-item GAD scale that has been demonstrated to have high sensitivity and specificity for detecting GAD (Kroenke *et al.*

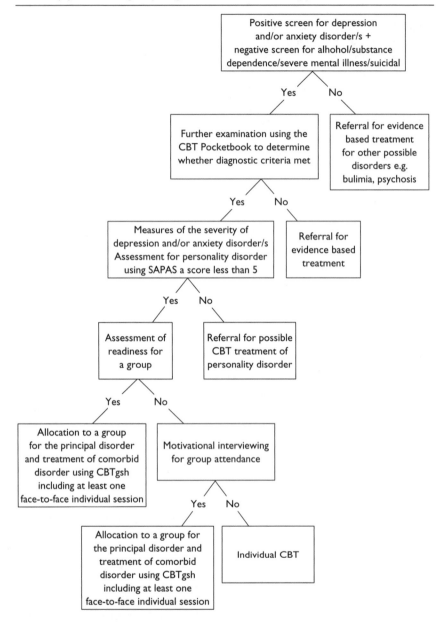

Figure 1.2 Assessment and treatment pathways for GCBT. The Standardised
Assessment of Personality – Abbreviated Scale (SAPAS), Appendix G; 7
Minute Mental Health Screen/Audit – Revised, Appendix B; First Step
Questionnaire – Revised, Appendix C; CBT Pocketbook, Appendix A;
readiness for a group, Chapter 2; group programmes, Chapters 4–9; CBT
guided self-help (CBTgsh), Appendices H–M; motivational interviewing,
Chapter 2; individual treatment protocols, Scott (2009).

Table 1.2 Excerpt from the 7 Minute Mental Health Screen/Audit – Revised/
First Step Questionnaire – Revised: panic disorder

2. Panic Disorder and Agoraphobia	Yes	No	Don't know
Do you have unexpected panic attacks . a sudden rush of intense fear or anxiety?			
Do you avoid situations in which the panic attacks might occur?			
Is this something with which you would like help?			

2007). However, at this time the screening questions for other disorders have only a face validity. The self-report version of the screen 'The First Step Questionnaire – Revised' similarly awaits validation; its strength is that it takes the client 2–3 minutes to complete and it takes the therapist only a minute to interpret using the guidance given for the correspondingly numbered items in the 7 Minute Mental Health Screen. If a screen/ questionnaire response for a disorder is positive then more detailed enquiry can be made for that disorder using the questions in Appendix A, the Pocketbook.

The First Step Questionnaire – Revised/7 Minute Mental Health Screen – Revised has an advantage in screening for multiple common psychiatric disorders rather than for just depression or anxiety alone. Gaynes et al. (2010) in their study of another multiple psychiatric disorder screening measure, the M-3, pointed out that in a typical sample of 100 patients in primary care, if the clinician administered only the nine-item PHQ-9 (Kroenke et al. 2001) it would identify 14 of the 16 depressed patients. The PHQ-9 would not identify the 9 patients experiencing anxiety alone, however, and would misidentify 5 bipolar depressed patients as having a unipolar major depressive disorder. Similarly, using only the seven-item GAD-7, whilst 7 of the 9 patients with an anxiety disorder alone would be captured, it would miss approximately 20 patients with major depressive disorder or bipolar disorder.

The First Step Questionnaire – Revised/7 Minute Mental Health Screen – Revised has an advantage over the M-3, in that it casts a wider net, screening in addition for alcohol/drug abuse, bulimia and psychosis. In Table 1.3 the diagnostic accuracy of the depression and PTSD questions (the * indicates that these questions were asked minus the 'Is this something with which you would like help?' question) from the First Step Question-naire – Revised/7 Minute Mental Health Screen – Revised are compared with the accuracy of disorder-specific measures, the PHQ-9 (Kroenke et al. 2001) and the Self Rating Inventory for Post-Traumatic Stress Disorder (SRIP) (Gaynes et al. 2010), and also compared with the accuracy of the depression and PTSD items from the M-3 (Gaynes et al. 2010). The First

Table 1.3 Comparison of sensitivity and specificity of First Step Questionnaire – Revised/7 Minute Mental Health Screen – Revised with other standard instruments

	Depression	PTSD
	First step Depression	First step PTSD
Sensitivity	0.79	0.78*
Specificity	0.94	0.87*
	PHQ-9	SRIP
Sensitivity	0.88	0.74
Specificity	0.88	0.84
	M-3	M-3
Sensitivity	0.84	0.88
Specificity	0.80	0.76

Step Questionnaire – Revised/7 Minute Mental Health Screen – Revised is at least as accurate as the disorder-specific measures and the multiple psychiatric disorder screening measure, the M-3, whilst being broader in scope than both.

The importance of a provisional diagnosis has been stressed by IAPT (2010a): 'Provisional diagnoses are needed as specific treatments have been developed to assist people with particular symptom patterns and NICE guidelines are diagnosis based. We can therefore only ensure that patients receive the best treatments in line with NICE recommendations if provisional diagnoses have been obtained. Provisional diagnosis should not be viewed as a pejorative label. Many patients feel diagnosis is useful to reassure them that there are others with similar patterns and difficulties.'

There are two alternative diagnostic classification systems, DSM-IV-TR (American Psychiatric Association 2000) and ICD-10 (World Health Organization 1992) and IAPT have drawn on the latter to produce a set of Screening Prompts (freely available from the IAPT website www.iapt.nhs.uk), IAPT (2010b) to give a slightly different way of screening clients, but it is not as broad based a screening as the 7 Minute Mental Health Screen – Revised.

Structured interview

Clients who screen positive for a disorder are then assessed using a structured interview to determine whether in fact they meet diagnostic criteria for a disorder/s. Diagnosis provides a common language and structured interviews such as the SCID (First *et al.* 1997a, 1997b) are the most reliable way of determining diagnoses. The interview questions in the CBT Pocketbook, Appendix A, directly access each of the symptoms of the depression and anxiety disorders considered in this volume. Whether or not a particular symptom is endorsed as present or not depends on the therapist's judgement not only of the client's response but also on the basis of all other information available, e.g. records, information from relatives. The therapist has also to determine whether a symptom is present at a clinically significant level, i.e. whether it produces functional impairment. For example, mere dreams of a trauma would probably be below the threshold but dreams related to the trauma that woke the person for more than a few minutes would be regarded as being above the threshold. The questions in the CBT Pocketbook should not be regarded as a symptom checklist and should not be presented as an interrogation. The questions are simply an aid to eliciting details regarding particular symptoms and supplementary clarifying questions may be needed depending on a client's responses.

Personality disorder?

The third step in assessing referred clients is to screen them for personality disorder. GCBT programmes for depression and the anxiety disorders have excluded those with cluster A and B personality disorders (DSM-IV-TR; American Psychiatric Association 2000). Cluster A personality disorders, termed the 'odd' personality disorders, refer to those with paranoid personality disorders, schizoid personality disorders and schizotypal personality disorders. Such is the pervasive level of mistrust among clients with 'odd' personality disorders that they are very unlikely to agree to participate in a group. If clients with an 'odd' personality disorder were included in a group they would present the therapist with an extreme challenge to make them feel included and this would be at the expense of focus on other group members. Cluster B personality disorders refer to those with antisocial, borderline, histrionic and narcissistic personality disorders, termed the 'dramatic' personality disorders, and again they are likely to make disproportionate demands on the therapist's time and other group members are likely to be alienated from the group. However, clients with cluster C personality disorders, dependent, avoidant, obsessive-compulsive personality disorders, are usually manageable in groups focused on depression and the anxiety disorders.

The Standardised Assessment of Personality – Abbreviated Scale (SAPAS), Appendix G, is a screen for personality disorders (Moran et al. 2003), consisting of just eight items, each item answered with a 'yes' or a 'no'; example items are 'Would you normally describe yourself as a loner?' and 'In general do you trust other people?' A score of 3 or more identifies 90% of those with personality disorders. However, for the purpose of screening clients for a group, probably the most appropriate cut-off is a score of 5 or more. Use of this cut-off in the Moran et al. (2003) study meant that no one who did not have a personality disorder was identified as having one, i.e. there were no false positives. Using a cut-off of 5 or more, Moran et al. (2003) identified three out of five of those who did have a personality disorder, thus letting some of those with a personality disorder through the gate but probably those with a more manageable personality disorder from the point of view of group treatment. It is of course possible to use the cut-off of 3 or more on the SAPAS and for those who screened positive to be followed up with a 'gold standard' assessment of personality disorder using the SCID II (First *et al.* 1997), but this takes over an hour to do and whilst it would be appropriate in a research context, a busy practitioner might well content themselves with using a SAPAS score of 5 or more.

Clients who are actively suicidal have also been excluded from GCBT as they require special individual attention (see Brown *et al.* 2005). A frame-work for risk assessment is detailed in Scott (2009). Alcohol/drug abuse is a common concomitant of depression and the anxiety disorders and can usually be dealt with in the context of the programmes outlined in this volume but the programmes are probably inappropriate for those who are dependent. Clients with more than very slight learning difficulties are likely to feel frustrated and demoralised in a group composed of those without learning difficulties and probably best served by ICBT with a stress inoculation focus (Meichenbaum 1985).

Highly autonomous individuals, i.e. those who base their sense of worth on their achievements, with cognitions of the type 'if I am not the top I am a flop', have been found to do less well in GCBT than in ICBT (Zettle and Herring 1995), but may benefit sufficiently if offered a number of individual sessions as well.

Psychometric tests

A full range of established psychometric tests for depression and the anxiety disorders is available free of charge for personal use in the IAPT *Data Handbook Appendices v 1.0* (IAPT 2010b), www.iapt.nhs.uk. They include the PHQ-9 (Kroenke *et al.* 2001) for depression, GAD-7 (Spitzer *et al.* 2006) for generalised anxiety disorder, Panic Disorder Severity Scale (Shear *et al.* 1997) for panic disorder, Fear Questionnaire (Marks and Mathews 1979) for agoraphobia, Impact of Event Scale – Revised (Weiss and Marmar 1997) for post-traumatic stress disorder, Social Phobia Inventory (Connor *et al.* 2000) for social phobia and the Obsessive Compulsive Inventory (Foa *et al.* 2002) for obsessive compulsive disorder. These tests are very useful as measures of changes in the severity of a disorder during treatment. Tests which identify the cognitions or behaviours that maintain a disorder also have a clear clinical utility and in Table 1.4 there are example tests of severity and cognitive measures for each disorder.

Clients should be asked to complete a measure of the severity of their disorder/s at each session so that progress can be charted (Appendix F) and also complete a cognitive measure. Psychometric tests are, however, not a substitute for diagnosis, as generally speaking psychometric tests yield false

Table 1.4 Commonly used tests

1   Depression – PHQ-9 (Kroenke *et al.* 2001), Dysfunctional Attitude Scale (Weissman and Beck 1978)
2   Panic disorder and agoraphobia – Beck Anxiety Inventory BAI (Beck and Steer 1993), Agoraphobic Cognitions Questionnaire (ACQ; Chambless *et al.* 1984)
3   The PTSD Checklist (PCL; Weathers *et al.* 1993), Posttraumatic Cognitions Inventory (PCTI; Foa *et al.* 1999)
4   Generalised Anxiety Disorder – GAD-7 Scale (Spitzer *et al.* 2006), Anxious Thoughts Inventory (AnTI; Wells 1994)
5   Social phobia – Social Phobia Inventory (SPIN; Connor *et al.* 2000), Social Cognitions Questionnaire (SCQ; Wells *et al.* 1993)
6   Obsessive compulsive disorder – Yale-Brown Obsessive-Compulsive Disorder Inventory (Y-BOCS; Goodman *et al.* 1989), Obsessive Belief Questionnaire (OBQ; Obsessive Compulsive Cognitions Working Group 2005), Personal Significance Scale (Rachman 2003)

positives, which means that sole reliance on them can result in targeting the wrong disorder.

The client's view

As well as diagnostic interviews and psychometric tests it is important to get the client's perspective on treatment; this can be garnered using the Satisfaction With Therapy and Therapist Scale – Revised (STTS-R; Oei and Green 2008). One additional item on the STTS-R relates to outcome and is probably particularly salient; it asks 'How much did this treatment help with the specific problem that led you to therapy?' and the responses are on a 5-point scale, Made things a lot better (1), Made things somewhat better (2), Made no difference (3), Made things somewhat worse (4) and Made things a lot worse (5).

Chapter 2

Engagement

It is likely that most clients, given the choice, would initially opt for individual rather than a group intervention. Thus even in those prepared to engage in group therapy there is likely to be a certain reluctance, a few are likely to be positively antagonistic and for others their motivation to participate in a group is somewhere in between. GCBT has therefore to be positively marketed, and client reservations anticipated and appropriately dealt with. Whilst the focus of this volume is on GCBT for depression and anxiety disorders, the same issue of preparedness to join a group appears to raise its head for other disorders and difficulties. For example, in a study of CBT for back pain (Lamb *et al.* 2010) only 63% of participants attended three or more of the six group sessions but the GCBT was still superior to standard advice. During an assessment session a client can be asked to complete the readiness for a group form (Table 2.1).

For clients with a determination to attend a group, i.e. a score of 8–10 on the 'ruler' (Table 2.1), their motivation to attend a group may be buttressed using a simple 10-minute pre-treatment procedure shown by Buckner *et al.* (2009) to increase treatment sessions attended and to lower treatment severity at termination. Clients are asked to picture themselves acting out their first four group therapy appointments and to spend a couple of

Table 2.1 Readiness for a group

Please circle a number, on the ruler below, to indicate how ready you feel to join a group of others with your difficulties, to learn new ways of handling your problems.

No			Maybe				Yes		
1	2	3	4	5	6	7	8	9	10

If you indicated a 'No' or 'Maybe' number above, what is it that puts you off joining a group?

. . . .

. . . .

. . . .

minutes going through the specifics, going into the building, meeting the leader or co-leader, leaving, returning the following week. Next, clients are asked to explain why they personally would continue with therapy for at least four sessions. These reasons are solicited in two ways. Clients are asked to select reasons from a list (e.g. I like to finish what I begin) as well as write a paragraph listing traits and qualities about themselves that would explain why they would 'stick' with therapy.

For clients with reservations about joining a group, individual sessions can be scheduled immediately prior to the start of the scheduled group to address their fears. Tolin and Maltby (2008) have described a four-session 'Readiness Intervention (RI)' for clients about to undergo treatment for obsessive compulsive disorder. Their intervention consisted of providing psychoeducation, motivational interviewing, video of a simulated session using actors, introduction to the type of materials they would encounter for use with the type of problems they had, and telephone contact with a client who had already completed a programme. They found their RI facilitated engagement in treatment and it is used in this volume as a model here for engaging clients in GCBT. An alternative way of motivating clients to attend a group is to construct a five-minute video of a client who has responded to the envisaged group programme. In this interview the ex-client can be depicted answering the following questions: (a) How did you first feel when invited to attend a group for your difficulties? (b) What was it like as you went through the group programme? (c) Looking back what did you find most useful? (d) What would you say to others doubtful about attending a group like the one you were in? Clients can be asked: 'To help people make a decision about whether or not to give a group a try, we have made a five-minute video; could you let me know what you think after we have watched it? The testimony of an ex-group member is likely to be a more credible source of persuasion than the therapist. Motivational issues are also important in the early group sessions and where possible an ex-group member should be invited along to provide their testimony live, using the structure of the above questions. It is recommended that the individual sessions that are conducted as a prelude to the group take place as close as possible to the beginning of the scheduled group as the newly found motivation to attend the group may be short-lived, 'striking whilst the iron is hot' as Tolin and Maltby (2008) suggest.

Readiness for change, be it joining a group, overcoming substance abuse, tackling a specific problem such as anger, can be conceptualised in terms of Prochaska, DiClemente and Norcross's (1992) stages of change model. First there are those in Precontemplation, not ready to think about change seriously. Somewhat more motivated are those in the Contemplation stage, ready to think about change, weighing up the pros and cons. More motivated still are those in the Determination phase who are preparing to make plans for change. The ruler in Table 2.1 can be regarded as a measure of where an individual is with regard to these first three stages. The same measuring instrument can be applied to whether a client wants to work on, say, a comorbid alcohol abuse problem or applied to say whether a PTSD client sees their post-trauma anger as a problem they wish to address or not. Thus the same person might score differently on the ruler depending on the 'object being measured' (group/substance abuse/anger). Those scoring 1–3 on the ruler may be regarded as in Precontemplation, whilst those scoring 4–7 are in Contemplation, with those scoring 8–10 in Determination. The fourth stage of Prochaska *et al.*'s (1992) model is Action, in which the client is implementing change. The fifth and final stage of the model is Maintenance, ensuring that the change in behaviour becomes habitual. Thus a client who has attended say the first two group sessions might be regarded as in the Maintenance phase but then misses the third session; it might be discovered via a phone call to the client or at a concurrent individual session that the client has reverted to say the Contemplation phase with regard to attending the group. There is thus a fluidity between stages and Miller and Rollnick (2002) suggest that different interventions are necessary at different stages and these comprise motivational interviewing. However, Tolin and Maltby (2008) have reflected that their Readiness Intervention delivered as a prelude to intervention may have affected fear of treatment to a greater extent than it did stages of change or expectancies for improvement.

Using a framework developed by Murphy *et al.* (2002) and applying it to readiness for a group, it is suggested those in a precontemplative stage are best served by (a) discussing what is involved in group attendance, e.g. times, extent of need for self-disclosure, confidentiality, (b) familiarising clients with the Survival Manuals for each of the disorders from which they suffer (Appendices H–M), explaining that they are the focus in both individual and GCBT and discussing issues arising from the client's reading of them and (c) asking open questions about their reasons for not wishing to join a group. Those in a contemplative stage would be asked in addition to (a) consider the pros and cons both short and long term for attending a group, (b) contact a former group member to chat about the possibility of attending and (c) watch a simulated video of a group session. Clients in the determination phase would be encouraged to attend a group session on an experimental basis, recording their expectations and contrasting them with their experience. In the action phase clients begin learning skills in the group and are committed to trying them out at home.

Individual sessions

The marketing of the group is made much easier by the offer of complementary individual sessions; this latter tends to be particularly important the more severe the disorder, for those with greater additional disorders (comorbidity) or highly personal concerns. The focus in the individual session/s is twofold: Motivational interviewing (MI) with regard to group attendance and the tackling of any comorbid disorder/s. To address motivational problems individual sessions can begin before the group programme. If clients default from a group programme it is usually in the early sessions, so the provision of prior or simultaneous individual sessions can act as a buttress against clients dropping out.

The following exchange illustrates the marketing of GCBT:

THERAPIST: We usually provide a combination of group and individual sessions for your type of difficulties.

NATALIE: Group?

THERAPIST: Yes, if I see people just by themselves they usually think there's something odd about them to be seeing someone like me. Even if I say lots of people have this problem, they still think of themselves as odd. In a group it's just like a night school class for your nerves, you can say as little or as much as you want.

NATALIE: I was never much good at school.

THERAPIST: If anything is not clear in the group there is a time to have a chat about it afterwards, or in an individual session or just before the start of the next group session.

NATALIE: When is the group?

THERAPIST: We were thinking of Tuesdays at 6. p.m., how would that be?

NATALIE: I would have to get someone to mind the kids. Usually I would get mother-in-law but she would think I should just pull myself together. I suppose I could get my friend Angie.

THERAPIST: Would Angie think you should just pull yourself together?

NATALIE: No, Angie is great, she has had her own troubles.

THERAPIST: Hopefully there will be others like Angie in the group.

NATALIE: What if they are like my mother-in-law?

THERAPIST: Maybe we can stop 'mother-in-law types' being too 'toxic' and focus on 'Angies'.

NATALIE: OK I'll give it a go.

THERAPIST: By the end of the group people are usually really happy they have had the benefit of it, as well as individual attention.

NATALIE: It might help me think I am less of a 'weirdo'.

In the above transcript the therapist has recognised the client's ambivalence about attending a group, and then addressed her self-efficacy, i.e. her beliefs about her capacity and her beliefs about whether joining a group would make a worthwhile difference, increasing her motivation to attend. Supporting self-efficacy is one of the four pillars of motivational interviewing, which are summarised in Table 2.2.

Table 2.2 Pillars of motivational interviewing

1 Express empathy using reflective listening
2 Juxtapose the client's important values with their current behaviour (e.g. 'You say you really want to be able to be connecting with others but couldn't face attending a group?)
3 Sidestep resistance by responding with empathy and understanding rather than confrontation
4 Enhancing self-efficacy

A client's ambivalence about change can also be picked up from the initial screening instrument, The 7 Minute Mental Health Screen – Revised (Appendix B)/First Step Questionnaire – Revised (Appendix C). For example, when the therapist asked the questions in Table 2.3 from the Interview screen of Natalie whom we met earlier in this chapter, though she felt she should cut down on her drinking, acknowledged that her mother-in-law got annoyed about her drinking and sometimes felt guilty about her drinking, she indicated that she did not know whether she wanted help with it. The therapist was able to clarify that she drank excessively most Friday nights when her friend Angie visited, though very occasionally she had drunk too much on a Sunday night when she was by herself and missed work the next day. In terms of the DSM-IV-TR criteria (American Psychiatric Association 2000) Natalie was abusing alcohol rather than being dependent on it. The therapist addressed the issue using a motivational interviewing framework in the initial individual sessions:

Table 2.3 Extract from the 7 Minute Mental Health Screen – Revised

8. Substance abuse/dependence	Yes	No	Don't know
Have you felt you should cut down on your alcohol/drug?			
Have people got annoyed with you about your drinking/drug taking?			
Have you felt guilty about your drinking/drug use?			
Do you drink/use drugs before midday?			
Is this something with which you would like help?			

THERAPIST: Do you look forward to drinking on Friday night as your well-deserved break from the working week?
NATALIE: I suppose I do.
THERAPIST: But it causes problems with your mother-in-law?
NATALIE: It's not just her, sometimes it leaves me too disorganised on the Saturday morning to get the kids to dance class on time and they get annoyed.

THERAPIST: So you want a break for yourself but not to 'break' things up for the kids and mother-in-law.

In the above exchange the therapist is highlighting the discrepancy between Natalie's behaviour and her values. As the exchange continues, the therapist continues to express empathy, avoids confrontation and heightens the discrepancy between Natalie's behaviour and values further:

THERAPIST: So Angie enjoys a break at the weekend with you as well?
NATALIE: Yes, we have a good time on a Friday.
THERAPIST: What about on a Sunday, doesn't Angie drink then?
NATALIE: No, she has to get up for work the next day.
THERAPIST: Doesn't she drink in her own home on a Sunday?
NATALIE: No, because she is not an idiot like me.
THERAPIST: Is having a break stupid?
NATALIE: It's *when* you have a break, I hate ringing in work on Monday morning lying that I am not well.
THERAPIST: It seems that you want a break but without it affecting the kids or work; we could discuss this further at the next individual session if you like.
NATALIE: Yes, I need to do something about it.

In the above Natalie has moved from a Contemplation stage to the Determination stage. Given that there is strong evidence for MI as a brief pre-treatment in the area of substance abuse (Burke *et al.* 2003) and this is often a complication of depression and the anxiety disorders, it seems reasonable that initial individual sessions should be framed around MI. Some of the individual sessions may take place before the group programme. The exact number would depend on the motivational level of the client for the group, the client's willingness to address comorbid conditions and the number of comorbid conditions.

Motivational interviewing was originally developed with the addictions in mind but its scope has been extended so that it can be a useful adjunct to the treatment of depression and the anxiety disorders. Westra and Dozois (2006) found that MI pre-treatment (three sessions) enhanced the efficacy of GCBT for a mixed anxiety disorders group (45% panic disorder, 31% social phobia and 24% generalised anxiety disorder) compared to those who received only the group CBT. The MI pre-treatment group had greater homework compliance in GCBT and a significantly higher number of responders. (In a subsequent study Westra *et al.* [2009] found that MI pre-treatment significantly improved the efficacy of an individual CBT programme for generalised anxiety disorder.) Adding two individual sessions of motivational interviewing and thought mapping before GCBT for obsessive compulsive disorder has also been found to be more effective than

GCBT alone (Meyer *et al.* 2010). However, in this study it is not possible to determine whether the added benefit of the two pre-treatment individual sessions arises from the motivational interviewing or the thought mapping. More generally it is not known whether any type of pre-treatment enhances outcome or whether the increased potency is specific to MI.

There appears to be no reason why MI sessions in relation to the disorder that is the group focus could not be run concurrently with the group. In practice the distinction between MI for a comorbid disorder and MI for group attendance is often blurred. For example, in relation to the client Natalie, discussed earlier, the therapist felt that depression was Natalie's primary problem and it was agreed that she would attend a depression group. At her third individual session, which occurred just before attending the group, the following dialogue ensued:

THERAPIST: How do you see alcohol fitting into your life when you are attending the group?

NATALIE: I'll just drink on Fridays, I only drink on Sundays because I get low by myself.

THERAPIST: Alcohol is a depressant, possibly not the best way of managing a low mood.

NATALIE: Don't I know it, maybe I'll find better ways of handling my low mood in the group.

THERAPIST: Yes they are like having driving lessons for low mood, some people get the hang of it quicker than others but it is more to do with practice of what you learn outside the lesson that really makes the difference.

In this exchange the therapist has shifted from motivational interviewing focused on alcohol abuse to MI for attending the group, underlining that the latter can be a credible vehicle for change.

Sharing of provisional case formulations of each identified disorder

At the individual sessions the therapist should distil and refine the case formulation for each client for each of the disorders that they are suffering from, drawing not only on what the client has said in the individual session but also on what they have verbalised in the group. The case formulation is the therapist's working hypotheses of how the client came to be suffering from their current problems and to present at this particular point in time.

The development of a case formulation is illustrated with regard to Natalie, whose difficulties were described earlier in this chapter. Using the 7 Minute Mental Health Screen – Revised, Appendix B, Natalie screened positive for depression, social phobia, panic disorder and alcohol abuse;

whilst she wanted help for the first three conditions she was ambivalent about help for her alcohol problem. The screens were confirmed by directly accessing each of DSM-IV (DSM-IV-TR; American Psychiatric Association 2000) symptoms for each disorder using the diagnostic questions in Appendix A. The disorders from which a person suffers can be regarded as reciprocally interacting, and determine overall psychological and social functioning; this is depicted in Figure 2.1 for Natalie. Her panic disorder and social phobia each led her to avoid a wide range of everyday activities which in turn served to maintain her depression. In the depressed state she was less motivated to dare herself to encounter the situations she feared and thereby learn that they pose little threat, leading to maintenance of her panic disorder and social phobia. Initially she was ambivalent about whether alcohol was affecting her functioning and so it was excluded from the initial presentation of Figure 2.1, but alcohol abuse was included as a fourth ball/stream in the funnel after the third individual session.

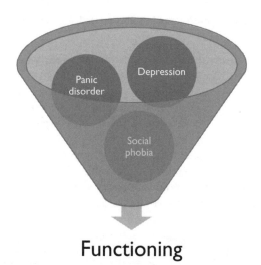

Functioning

Figure 2.1 Functioning as a product of the reciprocal interaction of disorders – Natalie as an example.

The inputs for the 'funnel' (Figure 2.1) arise, from the three 'P's, described by Weerasekera (1996), predisposing factors, precipitating factors and perpetuating factors. In Figure 2.2 this framework is applied to Natalie.

Much of the detail for Figure 2.2 emerges from an intake questionnaire (Appendix E) and an open-ended interview conducted at the first individual interview. Further details can be added as they emerge at subsequent sessions. It was explained to Natalie that treatment would focus on negating the perpetuating factors, so that 'nothing was poured into the funnel that

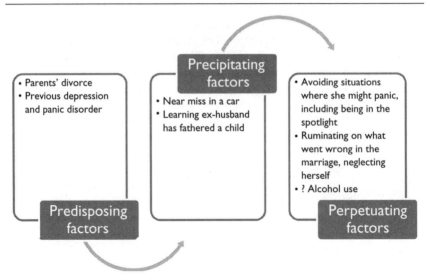

Figure 2.2 The process by which disorders are distilled – Natalie as an example.

would produce malfunctioning'. The particular aspects of the perpetuating factors that lead to the specific disorders are shown in Figure 2.3, with regard to Natalie.

A case formulation is a specific example of the cognitive model of a disorder; these models are detailed in the disorder-specific chapters in this volume.

Weerasekera (1996) refers to a fourth P, protective factors which may mitigate or prevent the effects of a disorder. Such protective factors in Natalie's case might be the tangible support she received from her mother-in-law and the emotional support she received from her friend Angie.

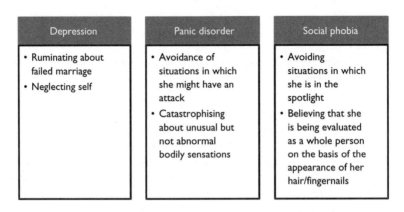

Figure 2.3 Perpetuating factors for each disorder – Natalie as an example.

Group and individual sessions

GCBT sessions are usually one and a half to two hours in length and programmes have typically run for about 15 sessions. However, the optimal number of sessions has yet to be determined. Scott and Stradling (1990) looked at the cost efficiency of a twelve-session group programme for depression including up to three individual sessions and computed a Counsellor Efficiency Score (the mean percentage change on the Beck Depression Inventory divided by the amount of counsellor time needed to achieve that change, per client [average per cent change per client per hour of counsellor time]) and arrived at a score of 14.5. In a later work Scott *et al.* (1995) conducted a seven-session group programme plus an individual session 'if you really need it' and the Counsellor Efficiency Score was 13.3. Scott and Stradling (1998) have also computed a Counsellor Efficiency Score for individual CBT based on published depression studies of 5.25 and for other psychotherapeutic modalities a score of 4.3. Reflecting on these depression studies the author considers that ten-session group programmes are probably the most cost-efficient but they do need to include typically up to six individual sessions and in the absence of data to the contrary it is not unreasonable to assume that this format may prove most cost-efficient for the other common disorders.

The individual sessions provide an ideal setting to address comorbid disorders. Clearly the group leader will have to be very familiar with the protocols for each of the disorders. However, inevitably aspects of an individual's comorbid disorder will crop up in the group session and the leader and co-leader will have to strike a balance between respecting expression of the individual's need and not losing focus on the common problems of group members.

The structure of a group session

The agenda for group CBT sessions typically follows the format shown in Table 2.4, and places a special emphasis on the use of self-help and computer-assisted materials.

The session in fact begins as soon as a client arrives and before the group is called to focus on the day's materials. In this more informal setting over drinks the leader and co-leader work to identify any major issues that might have arisen to prevent the client focusing on the new materials to be introduced. Exceptionally the leader or co-leader might invite the client to stay behind for a few minutes at the end of the session to have a chat about the pressing concern. In this way the leader/co-leader are increasing the client's readiness for the group.

Compliance with homework has been found to be a predictor of outcome in group cognitive therapy for depression (Neimeyer and Feixas 1990) and

Table 2.4 Structure of a group session

1   Welcome over coffee/tea/fruit juice
2   Review of homework
3   Introduction of new material
4   Setting of individualised homework incorporating new learning

a review of homework at the start of a session is mandatory. It is essential that the group leaders problem solve any difficulties in implementing the set homework or any unexpected adverse consequences of doing the homework. The therapist's task is to foster a group norm about the completion of homework and thereby enhance commitment to homework; thus a group member's assertion that they were too busy or too tired to do their homework cannot be allowed to go unchallenged. It is imperative that the group norm does not become 'you do homework if you feel you are up to it'. The emphasis has to be that what is practised between group sessions is more important than the sessions themselves.

This informal gathering is also something of a laboratory which can be used to highlight the client's concerns. For example, members of a social phobia group might be challenged on whether any of them make a point of arriving just on time to avoid the ambiguity of interacting over coffee beforehand or members of a depression group can be challenged as to whether they talk little of themselves to others in the group for fear of being found wanting. In essence the Welcome recognises clients' individuality but is also a vehicle for stressing commonalities, thereby normalising responses and lessening stigmatisation.

Most clients attending group sessions are likely to be highly anxious, on the one hand trying to take in the material presented but on the other bedevilled by task-interfering thoughts such as 'I'm too stupid to take this in, never was much good at school', 'Will this really make any difference?' In some groups for generalised anxiety disorder and social phobia, these TICs (Task Interfering Cognitions) can be a particular focus and clients are taught how to swap TICs for TOCs (Task Oriented Cognitions) using the mnemonic TIC/TOC. But in view of the sabotaging effects of the TICs it is important that clients have an easily understood record of what is being taught. The material is summarised in disorder-specific Survival Manuals, Appendices H–M. This material may be supplemented by self-help books.

Therapist-guided self-help

Therapist-guided self-help using CBT material is a NICE recommended treatment for mild and moderate depression (NICE 2009). In a study of mildly and moderately depressed over-55-year-olds (Scogin *et al.* 1989) one half of the sample was asked to try completing reading the book *Feeling*

Good: The New Mood Therapy (Burns 1999) within four weeks and provided with blank self-help forms, and the other half was placed on a waiting list. Both groups were contacted by telephone each week for 10 minutes and asked to complete a measure of the severity of depression; in addition, those in the book group were encouraged to complete reading the book. No therapy was provided yet despite this those in the book group produced changes comparable to those in individual CBT for depression. However, 41% of the sample had degree level or above education. This raises questions as to whether the results would generalise to other depressed populations or indeed other disorders. Ehlers *et al.* (2003) evaluated the efficacy of a 64-page booklet (18,000 words), *Understanding Your Reactions to Trauma* by Claudia Herbert (1996), combined with one 40-minute session of guidance in the use of the booklet, in the remediation of PTSD. Unfortunately the booklet was no more effective than a repeated assessment. It may be that the booklet was descriptive rather than prescriptive, as in Scott's *Moving on After Trauma* (2008), and/or that therapist guidance has to be more often than a single session. The optimal way of delivering guided self-help and the optimal materials have yet to be determined. It is suggested in this volume that guided self-help may be a cost-effective way of addressing comorbid disorders when the principal disorder is being treated in a group. The self-help Survival Manuals in this volume are each about 6,000 words (about 20 pages).

Key competences in GCBT

The aspect of CBT therapist competence that most relates to outcome is structure (Shaw *et al.* 1999); this refers to the setting of an agenda, assigning relevant homework and pacing the session appropriately. Pacing is likely to be particularly important in GCBT because the therapist can be distracted from the agenda for the session not only by the off-task comments of a client but also by an off-task discussion among group members. At the same time the therapist wishes to produce a group cohesion, so that members are supportive of each other and this may necessitate a degree of off-task focus. It is only with a foundation of empathy that clients can begin to understand how other group members are disturbing themselves and offer remedial help on the basis of what they have learnt in therapy. Arguably the member of the group the client is trying to assist becomes a role model for altering their own self-talk and behaviour on a 'physician heal thyself basis'. GCBT may offer some additional mechanisms for change not available in individual CBT.

In presenting new material the leaders should do so in as least abstract form as possible, using metaphor where possible; this is illustrated by the conceptualisations of the different disorders, presented in the CBT Pocketbook, Appendix A. For example, rationales for depression include 'being on strike for better pay and conditions, refusing to invest because the dice are loaded against me, not surprisingly there is no return'. Such use of metaphor invites ready discussion and engagement, carrying with it treatment implications. However, the therapist must not make the mistake of assuming that simply because they have used metaphor all group members have understood. On occasion the metaphor can get in the way for an individual, for example a member of a depression group who replies to the above treatment rationale for depression with 'that's how I come to be here, what I was investing for my retirement went pear shaped with the stock market, look where I am now'. It is crucial to check out that each group member has understood the teaching point and that if necessary it is rephrased to form a therapeutic alliance with the client; thus with the above-mentioned client the therapist drew a basket with just one item on and said 'from here on in we want to make sure that all your eggs are not in one basket'.

A client is unlikely to complete a homework assignment if they have low self-efficacy, i.e. they believe that they do not have the capacity to perform the task or they believe the task will not produce a worthwhile outcome. In the setting of homework the self-efficacy concerns have to be addressed so that the homework task becomes of a size they believe they can manage and there is a perception that it will make some difference.

The key skills underlining the competences are discussed in the next chapter.

Chapter 3

Content and process

In keeping with Beck's axiom that the different disorders are characterised by their differing cognitive content (Alford and Beck 1997), different therapeutic targets have been identified. The matching technical treatment strategies for these targets, for depression and the anxiety disorders, are summarised in the Cognitive Behaviour Therapy Pocketbook, in Appendix A. A case formulation is a specific example of the cognitive model of a disorder. Group members have in common that they are a 'case' of a particular disorder and to a degree this limits the extent to which the therapist/s have to adapt the programme to the idiosyncrasies of the individual. The use of formulations which are not disorder specific may place an impossible burden on group leaders.

A therapist's competence in delivering CBT is not just a matter of technical competence (knowing which technique is appropriate for which problem), but also of having general therapeutic skills, empathy/warmth etc. The technical and general therapeutic skills of a cognitive behaviour therapist have been embodied in the Cognitive Therapy Rating Scale (CRTS; the Scale and Scale Manual are freely from the Academy of Cognitive Therapy, www.academyofct.org). The CTRS has five items on Conceptualisation, Strategy and Technique and six items on General Therapeutic Skill (agenda, feedback, understanding, interpersonal effectiveness, collaboration and pacing). Thus the therapeutic relationship has always occupied an important place in CBT. However, in GCBT the therapist has to not only be able to relate to each group member but also be able to utilise their relationships with each other in a way that maximises therapeutic benefit. In addition, the therapist has also to effectively synchronise with a co-leader. Thus the GCBT therapist has need of a set of general group therapeutic skills. In Appendix D a set of General Group Therapeutic Skills has been codified. A therapist's competence in these skills is a measure of how well they manage 'process', the sum of the interactions in the group. Thus to assess the competence of a therapist delivering GCBT, Appendix D can replace the first part of the CTRS, to make the latter applicable to a group modality.

In individual therapy the extent to which a therapist develops a thera-peutic alliance with a client is predictive of outcome (Martin *et al.* 2000); so too in a group modality therapist process management skills are likely to predict outcome. However, in depression the alliance changes due to earlier symptom improvement (Feeley *et al.* 1999), calling into question whether there should be a focus specifically on the alliance. But a study of GCBT for depression by Oei and Browne (2006) suggests that group processes may yet be important. Oei and Browne (2006) found that the less support depressed clients felt they received from their group's leader, the more positive their clinical outcomes were at post-treatment, whereas the more perceived support, the worse the clinical outcomes. These findings suggest that there is an optimal level of support and that excessive support may be counter-productive. Further, it may have been the case that the group processes that were operating in the GCBT programmes overshadowed the therapist's contributions to the therapeutic relationship. It could be that other group members may have largely fulfilled the empathy and unconditional support that clients typically seek from the therapist. Thus whilst the therapist's contributions are undoubtedly important in the therapeutic process, it appears that group processes may play a similarly important role.

Though most of the GCBT studies have not focused directly on manag-ing process this does not mean that therapists have not implicitly exhibited general group therapeutic skills. It seems likely that such group skills are as important as the general individual therapeutic skills recognised in the first part of the CTRS. Overall the case is probably stronger for a dual focus on content and process in GCBT, rather than ignoring process. In making the group skills explicit it is possible for would-be GCBT practitioners to learn these skills.

General group therapeutic skills

The general group therapeutic skills are codified in Appendix D; each of the items is elaborated upon in turn below.

1. Review of homework/Agenda

The setting of an agenda is of key importance in GCBT, as the possibilities of being sidetracked in GCBT are much greater than in individual CBT. The sessions (beyond the first) should begin, however, with a review of how people have got on since the last session. To some degree how people have fared since the last session will have become apparent from some members as they have assembled, over tea/coffee. This informal group opportunity should be utilised to identify key issues for members. At the start of the group session itself the group leaders should make systematic enquiry of each member's functioning since the last session, encouraging them to ventilate their feelings. However, levels of emotion that are too high are likely to interfere with the functioning of the group, but at the other extreme levels that are too low are likely to be dysfunctional for the individual. As such the GCBT therapist has to operate something of a thermostat with regard to the levels of expressed emotion and this begins in the eliciting of members' functioning since the last session.

A review of the previous session's homework is another key aspect of setting the agenda. If a client's homework is not followed up and difficulties problem solved then they are unlikely to see the point of further homework assignments. In reviewing homework it is essential to make reference to a copy (using a carbon/photocopy/tablet PC) of what was set for the group member.

The competences involved in reviewing homework and setting an agenda are summarised in Table 3.1 (an extract from the General Group Therapeutic Skills Rating Scale [GGTSRS], Appendix D).

Table 3.1 Review of homework/Agenda from GGTSRS

0	Therapist did not set an agenda/did not review homework
2	Therapist set an agenda that was vague or did not involve group members/vague reference to previous session's homework
4	Therapist worked with group members to set a mutually satisfactory agenda/ difficulties with previous session's homework were locked onto
6	Therapist set an agenda that was suitable for the available time. Established priorities and tracked the agenda/difficulties with previous session's homework were effectively problem solved

The review of homework/setting of the agenda should usually not take more than 15 to 20 minutes. There should be a natural flow from picking up salient issues for members before the group session and at the start of the session, noting the apparent relevance of the previous session's homework to the identified concerns, and dovetailing these with the new material to be addressed in the session. From the therapist's point of view there is less flexibility about the content of the group programme, because to depart from the group programme will likely mean that important material will not be covered or more likely not be covered in sufficient depth. However, for the new material to be centrally processed by group members its relevance to the pressing concerns expressed by group members in the first 15 to 20 minutes of a session has to be acknowledged.

2. Relevance

The topography of clients' problems can appear very different; for example, in a depression group one member's depression may be related primarily to perceived underachievement whilst for another it is related primarily to a sense of isolation. The therapeutic task is to keep each group member engaged despite a diverse presentation. This can be achieved by applying the newly taught material to each of the domains of concern using each individual as an illustrative example. Thus, for example, if cognitive processes were on the agenda, the leader might suggest that an example of a mental filter would be a person very keen on achievement who focuses only on the classmates at school who have done better than him, whilst the co-leader might point out that an example of a mental filter might be the person who focuses on not having a close intimate relationship, ignoring the support of family and friends. The goal is not to be hooked by the details of each group member's difficulties, but to keep clients aware that a framework for addressing their concerns is being distilled and it will need their input to ensure it is moulded to their particular needs.

The competences involved in keeping the content of the group session relevant to each group member are summarised in Table 3.2 (an extract from the GGTSRS, Appendix D).

Table 3.2 Relevance from GGTSRS

0	Therapist did not ensure content was relevant to every group member at some point in the session
2	Therapist ensured content was relevant to most members most of the time
4	Therapist ensured content was relevant to all group members most of the time
6	Therapist ensured content was relevant to all group members throughout session

The danger of not addressing relevance is that the client peripherally processes what the therapist is saying, with rules of thumb such as 'this isn't for people like me, it's for people who are really bright' and they fade into the background in the group. The therapist has to be alert for non-verbal signs, such as a client doodling or avoiding any eye contact, that the content of the session has become irrelevant and check out whether it is germane. In this way the therapist is more like a skilled teacher than a barrister giving an oration; the former is simple, direct and straightforward.

3. Adaptation

Group members are likely to vary considerably in their ability to deal with abstractions and this is likely to be reflected in any written homework assignments. Similarly members' ability to benefit from self-help material will be affected by the reading age of the material. It is therefore necessary that the therapists have available alternative presentations of the same principles and are constantly checking that the material is appropriate for each group member. For example, one group member may well be able to complete a Thought Record, such as MOOD, when distressed, and make a distinction between observed thinking and objective thinking whilst another member has struggled to separate 'observed' from 'objective' and might be advised to use a simple STOP! THINK! strategy when upset, replacing first thoughts with better 'second' thoughts.

The competences involved in adapting content to each group member are summarised in Table 3.3 (an extract from the GGTSRS, Appendix D).

Table 3.3 Adaptation

0	Therapist did not check out group members' understanding of what was being taught
2	Therapist did some checking out of group members' understanding but failed to successfully adapt material for those who had some difficulty
4	Therapist checked out understanding of all group members and was able to suitably adapt material for most of those with difficulties
6	Therapist tailored explanations to the level of understanding of each group member

Historically, CBT has tended to concentrate on analysing discrete automatic thoughts that are considered to be playing an important role in a client's distress; thus, for example, a client with an anger problem might be taught to consider whether in their recent anger episode they had judged what another had done as truly catastrophic. However, it is possible to approach CBT not only at this micro level of automatic thoughts but also at a macro level of images/roles. Thus another member of the group might be better helped with their anger problem by recognising that when they get angry they become the 'growly bear' their young child has described and asked to consider thinking what other character they would like to play in their child's life. An ability to operate at both a micro and macro level offers the GCBT therapist an increased range of options for adapting material to each individual group member.

4. Inclusion

Although the groups described in this volume are homogeneous with regard to primary diagnosis, members may differ markedly in terms of culture, religion or sexual orientation. Thus it is usually the case that the therapists will have to pay special attention to the inclusion of at least one or two members. In addition, some clients have restricted self-expression either because of social inhibition or communication difficulties, e.g. a stutter, and again the therapist has to be especially alert to the importance of including the socially disadvantaged. To some degree space for the disadvantaged has to be bought by restricting the utterances of the most eloquent. However, a balance has to be struck between encouraging the emotional expression/verbalisations of the least eloquent and keeping to the agenda.

The competences involved in including each group member are summarised in Table 3.4 (an extract from the GGTSRS, Appendix D).

Table 3.4 Inclusion

0	Therapist allowed the most vociferous group members to dominate the group
2	Therapist made attempts to include less vocal members but was not able to give them sufficient space to express themselves verbally and emotionally
4	Therapist ensured all group members had reasonable air time but had some difficulties with some of the less vocal group members
6	Therapist ensured that all group members had sufficient air time to express both their thoughts and feelings, including commentary on the group session as a whole

It is difficult for a therapist to include all group members without an understanding of the culture/values of each; this is particularly the case if a therapist is antagonistic to the particular belief system of a group member. In essence the therapist may not know how to go with the grain of the individual's belief system. This may be made easier by consultation with a colleague from the same belief system.

In the interests of inclusion the therapists may have to be assertive with a vociferous group member in order to give space to those members who easily drift away, to express their views/difficulties. This can be achieved using the 'broken record' technique – just repeating the same line over and over despite interruptions, e.g. 'Just give x air time . . . just give x air time . . . just give x air time . . . and now how about some air time for y'. It is very easy for therapists to look back on a group session and find, to their chagrin, that they have been hooked by those who made vocal voluntary contributions to the session. Both therapists need to be very alert for this possibility.

5. Additional disorders

Clients suffering from a single disorder are the exception rather than the rule. Thus even in a group with a primary focus on one disorder, most clients are likely to express concerns related to additional disorders. The therapeutic response is to avoid extreme reactions on the one hand, stating that these concerns are not appropriate for the group, and on the other hand to effectively conduct an individual session within the group. The additional disorders can be addressed by having the therapist bear in mind the general problem-solving process (Nezu and Nezu 1989) of problem orientation, problem definition, brainstorming solutions, weighing up the advantages and disadvantages of the proposed solutions, choosing a solution and experimenting with the solution, and if unsuccessful trying another solution. Problem orientation refers to the individual's world view of problems; for example, a person may have a view that if they encounter a problem someone must be to blame. Problem definition refers to the gap between a person's actual and desired state and the obstacles in moving from one to the other. Brainstorming refers to generating as many possible solutions to a problem as possible. In a group session therapists can strike a balance between the needs of the individual to have all their disorders addressed and the needs of the group by, in the initial sessions, confining themselves to the first three stages of problem solving with regard to the additional disorder. Thus, for example, in a post-traumatic stress disorder group one member might express concerns about their panic attacks. The therapist might legitimise a focus (problem orientation) on the panic attacks by normalising them, perhaps responding by saying 'this is also a problem for one or two others in the group'. Then moving on to the second stage of problem solving, definition of the problem, by saying 'the problem is not so much the panic attacks but how seriously you take them'. But then within the group session only going as far as the third stage of problem solving, brainstorming, by suggesting that it is within the individual contacts with leader and co-leader (CBT guided self-help, CBTgsh) that coping strategies will be discussed. Thus within the group session the presence of the additional disorder is fully acknowledged and legitimated and a general direction for resolving it is indicated but the particular pathway is distilled outside of the group session, i.e. the final stages of the problem-solving process with regard to the additional disorder take place after the group session or at an individual session, but would nevertheless be the subject of a homework assignment, which could be reviewed before the start of the next group session by telephone/e-mail or at a face-to-face individual session.

The competences involved in addressing additional disorders within a group session are summarised in Table 3.5 (an extract from the GGTSRS, Appendix D).

The tackling of the additional disorders does presume that the therapist has a knowledge and experience of the evidence-based treatment protocol for that disorder. In instances where this is not the case, treatment of the comorbid disorder/difficulty might be postponed until it can be treated by someone else after the conclusion of the group programme. For example, cognitive behavioural marital therapy (Beach and O'Leary 1986) has been found to be as effective for depression as cognitive therapy, for married women, and whilst a therapist might feel proficient in delivering GCBT for

Table 3.5 Additional disorders

0	Therapist either did not acknowledge a group member's expression of difficulties with a disorder that was not the prime focus of the group or spent such time on these concerns that other members were losing focus, e.g. chatting amongst themselves
2	Therapist acknowledged a group member's additional difficulty but without signposting a direction from which appropriate help might come, e.g. an individual session, or tried unsuccessfully to address the additional difficulty but showed a lack of competence in this area
4	Therapist managed group members' expressions of additional concerns and was mostly able to offer succinct advice and reassure that these difficulties could be addressed
6	Therapist managed to address all group members' expressions of additional problems and suggest appropriate options for their resolution without losing focus on the main teaching for the session

depression they may have an unfamiliarity with marital therapy and referral to a more experienced colleague after the GCBT has finished might be an option.

6. Magnifying support and minimising criticism

In GCBT the therapist is not the sole source of influence on the client, other group members may also influence the client. Some group members may attend a group programme with a vivid memory of some humiliation in a group situation many years previously. Tversky and Kahneman (1974) have described the operation of an availability heuristic, in which the vividness of a memory can give a mistaken impression that it is very likely. Thus some group members may be hyper-alert for signs of a re-enactment of humiliation. If in the first few group sessions they perceive rightly or wrongly some slights, they could then operate on the anchoring heuristic (which is also described by Tversky and Kahneman 1974), and not process information which indicates that they are valued. The danger is that such individuals default after a couple of group sessions. The therapist has to be alert for the possible operation of these heuristics and help to short-circuit them by magnifying support and minimising criticism.

The competences involved in magnifying support and minimising criticism within a group session are summarised in Table 3.6 (an extract from the GGTSRS, Appendix D).

The goal in GCBT is not only for the therapist to develop alliances with each group member but to foster alliances between members. This can be done not only within the formal group session but also in the relatively informal periods before and after a session; for example, the therapist might point out to two members that they live near each other or do the same

Table 3.6 Magnifying support and minimising criticism

0	Therapist did not acknowledge the power of other group members to influence each other for both good and ill
2	Therapist paid minimal attention to expressions of emotional and tangible support from group members to each other
4	Therapist encouraged group members to come up with solutions to members' problems based on what had been taught in the sessions, underlying support proffered and ensuring that criticism was reframed in terms of different behaviours rather than an attack on the person
6	Therapist magnified group support for a member and short-circuited personal attacks, utilising the period during which the group was assembling and departing to enhance alliances between members and pick up on members' concerns

type of work. In this way the therapist can build bridges between members which serve as pathways for support which might be tangible, e.g. one group member giving a lift home to another member, and/or emotional, e.g. two members both working for the local council empathising with each other over impossible targets. But the influence of one group member on another may not be always benign; for example, a group member who is unemployed might have little patience with another who is complaining of work pressures, accusing the latter of 'moaning'. The therapist has to shield members from high levels of criticism in order to prevent a worsening of mood; thus in relation to the 'moaning' charge, the therapist might interject 'to some extent we are all "moaning" in that there is a gap between where we are and where we want to be and we are struggling to find ways of closing the gap'. The therapeutic task is not to nullify criticism but to use the therapeutic thermostat to ensure that it is expressed at a level that is manageable in terms of the coping skills taught in the sessions.

7. Utilising group members as role models

One of the advantages of GCBT over individual CBT is that in the former other group members can serve as coping models for a particular difficulty. For example, one group member may have completed a homework assignment such as writing about their accident, whilst another has been too fearful to write about their accident. In this situation the therapist can usefully explore the homework-compliant group member's fears about writing about the trauma and enquire whether these were similar to those of the non-compliant group member. If compliant and non-compliant members are found to have similar fears, the compliant member's experience of writing about the task can be used as evidence that anticipation is worse than experience. Other members of the group may be more powerful sources of persuasion than the therapist.

The competences involved in utilising group members as role models within a group session are summarised in Table 3.7 (an extract from the GGTSRS, Appendix D).

Table 3.7 Utilising group members as role models

0	Therapist focused entirely on himself/herself as the source of persuasion
2	Therapist made fleeting reference to the positive behaviour of a group member but without making it explicit to what other member/s that behaviour might be particularly relevant
4	Therapist, to large extent, tuned into the cultural/religious background, friendships in the group to build alliances that would reinforce the learning and application of material taught
6	Therapist adeptly tuned into the assumptive world of each group member and was able to draw on it to reinforce alliances between members and ensure application of material taught outside the session

Other group members can serve as role models not only because they have been set similar homework but because they have been helped to identify with other group members from a similar background, i.e. the attractiveness of the group has been enhanced. Thus a group member may attempt a coping skill partly as a result of a group norm. It follows from this that therapists have to work assiduously in the construction of these norms, e.g. that homework should be completed.

8. Therapist presentation skills

The GCBT therapist is a skilled teacher rather than a lecturer or lawyer. As in individual CBT, whilst the content of what is presented is of critical importance, so too is the manner of presentation. The GCBT therapist should present material in chunks, checking that one 'chunk' has been understood by all before moving on to the next chunk. Each chunk should be summarised on paper, with as few simple words as possible and a straight-forward diagram, so that the group member can take it home and make reference to it between sessions. The likelihood of reference to a summary of a learning point is increased if during the session the therapist has talked group members through the written material, it has been discussed and the individual group member has personalised it by adding their own notes during the presentation of the particular chunk. In the appendices (H–M) are the handouts for different disorders, which can be downloaded from the publisher's website and used as a presentation in the group session.

The competences involved in presentational skills within a group session are summarised in Table 3.8 (an extract from the GGTSRS, from Appendix D).

Table 3.8 Therapist presentation skills

0	Therapist/s gave a didactic presentation with no written summary of material covered. If, more than one therapist, there was no synchrony between therapists, they were not reinforcing what each said or coming to each other's aid at difficult moments
2	Therapist/s did provide written summary of material covered but it consisted largely of printed words and at a reading age above some of the group. When diagrams were provided they were overly complex. Role plays were not used or if used did not follow a format of therapist modelling, group member practice and therapist feedback. If more than one therapist, whilst they shared the burden of presentation, there was little humour or support between them and some defensiveness
4	Therapist/s provided written summaries, diagrams of materials covered at a level accessible to all group members. Role plays were used and appeared to have enhanced group members' understanding. If more than one therapist, the therapists synchronised with humour and encouragement, helping create an appropriate climate
6	Therapist/s provided written summaries, diagrams at a level accessible to all but also highlighted other resources, books, computer-assisted therapy that some members might derive additional benefit from. Role plays were used and followed a format of therapist modelling, group member practice and therapist feedback that accentuated the positives and problem solved the negatives. If more than one therapist, the therapists seemed to 'dance' very well, presenting material effortlessly with humour and without defensiveness

The presentational style of the group leaders should be like that of dance instructors, modelling the skill to be learnt, the members practising the skill, with first positive feedback for what has been done well and specific problem solving for what has not been done well as opposed to criticism. However, the humour and interactions of the leaders are of key importance in being able to carry the class and in making it attractive.

9. Addressing group issues

Whilst the GCBT therapists are like skilled teachers, the analogy becomes misleading if the therapist is concerned simply to 'get through the syllabus and get those who remain the highest grades'. The therapeutic task is to address the group issues without allowing them to significantly encroach on the group session; for example, the therapist might allow a brief discussion about whether the session should be scheduled 30 minutes earlier or later. In some instances the group issue might first have to be addressed in an individual session with the affected group member, for example where one member has allegedly breached another's confidentiality. This might lead to the importance of confidentiality being stressed at the next group session. The therapist should engage collaboratively in helping a group member problem solve difficulties; for example, a GCBT leader might be informed by a group member that another member of the group is being over-familiar and the leader would be guided by the individual as to whether they should say anything to the 'offender' or whether the issue might be dealt with more generally by the leader stating that it is usually best to get over the disorder first in order to have the proper space for a new relationship. In some instances the therapist might place a possible group issue on the agenda for discussion, for example if typically two or three members out of a group of six attend regularly, with one or two members attending occasionally and one very rarely.

The competences involved in presentational skills within a group session are summarised in Table 3.9 (an extract from the GGTSRS, Appendix D).

Table 3.9 Addressing group issues

0	Therapist did not address any group issues that arose, such as timing of the group, number of sessions, difficulties in scheduling individual sessions, conflicts between group members, confidentiality, ambivalence about attendance, dropouts, ending of group and relapse
2	Therapist did address some group issues but was unnecessarily defensive
4	Therapist addressed most difficulties expressed by group members in a spirit of openness
6	Therapist addressed all group issues in a collaborative way with group members engaging them in a problem solving process

The group issues are not necessarily confined to the clients; it may be that there are issues between the leader and co-leader, for example a co-leader in a struggle for dominance scoring points off the leader, or the co-leader not setting SMART (specific, measurable, achievable, realistic targets, time frame) goals for homework. For the sake of group cohesion, difficulties between a leader and co-leader are best addressed away from the group session. It may be necessary, particularly if the therapists have never worked with each other in a group, to decide beforehand on the division of labour in presenting material. It is usually better for the therapists to sit opposite each other in the group, giving not only a more comprehensive field of view but allowing each to use a prearranged signal such as rubbing of chin to indicate that they would like input from the other because they are stuck as to how to respond.

If it is felt that one group member is dominating the group and this is having a deleterious effect on other group members, for example some group members are not contributing at all, the therapists can suggest a five-minute break for a 'cup of tea' and ensure one or other therapist sits next to the 'difficult' group member when they reconvene – this often has a moderating influence. The leaders need also to take stock and identify who may have been 'offended' by the miscreant and involve them.

The individual sessions at the beginning of the group programme are an ideal opportunity to nip 'bad behaviour' in the 'bud' by reiterating group rules about respect. Further, the therapist can question whether the particular behaviour, e.g. blocking the view of another group member in a heated exchange with one of the therapists or criticism of another member, is conducive to group cohesion – the group achieving its goals. The individual sessions can also be used to check with other group members the impact of high levels of emotion or criticism and secure agreement about what steps will be taken in future to circumvent this.

Use of the GGTSRS

The GGTSRS serves not only as a reminder of necessary general group therapeutic skills but can be used in supervision to indicate a therapist's strengths and weaknesses. Feedback using the GGTSRS should improve skills. In using the original Cognitive Therapy Rating Scale, therapists have often been judged as competent if they scored an average of at least 2.5 on the items that comprised the scale. Whilst such a procedure could be applied to the GGTSRS, it should be stressed that this rating scale has only face validity at this time as its predictive ability remains to be demonstrated.

Harnessing group power

A number of constructs have been distilled in an attempt to capture the active ingredients in group processes: climate (the atmosphere of a group), cohesion (a sense of belonging) and empathy (a sense of being understood) (Johnson et al. 2005). But different researchers have measured these constructs in different ways with unsurprisingly mixed results. Oei and Browne (2006) assessed the influence of group processes on clinical outcomes of clients with anxiety and depression following GCBT. Five group variables were measured: cohesion, leader support, expressiveness, independence and self-discovery, but only expressiveness and independence related to outcome. In a study by Ryum et al. (2009) utilising Free's (2007) GCBT manual for a mixed depression and anxiety disorders group, they used the Group Climate Questionnaire-Short Form (GCQ-S; MacKenzie 1983), which consists of three subscales: (a) Engagement (which includes items on self-disclosure, cognitive understanding and confrontation; (b) Avoidance – to what extent the group member avoids responsibility for their change process; and (c) Conflict – measures interpersonal conflict and distrust between group members as well as withdrawal. Whilst ratings on Engagement and Avoidance predicted status at 1-year follow-up, ratings of Conflict were unrelated to all follow-up scores. Engagement was regarded by these researchers as synonymous with cohesion.

Pathways to changing cognition

In CBT the advocated change strategies are principally via cognition (thoughts/images) or behaviour. However, Beck (Alford and Beck 1997) has also recognised that cognition, behaviour, emotion and physiology interact with each other. Thus it is possible to change cognition by altering physiology with for example the prescription of medication, or by replacing one emotion such as depression with another such as anger. An individual can be regarded as an 'island' with four ports of entry – cognition, physiology, emotion and behaviour, and other people (family, friends, therapist, other group therapy members) can access the ports, greatly influencing the 'climate' on the 'island' and thereby the wellbeing of the individual. Indeed the pressing need of some clients is for appropriate 'climate change'. The situation is summarised in Figure 3.1; for ease of illustration the climate is shown as influencing the individual via the cognitive port but could equally be viewed as operating via any port.

From a CBT perspective, depression and the anxiety disorders are maintained by specific anxiogenic/depressogenic cognitions and behaviours. It then remains to be determined which 'climate' is the best or most cost-effective way of nullifying those factors that play a pivotal role in the development and maintenance of an individual's depression or anxiety disorder.

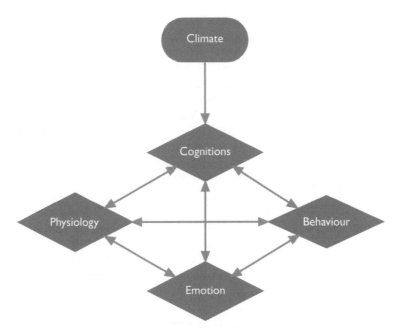

Figure 3.1 Intrapsychic and interpersonal determinants of emotion.

The synchronisation of GCBT

For GCBT to be effective, a necessary ingredient is a synchrony between the content of the programme and the diagnostic status of the individual; however, by itself this may be insufficient for a positive therapeutic outcome. The individual characteristics of the client, e.g. a highly autonomous individual, may sabotage this synchrony. Further, the synchrony may be sabotaged if the group leader does not have the group skills to ensure that each individual's needs are addressed sufficiently and 'toxic' influences from other group members are short-circuited and benign influences enhanced. The determinants of effective outcome are summarised in Figure 3.2.

Figure 3.2 makes it clear that the outcome of GCBT is not only a product of therapist endeavours. The interactions of clients can also make a difference and not only within the group session; these interactions can occur as the group is assembling or over coffee as people are departing. To a degree GCBT is something like a dance class, with leader and co-leader modelling behaviours and clients being asked to practise those behaviours; their successes, however limited, are praised and their difficulties problem solved. In some instances it is as if one member of the class takes another member to a side room and demonstrates a 'step'. Just as people are unlikely to continue to attend a dance class unless there is the right atmosphere, and a sense of humour, so too with GCBT.

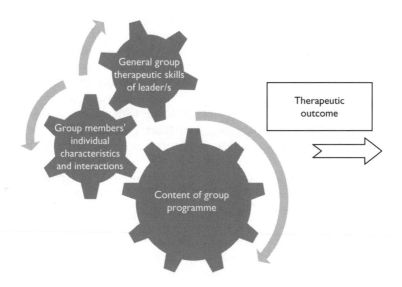

Figure 3.2 The determinants of effective GCBT.

Getting Started

Each group programme begins with the leader and co-leader introducing each other. The leader indicates the items on the agenda for that session (Table 3.10).

Table 3.10 Agenda for Session 1

1 Working arrangements
2 Introductions
3 Group Survival Manual
4 Other Survival Manuals
5 Self-help book
6 Explaining the disorder, outlining what can be done
7 Setting homework

The leader indicates that group members can bring up any pressing problems, but that time on them might be limited in order to get through the agenda. The leader makes it clear that the primary focus of the group is on a particular disorder and that any additional disorder/problems would be primarily addressed by a combination of individual face-to-face and telephone/e-mail contact between sessions and bibliotherapy.

The first item on the agenda, 'Working arrangements', embraces all the practical arrangements, e.g. tea/coffee from 15 minutes before session and at end of session, places to park, transport, but also includes an explanation of the rules that have to be kept to in order to ensure the group is viable, such as starting exactly on time and finishing by a prescribed time and importantly the issue of confidentiality, asking group members not to give any identifying details of any other member to others outside the group.

The leader and co-leader model introduce each other to the group, preferably with some humour, e.g. 'he/she is a good therapist and is almost human except for being a Manchester United supporter'. Group members are then asked to have a two-minute dialogue with the group member to their right, ask them their name and something about them, e.g. the area in which they live, how they spend their day, and each introduces the other to the group.

The introductions often result in some norming, e.g. a group member saying 'he/she comes from X as well' or 'he/she is a Manchester United supporter as well', and are a useful ice breaker. The Survival Manuals, Appendices H–M, provide a rationale for the development and main-tenance of each disorder and detail both the materials the therapists intro-duce and the handouts given to group members. It is recommended that sections of the Manual be given out as the material becomes pertinent to highlight its relevance to what is being taught and to ensure that the client has a tangible reminder of the new subject matter. To further ensure that the material is being centrally processed group members are asked to write their answers to questions posed in each section and are invited to discuss their responses in the group. Thus the 'you' questions in the Manual are both singular and plural.

Clients' comorbid disorders can be addressed using the disorder-specific manuals for CBT guided self-help (CBTgsh) via a combination of at least one face-to-face session and between-session contact by telephone and/or e-mail. The Manuals (Appendices H–M) also constitute workbooks for all clients. They are termed 'Survival' Manuals to indicate to the client that post-treatment they are likely to have an ongoing vulnerability to the disorder and likely will need recourse to the Manual to stop slips from becoming full-blown relapses.

For most disorders a self-help book can be recommended and ideally there should be 'library copies' of these texts available to members. The first session ends with the setting of homework pertinent to the principal disorder from which the client suffers. The setting of homework is governed by the mnemonic 'SMART', i.e. the tasks must be specific, measurable, achievable, realistic and have a time frame – before the next session.

Chapter 4

Depression

At any point in time about 1 in 10 of the UK adult population is suffering from a mix of depression and anxiety. The prevalence rates for comorbid depression are 71 and 124 per 1,000 in males and females respectively; however, for depression alone the corresponding prevalence rates are 17 and 25 (NICE 2004). Thus only a minority of depression sufferers, 31% in a study by Zimmerman *et al.* (2008), have no comorbidity.

The ubiquity of depression makes heavy demands on therapeutic resources, and attention has shifted to GCBT as a possible cost-effective intervention. NICE (2009) in its draft guideline recommends that GCBT should be considered for those with minor (subthreshold) and mild to moderate depression. They point out that depression below the threshold in DSM-IV can be distressing and disabling, particularly if persistent. For a diagnosis of subthreshold depression the therapist would have had to satisfy themselves on the basis of all the available evidence, including the client's self-report, that during the previous two weeks they had been sad, down or depressed most of the day nearly every day (question 1 under the depression heading in the CBT Pocketbook, Appendix A) and/or had lost interest or pleasure in the things they usually enjoyed (question 2 under the depression heading in the CBT Pocketbook, Appendix A). There is no rigorous definition as to how many of the symptoms from questions 3 to 9 are needed, it is a question of gathering the overall functional impairment from the answers, but one to three symptoms (of questions 3–9) would need to be endorsed. DSM-IV places depression on a continuum of severity from minor depression, to mild depression (few, if any, symptoms in excess of the minimum five symptoms with only minor functional impairment), moderate depression (symptoms or functional impairment are between 'mild' and 'severe') and severe depression (several symptoms in excess of the minimum five symptoms and symptoms markedly interfere with functioning; with or without psychotic features). NICE (2009) also states that treatment should be based on a treatment manual which should be followed with regard to structure and duration and that staff should evaluate adherence and competence.

The cognitive behavioural model of depression

The most recent exposition of Beck's (2008) cognitive model of depression is summarised in Figure 4.1; in this work he also delineates the neuro-biological correlates of the model.

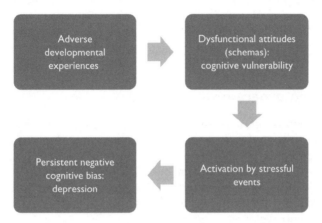

Figure 4.1 Beck's cognitive model of depression.

In Figure 4.1 early adverse events foster negative attitudes and biases about the self, which are integrated into the cognitive organisation in the form of schemas (templates for processing information). The schemas become activated by later adverse events impinging on the specific cognitive vulnerability. The events have to be congruent with the vulnerability, so that for example a sociotrope, whose sense of worth relies heavily on approval by others, might become depressed if they were rejected by others but not if they failed to achieve. Similarly an autonomous person whose sense of worth is based on achievement might become depressed if they fail to achieve but not if they were rejected by another person. The vulnerability may be likened to a lock which can be opened only by a particular key – a certain type of event. Or to put it another way, it is not the vulnerability per se that is a problem, it only becomes a problem in the presence of a matching event. Once the door to depression opens, a systematic negative bias operates. In Beck's model early traumatic experiences and the forma-tion of dysfunctional beliefs are predisposing events and congruent stressors in later life are precipitating factors.

The predisposing factors and precipitating events can be conceptualised as Beck has done at the micro level of individual attitudes and events but also as Champion and Power (1995) have done at a more macro level of roles and events. Champion and Power (1995) suggest that when a role has been overvalued, i.e. an individual has used the role to define their sense of worth, then an event that sabotages the continuance of that role may usher in depression.

In an earlier exposition of cognitive models of depression Beck (1987) presented an evolutionary model of depression, to explain the inactivity that is involved in depression. He suggested that from an evolutionary perspective depression was an attempt not to squander meagre resources.

The explanation of depression given to group members in the Depression Survival Manual, Appendix H focuses on the contributions of inactivity, negative spin (persistent negative bias) and the loss of valued role.

Depression programme

The depression programme outline is shown in Table 4.1. The material to be taught is in the form a client workbook, the Depression Survival Manual, Appendix H, and the particular sections covered in each session are indicated in the final column of Table 4.1. At the start of the programme clients are introduced to the self-help book *Feeling Good: The New Mood Therapy* by David Burns (1999) and asked to complete reading this in the first four weeks of the programme.

The full cast of the depression group that Natalie was involved in is summarised in Table 4.2

Sessions 1 and 2

After the introductions the leader and co-leader distributed the Depression Survival Manual, Appendix H, and the leader explained that it was group members own private workbook for getting through depression. The co-leader drew the group's attention to Figure 1, in Appendix H and suggested that depression often results from a combination of a loss of a valued role, say relationship or job, stopping investing in what may give a sense of achievement or pleasure and putting the most negative spin on everything. The following dialogue ensued at the start of the first session:

CO-LEADER: If a depressed person heard someone say 'that's a beautiful sunset', they would likely reply 'hmm, it's not going to last', that's an example of a negative spin.

SIMON: But they are right it is not going to last.

CO-LEADER: That is what makes negative spin difficult to deal with, there usually is some truth in it. It is a bit like when someone lies to you; if there is some truth in what they say it can take some time to find the truth of the matter.

MARGARET: Hmmm.

Table 4.1 Depression programme

	Therapeutic targets	*Treatment strategies*	*Materials – Depression Survival Manual, Appendix H*
Sessions 1 and 2	1. Depression about depression	Focus on responsibility for working on solutions and not on responsibility for problem	Section 1: How depression develops and keeps going and Section 2: No investments, no return
Sessions 1 and 2	2. Inactivity	Developing a broad investment portfolio, wide-ranging modest investments	
Sessions 3–5	3. Negative views of self, personal world and future	Challenging the validity, utility and authority by which views are held. Use of MOOD chart	Section 3: On second thoughts, and recap Sections 1 and 2
Sessions 6 and 7	4. Information processing biases. Dysfunctional attitudes	Highlighting personal biases and stepping around them using MOOD chart. Modifying dysfunctional attitudes	Section 4: Just make a start; Section 5: Expectation versus experience and recalling the positive; Section 6: Negative spin or how to make yourself depressed without really trying; 7: An attitude problem? Recap sections 1–3
Sessions 8–10	5. Overvalued roles	Valuing multiple roles, renegotiation of roles in social context	Section 8: My attitude to self, others and the future; Section 9: Be critical of your reflex first thoughts not how you feel. Recap sections 1–6
Sessions 9 and 10	6. Relapse prevention	Personally constructed Self-help 'manual', utilising key points from therapy and drawing on self-help books	Section 10: Preventing relapse. Recap sections 1–9

LEADER: Sorry, Margaret you were about to say something.

MARGARET: Oh nothing, it is just that I know someone who is a 'lying toad' and stupid me was taken in by him for a long time.

LEADER: That might be another example of negative spin, calling yourself stupid because you didn't spot the lie.

Table 4.2 Depression group members

Name	Thumbnail sketch
Natalie	Ruminates on marriage break-up, abuses alcohol, panic disorder and social phobia
Ian	Found work pressures as senior social worker impossible, off sick. No comorbid disorder
Margaret	Marriage strained, always been a worrier.
Simon	Made redundant, unable to get another job
Paul	Gymnastic teacher unable to work since injury
Colleen	Bullied at school, gay, self-harm, taken a year out at university because couldn't concentrate, lost part-time job. Panic disorder
Colin	Wife died suddenly of a brain haemorrhage, two of his adult children have left home, the third about to go to university
Sonia	Adult son has learning difficulties, worried about the future, social phobia

The above extract illustrates a synergy between the group leader and co-leader and the latter goes with the flow of a critical comment from a group member but uses it to underline the point that is being made about the pivotal role negative spin plays in depression. In terms of expressing the skills codified in the General Group Therapeutic Skills Rating Scale, Appendix D, the co-leader has kept to the agenda (item 1 of the GGTSRS) and the leader has locked on to an utterance of a group member to include (item 4 of the GGTSRS) her in the group but without pressing her to disclose more than she might wish. The session continued:

LEADER: We all put a negative spin on things from time to time, but the depressed person keeps on doing it, to such an extent that they become dizzy with the negative spin.

SIMON: So we keep lying to ourselves.

LEADER: Not exactly, it is more like you have decorated your room, a visitor comes and says how nice it is and you say 'yes but have you looked in this corner, the parts of these two flowers don't match up'.

SIMON: No problems like that in my flat, haven't decorated in years.

CO-LEADER: Are you like me, Simon, allergic to DIY, why do something yourself if you can get somebody else to do it?

SIMON: No, I used to like DIY, but I can't be bothered but then finances don't help since I was made redundant.

LEADER: This might be a good time to answer the questions under Figure 1 in your workbook; I guess Simon would put that he has stopped doing DIY and that he is put off doing it partly because of finances and partly because he can't be bothered.

SIMON: On the third question I wish I was on strike for better pay and conditions, at least I would have a job!

LEADER: If you look at Figure 1 the loss of a valued role, such as a job, often contributes to depression but so too does not investing your energy in anything because there can be no return. If you would take just a minute or two to write in your answers to the three questions that would be great.

In the above extract the leader continues further work on inclusion, by normalising negative spin and indicating that it is the excessive use of it in depression that causes the problem. The co-leader then picks up the theme of inclusion begun by the leader, by asking a group member whether they were alike in their distaste of DIY. In so doing the co-leader is also modelling self-disclosure, which is a major issue in social phobia and one of the comorbid disorders from which Natalie suffers. The leader shows good presentation skills (item 8 on the General Group Therapeutic Skills Rating Scale, Appendix D), not only making repeated reference to Figure 1, but ensuring that material was actively processed by having all members answer questions related to it in their workbook. The session continued:

IAN: I've never thought of it like that, but I suppose with my job I am on strike for better pay and conditions.

MARGARET: I suppose if I'm honest that is what I do in the marriage. He does his thing I do mine.

LEADER: A lot of depression arises when a person says to themselves I can't go on having business as usual, I've got to do a stocktaking, you've put a 'Closed for Refurbishment' notice up.

SIMON: But how long do you leave it up?

LEADER: I think the first step is not blaming yourself for putting the notice up in the first place, but as Simon indicates you can't leave it up for ever, 'it's bad for business'. But it is important not to get cross with yourself for getting depressed and to be responsible only for trying to work out better solutions. One of the first goals that people might consider is to have just one problem, depression, and not two problems, depression and depression about depression.

COLIN: I suppose I do blame myself for being depressed, the kids are virtually off my hands now, no financial worries, but I don't really do anything.

COLLEEN: That's like me; I have taken a year off from University, the others are getting their degree this year.

CO-LEADER: Sounds as if you are both at a crossroads, unsure of what investments to make, is it wrong to be unsure?

COLIN: I suppose none of us has a crystal ball, I didn't expect my wife to die without warning of a brain haemorrhage, just as we are about to have the freedom to do all sorts of things.

SIMON: But it is like I said before, how long can you go doing next to nothing?

LEADER: I think if you wait to be certain of an investment you wait forever, it is probably more important to try out a few things and see what happens. But getting started can be very difficult. It is like having a lead weight around your neck: to do anything is a major achievement and you have got to praise yourself for each little step. Take Simon for example: if he decided to decorate his flat he would probably be so irritable after twenty minutes with everything everywhere he might start slinging everything around and then feel guilty about the extra mess and go on permanent strike.

SIMON: You know me too well!

LEADER: If there is a task to do like say decorating, break it down into lots of little tasks, have a break after each small task, tick it off your list then do the next. Put all the small tasks in a queue outside of a turnstile, let one through at a time, complete it then have a break. Don't have an open door, doing lots of different tasks at the same time, if you do you will get totally stressed out.

IAN: I used to be able to juggle things all the time at work, now I just can't cope.

LEADER: Maybe a negative spin there Ian, maybe you can cope but just using a different method, a turnstile instead of an open door.

In the above extract the leader and co-leader are tracking client's concerns and difficulties to promote group cohesion but using them to illustrate the items on the agenda. One of the strengths of a group modality is that members can identify with each other, lessening the sense of isolation. A further advantage is that the exposition of the cognitive behavioural model of a disorder can be made less abstract by locating it as a solution to a particular group member's difficulty, as in the case of Simon above. Additionally this makes the teaching more relevant (item 2 on the General Group Therapeutic Skills Rating Scale, Appendix D).

About three-quarters of the way through the first session the group were asked to spend a few minutes answering the questions at the end of Section 1 of the Depression Survival Manual. They were then asked whether anything struck them from answering these questions and the following dialogue took place:

COLLEEN: Friends see me as great but I'm just putting on a front.

LEADER: One of the major things we will be looking at in future sessions is how we get a very different view of things depending on whose eyes we look through. For Colleen looking through her own eyes at herself, she felt pretty low but looking through others' eyes it is a different story. We will be looking at what is the most useful or valid story.

In the above extract the leader has used the dialogue to plant the seeds of the cognitive perspective. Towards the end of the first session the co-leader noticed that Natalie had not said a word throughout the session and in the interests of inclusion (item 4, on the GGTSRS) engaged her in the following exchange:

CO-LEADER: Natalie how do you feel about what we have been discussing today?

NATALIE: A bit down, I should be grateful for what I have got when I hear of others' difficulties.

CO-LEADER: I know what you mean, I feel like that when I see starving children on the TV, trouble is it doesn't last more than five minutes.

NATALIE: I've just got to get on and do things and leave off the blame.

CO-LEADER: Any other comments about today's session?

Natalie, whom we met in Chapter 2, was one of the nine clients scheduled to attend the depression group; she was additionally suffering from social phobia, panic disorder and alcohol abuse. Her ambivalence about attending the group and addressing her alcohol abuse were tackled using motivational interviewing in three individual sessions that took place prior to the group. It was decided that her social phobia and panic disorder would be addressed in the following ways: (a) she was given the Social Phobia Survival Manual/ workbook (Appendix K) and the Panic Disorder and Agoraphobia Survival Manual/workbook (Appendix I); (b) progress in the application of the additional Manuals would be monitored primarily by telephone contact and e-mail as the demands of work and domestic life precluded attendance at more than one further individual face-to-face session.

At the close of the first session the leader and co-leader negotiated individualised homework assignments. For example, although Margaret was, like other group members, asked to schedule in potentially uplifting events to her week and engage in events to give her a sense of achievement, in small doses, it was known that marital difficulties were a major problem for her and she was given the additional task of reading 'Restoring relationships', Chapter Seven in *Moving On After Trauma* (Scott 2008), and it was agreed the co-leader would briefly telephone her before the next session to see how she was getting on. Whilst it is the case that the majority of depressed clients treated with cognitive therapy respond to treatment, there is a lack of improvement in relationship satisfaction (Atkins *et al.* 2009) and ongoing relationship distress may be a risk factor for future relapse or recurrence of depression, hence the need to pay particular attention to this client's wider problem.

All group members were asked to begin reading the David Burns book *Feeling Good* (1999) and to complete the PHQ-9 (Kroenke *et al.* 2001), a measure of the severity of depression (this is freely available on the IAPT website, www.iapt.nhs.uk, for personal use); scores of 5, 10, 15 and 20 on the PHQ-9 represent cut points for mild, moderate, moderately severe and severe depression, respectively and can be used as benchmarks for a client's progress in therapy. The Dysfunctional Attitude Scale (Weissman and Beck 1978) can also be administered. It is a 40-item questionnaire designed to assess maladaptive cognitions including concern with evaluation, perfectionistic standards of performance, causal attributions and rigid ideas about the world. It is recommended that these measures are administered after each session to monitor progress, (Appendix F).

Post-mortem on Session 1

Although nine clients were due to attend the first session only seven turned up. It was agreed the co-leader would contact the non-attenders, and after the first session the co-leader telephoned them. One of the non-attenders, Sonia, said that her adult son who has learning difficulties was ill. At one level the co-leader thought this was reasonable but he wondered whether her non-attendance might also be related to her social phobia and the following exchange took place:

CO-LEADER: Do you think you might have been able to come along if it was just an individual session?
SONIA: I might have done, could have rearranged the time.
CO-LEADER: Is the thought of being in the spotlight getting to you?
SONIA: I think it is a bit.
CO-LEADER: You can say as much or as little as you want and I'll be there.
SONIA: He should be OK for next week, I'll give it a try then.

The above transcript illustrates the fluidity of motivation and the way in which clients can make apparently irrelevant decisions (AIDs) to circumvent engagement in group treatment. The often plausible AIDs need challenging but in the style of the TV detective Columbo of bemused/befuddlement, not in the manner of a barrister conducting a cross-examination. The second non-attender, Paul, had the following telephone conversation with the co-leader:

PAUL: I was in too much pain to attend the group.
CO-LEADER: How come?
PAUL: I think I had done too much yesterday when I went shopping with my wife. I was exhausted when I came home and irritable, then we had a massive row, because I hadn't let her know when it was too much.
CO-LEADER: So this morning was it the pain that stopped you coming to the group or that you were too fed up to bother after last night?
PAUL: Too fed up really.

CO-LEADER: How has not attending the group made you feel?

PAUL: I just feel that I have let you and everyone down.

CO-LEADER: One of the things we talked about in the group was the importance of investing and doing things and it sounds as if you have already made a good start on this by going shopping, but there are some special ways of pacing yourself with pain and I can give you some self-help material on this (Chapter 9 from *Moving On After Trauma*) and review how it works out. Would it be impossible to attend the next few sessions of the group and test out whether it had anything to offer?

PAUL: OK I'll come, thanks for your concern.

In this extract the co-leader is concerned to point out that though the prime focus is the depression group it is intended that the totality of the client's concerns will be addressed, i.e. that it will be totally relevant (item 2 of the GGTSRS).

Session 2

At the beginning of the second session the questionnaires were collected and inspected by the co-leader, with a particular focus on question 9 of the PHQ-9 which focuses on suicidal intent. No group member endorsed this item so no detailed individual discussion was scheduled on suicidal intent.

Before the start of the second session Sonia and Paul (the missing attendees) were asked by the co-leader if they would have a word with each other so they could introduce each to the group and they duly agreed. They were also each given Depression Survival Manuals, Appendix H. At the start of the session the leader welcomed them and they made the introductions. The leader then, with reference to the Depression Manual, briefly summarised what was taught at the first session and proceeded to ask the group how they had got on with their homework exercises. The session began:

SIMON: I made a start decorating, then my dad visited, poked his nose in, wanted to take over and we had a blazing row, after that I didn't bother.

LEADER: What stopped you carrying on after the argument with your dad?

SIMON: I couldn't settle.

LEADER: What was stopping you settling?

SIMON: It was when he said I could have done better than work in a bookshop, as if it was my ****** fault that the book chain closed down and I've not been able to get another job.

LEADER: Is it just with your dad that you go on strike when there is criticism?

SIMON: I just go so into myself when there is criticism.

IAN: That's like me in work when I was criticised by my boss for restricting the caseloads of the social workers under me because they are already overloaded, then I worry about unallocated cases.

SONIA: I've found Social Services useless finding proper Day Centre Care for my son with learning difficulties.

At this point the leader and co-leader notice Ian literally curl up and put his eyes down and there is a difficult pause broken by Sonia thus:

SONIA: *looking at Ian*, sorry I wasn't having a go at you, I just get so frustrated.

At this point the leader and co-leader feel they are walking a tight rope; on the one hand they want to encourage emotional expression so that relevant 'hot' issues are addressed but on the other hand there is a concern to minimise criticism (see item 6, General Group Therapeutic Skills Rating Scale, Appendix D). The leader moderates the level of expressed emotion by using the material to make a teaching point:

LEADER: It is well known that people who are prone to depression react badly if there is over-involvement like Simon's dad or if there is excessive criticism like Ian's boss [Hooley *et al.* 1986] and we are going to look at how you can focus your camera in such situations so that you are not out of the game.

SIMON: I just get cross with myself that I've let such a ***** get to me.

IAN: That's what I do, *laughing* I could even find myself going over and over what Sonia said even though I know she's not really having a go at me.

CO-LEADER: It seems like you are both addicted to approval, Simon and Ian, and that makes people vulnerable to depression, one of the things we want to look at in the programme is weaning off addiction to approval, but for now I would like to see how others got on with their homework.

The above extract illustrates the inevitable drift that occurs in GCBT, but it should be like that of a boat attached to its moorings, a return to the agenda and the using of 'off-task' material to flag up future learning points. The session continued:

COLIN: I did telephone a friend and he was pleased I rang, but I was going through the motions asking about football and thinking for ***** sake my wife is dead.

CO-LEADER: I think there is a lot of going through the motions before the taste of life returns and often it is something unexpected that lifts your mood.

PAUL: Yes I was pleased an old friend from schooldays contacted me and that lifted me but he wants to meet up sometime but I'm too embarrassed.

CO-LEADER: About what?

PAUL: Well if we go for a meal I can only sit for about 15 minutes with my injuries.

CO-LEADER: Are you bothered here getting up after 15 minutes?

PAUL: No.

CO-LEADER: Why would your school friend be bothered?

PAUL: Well he knew me the way I was a gymnast.

CO-LEADER: Would he think any less of you?

PAUL: No, I suppose it's me really.

LEADER: People often get depressed, like Paul when they lose a valued role like Paul being a gymnast.

IAN: I feel useless being off work.

SIMON: I feel useless not being able to get work, maybe we are just a bunch of losers.

COLLEEN: Sounds about right.

LEADER: It is easy to feel that way if you leave your camera on what hasn't worked out and there are clearly different things that haven't worked out for different people, but when you heard other people's stories did you think 'loser'?

NATALIE: No, when I heard what Sonia has been through, I think my God.

COLLEN: And me too.

IAN: Me too.

CO-LEADER: How do you mean?

IAN: Sonia has shown such commitment to her son, *at which Sonia wipes a tear away.*

SIMON: No, I don't think we are all losers.

LEADER: In depression you may be harder on yourself than most other people would be.

NATALIE: Hmm I think it is OK for Paul to get up and walk around but I'd be too embarrassed to keep getting up in a restaurant, in fact these days I will not even go in a café for a coffee.

CO-LEADER: Yes, we will give you some extra help for your 'spotlight' difficulties but it is great that despite them you have joined in today's session.

In the above extract the leader has addressed openly the group issue (item 9 of the General Group Therapeutic Skills Rating Scale, Appendix D) of whether the members are 'losers' and has helped cement alliances between group members by allowing them space to comment about each other. This sets the scene for other group members to become credible sources of persuasion. The therapists have again utilised material to flag up the cognitive components of the programme to be addressed later, whilst staying focused on the behavioural activity scheduling. In the second session the behavioural material was addressed further by reference to the Depression Survival Manual, Appendix H, asking group members to try and anticipate likely low spots in the week and schedule in specific activities to offset them. Further, group members were asked to track their mood using a 0–10 scale, where 10 is extreme distress, to see if their mood was any better if they were active. It was suggested they rate their mood and document their activity morning, afternoon and night using Table 4.3 and the ruler below:

Table 4.3 Activity and mood

0	1	2	3	4	5	6	7	8	9	10

No distress		Extreme distress

	Monday	Tuesday	Wednesday	Thursday	Friday	Saturday	Sunday
Morning 0–10 Activity							
Afternoon 0–10 Activity							
Evening 0–10 Activity							

At the end of the second session the co-leader was concerned that Colleen had participated little in the session and, given her previous self-harm, felt that an individual face-to-face session should be scheduled and at which her comorbid panic disorder could be addressed using the Panic Survival Manual. Colleen was pleased that an individual face-to-face session was scheduled. At this individual session Colleen brought up her fears that her bisexuality might mean she was not acceptable to the group. It was agreed to keep weekly telephone contact between group sessions for a few weeks to address these concerns and that thereafter she was free to make contact if self-harm was becoming an issue.

The leader and co-leader conducted a post-mortem after the second session and reviewed, using Table 3.2, the extent to which they were meshing the content of the programme with the individual characteristics of group members and utilising the general group therapeutic skills embodied in the General Group Therapeutic Skills Rating Scale, Appendix D.

Sessions 3–5

The third session begins with a focus on the Activity and Mood Forms, Section 2, Appendix H. The leader used these to recap what was taught at the previous session, noting that Margaret was particularly low on a Sunday afternoon, and the following exchange ensued:

LEADER: I notice that you felt particularly low on Sunday afternoon, Margaret.

MARGARET: It is always the same, I have looked at the papers, he's nodded off in the chair, I'm channel hopping; you would think with 80 stations that there would be something on.

LEADER: So your investment plan for Sunday afternoon was to do what you always do?

MARGARET: Yes.

LEADER: Does that work?

MARGARET: Well, no.

LEADER: What stops you doing something different?

MARGARET: You shouldn't have to, you should just be happy.

CO-LEADER: Who says so?

MARGARET: It is what being married is about.

NATALIE: It is what I thought marriage was about, but looking back we should have been doing things more, he used to ask me to go and play badminton but I've never been into sport.

MARGARET: *muttering* The only sport mine is into is 'playing away'.

NATALIE: What about visiting old friends?

MARGARET: I suppose we could do better than looking at the four walls.

The therapists have let the above exchange run its course to allow other group members to act as role models and therapists to each other (item 7, General Group Therapeutic Skills Rating Scale, Appendix D). The session continued:

NATALIE: I had a go at making cards again on Sunday afternoon but I kept getting interrupted by my daughter so I gave up.

CO-LEADER: How long did you do before you were interrupted?

NATALIE: About 20 minutes whilst she watched her DVD.

CO-LEADER: On your Activity and Mood Form you were pretty low on Sunday afternoon.

NATALIE: I just got so frustrated.

CO-LEADER: Maybe we can do slow motion action replays of the Sunday afternoon events to see if there are often different ways of thinking about upsets that are more helpful.

SIMON: Perhaps we should all go down to the **** River on a Sunday afternoon and throw ourselves in?

COLLEEN: If we do I am not throwing you a lifebelt!

IAN: It is OK Simon I'm quite a good swimmer.

SIMON: *with laughter* Just what I need – some **** rescuing me!

The therapists were pleased about the support shown by Natalie to Margaret and by Ian to Simon. However, the tone of Colleen's comment suggested irritation with Simon who despite the humour was probably struggling greatly and in many ways was not dissimilar to Colleen. Though the leader had intended by this stage in the third session to have begun psychoeducation on the pivotal role cognition plays in emotion, he chose to suspend this and address the sense of hopelessness expressed by Simon and probably also present with Colleen. Hopelessness has been found to be a major predictor of suicidal intent (see McMillan *et al.* 2007). The exchange continued:

LEADER: The water is probably very cold in the river! Sometimes it is useful to think of what has stopped us doing drastic things and remind ourselves of them, maybe even write them down.

NATALIE: I get like that sometimes but I just think of my daughter, I couldn't do that to her.

MARGARET: I never get quite that bad.

CO-LEADER: You can never be sure that good times will not happen again or that there will not be a good or improved relationship.

COLLEEN: Sometimes it is hard to keep going.

CO-LEADER: It is often a bit of a marathon with some surprises for good and bad.

SIMON: It is when the bad comes altogether you just want to give up.

CO-LEADER: One way of looking at it is to divide your life up into say 5 year chunks and look at how you were in those periods and ask yourself 'can I be sure one of the good chunks will not come again?'

SIMON: It was good at university, but I have had only dead end jobs since.

CO-LEADER: In depression people tend to remember the good things in a vague way; if you keep a diary of positive experiences you have greater access to them and can lift your mood. For homework I would like people to keep a diary of positive experiences and record a detailed account of them. There is an example given if you turn to Section 2 of the Depression Survival Manual, just for 2 minutes try and recall a similar example to it, *pause* Any comments?

PAUL: I remember with some friends putting a bench in the school swimming pool to see if it floated!

IAN: Delinquent! I was a good little boy at school!

In the above exchange the leaders have noted a possible group issue (item 9 of the General Group Therapeutic Skills Rating Scale, Appendix D), hopelessness, and addressed it. The co-leader has also used the opportunity to advocate detailed, graphic recall of ongoing positive experiences as an antidote to low mood; this has been part of the effective GCBT protocol, used by Bockting *et al.* (2005), to prevent relapse/recurrence in people who had suffered recurrent depression. This strategy also lightens the tone of the group, making for greater cohesion.

The new material for Sessions 3–5 is introduced using Section 3 of the Depression Survival Manual. Group members are asked to spend a few minutes completing the questions, and the leader then asks whether anything struck group members in answering the questions, resulting in the following dialogue:

SIMON: I nearly wasn't going to come this morning, but I'm better for being here, hearing of Paul's delinquency, than sitting at home

CO-LEADER: Does that often happen, where your first thoughts are that something is going to be awful but your experience turns out to be not that bad?

SIMON: I suppose it does.

CO-LEADER: What could you say to yourself next time when the exaggeratedly negative thoughts first spring to mind?

SIMON: This is a game I play on myself always assuming the worst.

CO-LEADER: So your second thoughts before next week's session could be 'stop assuming the worst'.

SIMON: Yes.

LEADER: But why do you assume the worst?

SIMON: So I am not disappointed.

LEADER: So it sounds as if part of your first thoughts before coming to the group are 'I can't be bothered, I will be disappointed' but the other part is something like 'I could not stand being disappointed'.

SIMON: Yes my first negative thoughts are a bit more involved than I would have thought.

LEADER: If you do a little bit of digging you usually find there is a little more to your first negative thought than you first thought, and you can only properly uproot it when it is fully exposed.

In this dialogue the therapists have attempted to use 'hot' cognitions, i.e. current cognitions about the present, to more powerfully explain cognitive restructuring. Further, the therapists have used metaphor to make explicit the need to clarify the reflex automatic negative thoughts before proceeding to develop appropriate second thoughts. The use of 'hot cognitions', metaphor and regular reference to a Survival Manual, are part of the Presentation Skills, coded in item 8 of the General Group Therapeutic Skills Rating Scale, Appendix D. The group are then introduced to the MOOD chart in the Survival Manual and members are taken through the two examples given in Appendix H.

In teaching any new skill the therapists first model the behaviour, invite a group member to try out the skill and feedback is given in which any approximation to the desired behaviour is praised and any shortfall is problem solved. The group member who attempts the skill can serve as a coping model for other group members and may lessen any perfectionism on the part of group members. This is illustrated in the following dialogue:

LEADER: My mood dipped on the way here this morning as I was driving and I thought, did I put the memory stick for this session in my bag? Felt panic, couldn't stop with traffic and would be late if I went home and thought it will be a mess if there are no visual aids. So in the first column of the MOOD chart, I could write panic driving here, in the second column I could write no memory stick, I'm going to make a mess of this. Can you guess what my second thoughts were, what I put in the third column?

SIMON: We are all such a lovely group they won't be bothered at all!

LEADER: *laughing* Hmm, not quite, it was more it would be good to have overheads but it is not the end of the world, everyone will have the Depression Survival Manual so it will not matter that much. In my mind I put that in the third column and in the fourth column I decided to carry on driving here and tolerate the uncertainty of not being sure I had put the stick in my bag. Any questions on that?

CO-LEADER: No, OK, so that second thoughts can be quite different, you could have thought along the lines that Simon indicated or look at it the way you did?

LEADER: Yes, there are different ways of taking a better photograph of the situation. One way is to ask 'how true are my first thoughts?', that is to question the *validity* of the thought, e.g. 'how true is it that I have forgotten my memory stick?' A second way is to ask 'how useful is this way of thinking?', that is to question the *utility* of the thought, e.g. 'how useful is it to keep agonising that I have forgotten it?' A third way is to ask 'who says I should look at this situation in this way?', that is to question the *authority* of the thought, e.g. 'who says I should be agonising about this, isn't it only me? So you can cross-examine your reflex automatic negative thoughts using validity, utility and authority.

CO-LEADER: Simon, if you were putting your thoughts about coming here today through the filter of the MOOD chart, what would you put in the different columns?

SIMON: I guess in the first column felt like ***** when I got up this morning, then in the second column, I just cannot be bothered getting ready to go the group, then in the third column I would put no point in sitting around all day in my flat moping, not sure that I decided to do anything, so don't know what I would put in the fourth column.

CO-LEADER: You have done the first three columns really great, any comments on what Simon could put in the final column?

IAN: Simon is here now so it sounds like he did decide, he didn't arrive by magic.

SIMON: Yes, I suppose I did decide.

CO-LEADER: It is a decision to do nothing or to do something.

MARGARET: Maybe Simon could decide not to swear all the time!

SIMON: *somewhat sheepishly* Sorry *a long silence which the leaders did not break allowing space for group processes to resolve the conflict.*

COLLEEN: Sometimes I'm so fed up with what is going on swearing is the only thing to do.

NATALIE: I think now and again is OK but not all the time.

In the above exchange the therapists have focused on a group issue, swearing (item 9 of General Group Therapeutic Skills Rating Scale, Appendix D), but using group processes to establish group norms rather than impose 'rules of the group', and in so doing have involved most group members (item 4 of the General Group Therapeutic Skills Rating Scale, Appendix D). In addition the leaders have utilised a group member as a coping (as opposed to masterful) role model (item 7 of the General Group Therapeutic Skills Rating Scale, Appendix D).

Locating a client's experience within the context of the Survival Manual helps reduce isolation and helps ensure that the Manual will be used as a resource post-treatment. It also has the advantage of not having to expound the content of the Manual in a somewhat abstract way, as the following exchange illustrates:

LEADER: Simon, I think maybe there is a picture of you, as you were getting up this morning, in Figure 5 of the Survival Manual.

SIMON: *looking at figure in Figure 5 with a ball and chain,* Ah yes, that's about it.

COLLEEN: I can see the resemblance, looks like a convict!

LEADER: Well depression is a bit like being held in a prison, the great thing is that Simon did something, coming here despite the ball and chain; you can see the gap between Simon's expectations and his experience in Figure 6 of the Manual. Once you know you have an expectation experience gap you can begin to take your expectations with a pinch of salt. Maybe think of expectations as a meal that you have to sprinkle salt on.

MARGARET: I put too much salt on everything.

CO-LEADER: Maybe it is just having a few special things that you put salt on like an expectation pie.

MARGARET: I see what you mean.

The above exchange illustrates that graphic use of metaphor can be a powerful teaching aid but it can need careful adapting (item 3 of the General Group Therapeutic Skills Rating Scale, Appendix D) for some clients who take the metaphor too literally. At the post-mortem following the third group session the leader and co-leader discussed how they had failed to bring Sonia into the exchanges in the group and they reflected that this might be in part because of her social phobia (difficulties in being in the spotlight) but also wondered whether the MOOD chart was in fact too abstract for her. It was agreed that the co-leader would utilise a pre-arranged telephone contact with regard to her social phobia to ask how she found the discussion of the MOOD chart and if necessary discuss an alternative (item 3, Adaptation of the General Group Therapeutic Skills Rating Scale, Appendix D). Sonia said that she had not really understood the MOOD chart and had switched off and had been thinking about how her son would manage if he had to attend a different Day Centre. The co-leader focused on this concern to illustrate a Stop! Think! strategy as an alternative to the MOOD chart. Sonia was asked whether dwelling on what might happen to her son had been useful and she replied that it hadn't, but just made her feel ill. The co-leader suggested that instead of using the MOOD chart, when there was a worry, imagine herself as a tortoise and when she spots the worry tell herself to STOP, pull her head inside the shell telling herself to THINK it out properly, then pop her head out again and get on with doing, don't stay in the shell agonising, just think it out, then move on. Sonia reflected that she had spent the whole of the last session in her shell. The co-leader said that at the next group session the STOP! THINK! strategy would be mentioned as an alternative to the MOOD chart; the co-leader was thereby addressing the issue of inclusion (item 4 of the General Group Therapeutic Skills Rating Scale, Appendix D) with regard to Sonia.

Sessions 6 and 7

These sessions address the information processing biases that can serve to perpetuate depression. The sessions begin, as with the previous sessions, with a review of homework, and the sixth session began as follows:

PAUL: I am finding it really useful using the MOOD charts for the dips in my mood, I upset myself over the stupidest things.

LEADER: Lots of depression is a snowball of minor hassles, one minor thing upsets you like being late because you could find nowhere to park, then you might think people weren't really listening to what you said, then your partner might make you a cup of coffee instead of the tea you asked for, you get angry, your partner gets angry and you go to bed very depressed but then you are even more depressed because nothing really bad has happened that day to justify being low, depression about depression.

PAUL: Have you been in my house?

SONIA: I think you have been in my house as well!

CO-LEADER: It's really a question of getting yourself to STOP and THINK after each hassle, you do this by imagining you are a tortoise and something happens like getting a cup of coffee instead of tea, you are about to take off, you tell yourself STOP!, pull your head in the shell and THINK, 'is it really the end of the world that my son has brought me coffee?', then put your head out again and go and make the cup of tea. You can use the 'tortoise' or the MOOD chart after each hassle to stop things escalating.

PAUL: My mood has been better during the day using the MOOD chart, but it is still taking me hours to get to sleep.

LEADER: Do you use the MOOD chart as you are trying to get to sleep?

PAUL: No, you can't be writing it down as you are trying to get to sleep.

LEADER: I agree certainly in the last 30 minutes before you go to sleep you would not be writing things down, but you could use the same framework just mentally.

PAUL: I suppose I could, I think when I'm going to bed I'm thinking I'm 'off-duty' deserve a break and don't have to use the MOOD chart.

LEADER: The MOOD chart or tortoise is like a filter in a water purification system, it has to be used all the time if you are not going to get ill.

IAN: It's remembering to be bothered all the time.

CO-LEADER: It is an effort, and to do anything with depression is a major achievement but if you choose not to bother with the 'bottled water' you will be ill. If you are not asleep in 30 minutes, most people get annoyed with themselves and this makes sleep even more difficult, so just get up and only go back to bed when you are really tired.

In the above dialogue the therapists have continued to use metaphors such as 'tortoise', 'water purification system', 'bottled water' to explain basic cognitive behavioural principles and have avoided unnecessary abstractions, mindful of the varying capacities of group members to handle such material. So far in the group programme the focus has been on identifying and modifying the content of maladaptive cognitions. In Sessions 6–8 the focus shifts to helping group members identify their characteristic ways of putting a bias (negative spin) on information processing. The group's attention is drawn to the Depression Survival Manual, Table 2, Information processing biases, in Appendix H, which details ten ways in which a person might be biased. Any one person is likely to characteristically use two or three of the biases. It seems likely that a person who is depressed uses their particular biases more habitually than their non-depressed counterparts and that it is not the case that the latter are free from biases. After running through the content of Table 2, the following dialogue took place:

LEADER: Perhaps we could look at one of the situations that you filtered through the MOOD chart and inspect it further to see if one or more of these ten biases was operating. I noticed on the MOOD chart you handed in, Margaret, there was a problem over the three piece suite that you had delivered, is it OK if we put that situation under the microscope and see what we come up with?

MARGARET: Fine, no problem.

LEADER: Would you tell the group what happened.

MARGARET: Well I had a three piece suite delivered, waited 6 weeks for it, when it arrived my husband said how great it looked and I said 'hope so, I wonder can we keep it clean it is so light?' My husband then got annoyed with me for moaning and I stormed out of the house and didn't speak for days.

NATALIE: Did you choose the suite together?

MARGARET: Yes, we were fine about it.

CO-LEADER: Any offers as to which of these biases might have been operating?

IAN: I think it is the second one in Table 2, mental filter, Margaret has focused on the negative, the suite might get easily dirty, ignoring the positive that it was probably great to finally have a nice suite.

NATALIE: Margaret you have done what I used to do with my ex, storm out.

COLLEEN: Maybe there is also some Jumping to Conclusions, no point in staying in and discussing it with him, never get anywhere.

SONIA: At least he did go with you Margaret to choose the suite in the first place, my ex never did anything, as soon as he found my son had learning difficulties he was off.

LEADER: Sonia has given a clue to another bias that might be operating.

PAUL: Looks like magnification and minimisation; Margaret has minimised her husband's good points and magnified his failings, the criticism.

MARGARET: Now I feel really stupid; mental filter, jumping to conclusions, magnification and minimisation, I've probably done all ten!

CO-LEADER: But what bias might your husband have used as well?

MARGARET: He has jumped to conclusions that I was 'moaning', I wasn't.

CO-LEADER: When two people are both using the biases, it is like sloshing petrol on a fire and communication training is useful to stop them both worsening a situation; there are some communication guidelines in *Moving On After Trauma* that you might want to read, Margaret, and I'll give you a ring to see if you find them helpful.

MARGARET: Fine.

LEADER: Earlier when Margaret said 'I've probably done all ten', which of the negative spins do you think she was using?

SIMON: I think number 3, personalisation, I've made mistakes using at least three biases so it is all my fault. I must admit I used personalisation when Margaret criticised me for swearing, after the session I was very low.

MARGARET: I'm sorry I didn't mean to.

SIMON: It's OK I shouldn't personalise it when there is a criticism, you were just pointing out a mistake of mine.

LEADER: Do you use Personalisation in any other situations?

SIMON: Yes probably with my dad. I think I'm still like a child wanting his approval.

SONIA: You are a big softie inside.

SIMON: Thanks, I'll take that as a compliment.

LEADER: For homework when you are using the MOOD chart, run through Table 2 to see if you are using any of the biases, and then step around them. The biases are fairly ingrained, you can't stop them popping up but if you are aware of them you can make sure that they do not have the last word.

Sessions 8–10

The new material introduced in these sessions focuses on the clients' underlying assumptions/core beliefs (it can be introduced slightly earlier if time allows). Depressogenic cognitions are reflected in the Dysfunctional Attitude Scale (DAS, Weissman and Beck 1978), which should be administered after each session. Group members' attention is drawn first to Section 7 of the Depression Survival Manual, 'An attitude problem?', Appendix H, and in essence the cognitive vulnerability model of depression is described. However, the model is simplified by reference to a visual aid and a description of the interaction of key event/s and past attitudes as often being the springboard for today's upset. Group members are invited to discuss the extent to which they see themselves as a sociotrope, autonomous, perfectionist and excessively rigid. The group responded as follows to Section 7 of the Depression Survival Manual:

NATALIE: That is me, I thought I was just daft bending over backwards to please everyone, exhausting myself, but now I know I am a 'sociotrope'!

SIMON: Well you might be a daft sociotrope!

COLLEEN: You are all heart, Simon!

LEADER: Using the MOOD chart, Natalie, if your mood dipped when you were called 'daft', your first thoughts might be 'he thinks I am daft, he doesn't like me, it's terrible'. But recognising your addiction to approval, for objective thinking you might put what?

NATALIE: Maybe, 'not everyone's approval is important, it is only Simon'.

SIMON: Thank you, Natalie, anyway you would be using Jumping to Conclusions if you thought I did not like you just because I though you were daft.

NATALIE: Oh, you do like me then?

IAN: Let's not go there!

NATALIE: Looking at Table 3, the other one I do is excessively rigid, I always had the idea of wanting to be happily married, now I think there was nothing wrong in that but my mistake has been turning it into a 'must'.

COLLEEN: I think 'excessively rigid' has been a problem for me, 'I have got to be just like others, not bi-sexual', I have got to accept me and just work out the difficulties as best I can.

LEADER: If you are weighed down by a poor opinion of yourself, you may try to lift it as in Figure 8 in the Depression Survival Manual by being a sociotrope or a perfectionist or highly autonomous or very rigid but these characters can only lift it temporarily. The rigidity might be expressed by not just valuing a role, for example Natalie wanting her marriage to work out, but overvaluing it 'it hasn't worked out so I'm nothing'. One way or another all roles pass and it's therefore a problem if we use them as 'proof' of our worth.

SIMON: It's easy for you to say when you have got a job.

PAUL: I can't teach gymnastics now, but I can still be a worthwhile person.

SIMON: How do you mean?

PAUL: Well, I've just started learning sign language as part of a Signing Choir of deaf and not deaf people, it's good fun.

SIMON: And that pays the bills?

PAUL: No, but there are no pockets in a shroud.

SIMON: Point taken.

The above dialogue illustrates one of the strengths of GCBT in that other group members can become more credible sources of persuasion than the therapist, but have to be given the space to be so, item 7 of the General Group Therapeutic Skills Rating Scale, Appendix D. Again throughout these sessions the therapist's presentation skills (item 8 of the General Group Therapeutic Skills Rating Scale, Appendix D) have been enhanced by reference to and explication of the members' own Survival Manual. Importantly the new material is integrated with previous material (e.g. MOOD charts), thus reinforcing the significance of the latter. Some group members tend to fade into the background in a group more than others and it is particularly useful for these (item 4 of the General Group Therapeutic Skills Rating Scale, Appendix D) to ask all group members to take a few minutes to work through Section 8 of the Survival Manual to obtain a better understanding of the historical origins of their negative view of themselves and perhaps others and to begin to consider alternative perspectives on themselves and others. After a few minutes silence, the leaders noticed that a member was crying and the following exchange took place:

CO-LEADER: Are you OK, Sonia?

SONIA: *through tears* Yes I'm fine.

MARGARET: *leaning over and holding Sonia's hand* You're not, love.

CO-LEADER: Sometimes when we go back to how we came to look at ourselves negatively, it's like we are back there not just remembering it and it can be quite upsetting.

SONIA: I just remember a teacher telling me the best I could hope for was to work in a shop and I have felt stupid ever since and stupid for marrying my son's father, my mother warned me against him.

MARGARET: *still holding Sonia's hand* It's easy to be stupid over men.

NATALIE: Tell me about it!

COLLEEN: *laughing* That's why you should try women as well.

SONIA: *laughing* I might pass on that! I'm stupid for getting upset.

LEADER: The next section of the Depression Survival Manual that I wanted the group to focus on is Section 9 and Sonia, it's about not criticising yourself for what you feel or how upset you get but just criticise the first thoughts that lead to the upset. If we take a few minutes to read through Section 9 and if anyone has comments it would be great to hear them.

In this exchange the therapists have recognised that historical material can produce powerful affect and have not restricted the expression of emotion. Nor have the therapists rushed to the rescue, allowing instead the group cohesion and members of the group with greater credibility to provide support. Section 9 also introduces the idea that it is not upset per se that is a problem but the evaluation of it, i.e. the problem is more meta-cognitive than cognitive, albeit that this somewhat technical language is probably best avoided. Figure 12, in Section 9, is used to illustrate that a client's acceptance of their emotional state is the first step out of depression, but acceptance is not the same as resignation and further steps are then taken culminating in investing in life. In many ways Figure 12 is a summary of the main points that have been made in the programme.

Finally the group is asked to address Section 10 of the Depression Survival Manual, 'Preventing relapse', and to spend a few minutes quietly running through it before any questions about it are discussed in the group. After a couple of minutes the following exchange took place:

NATALIE: When I was doing Figure 13, I put an early warning sign for me is drinking.
CO-LEADER: How is drinking fitting into your life now?
NATALIE: I just don't.
CO-LEADER: Because . . .
NATALIE: I look at my daughter and I'm not going to ruin her life.
CO-LEADER: How would you handle any slips?
NATALIE: Contact my friend Angie.
CO-LEADER: What if you began to get depressed but you weren't drinking?
NATALIE: Again, contact Angie, I might even pester some of the group.
MARGARET: That would be great Natalie.
SIMON: Me as well Natalie.

The final treatment session is best arranged for about a month after the penultimate session, allowing group members greater opportunity to test out their new-found skills and to gradually let go of the group. At the same time the final session gives a further opportunity to refine skills and is seen as something of a safety net.

During these sessions arrangements are made to formally reassess each group member individually using the CBT Pocketbook. Clients who have not recovered from their depression should be offered individual CBT.

Concluding comments

GCBT for an anxiety disorder appears much more common than for depression. It may be that sufferers from depression are more reluctant to join a group than anxiety sufferers but the author knows of no empirical evidence on this and it is not his clinical experience. The answer may be that therapists feel that a group of depressed clients is a much more daunting challenge than a group of anxious clients, fearing that they will be weighed down by the experience. In the author's experience certainly the first session or two can be heavy, but once past this, as I hope the above transcripts indicate, it can be a lot of fun as well as importantly offering effective help to a greater number of depressed clients.

Chapter 5

Panic disorder and agoraphobia

The essence of panic disorder is a 'crescendo of fear' (ICD-10; World Health Organization 1992) occurring unexpectedly. Many anxiety sufferers, such as clients with generalised anxiety disorder, suffer from periods of heightened anxiety, but the distinguishing feature of panic attacks is that symptoms reach a peak within ten minutes of experiencing the first symptoms (see CBT Pocketbook, Appendix A, which directly accesses each of the symptom criteria for the condition in DSM-IV-TR [American Psychiatric Association 2000]). Although panic attacks are a necessary feature of panic disorder, panic attacks are not on their own enough to make the diagnosis. Panic attacks may happen in the context of specific situations such as social or specific phobias which are different from panic disorder. Panic disorder is classified by the DSM-IV-TR (American Psychiatric Association 2000) as recurrent, unpredictable panic attacks followed by at least a month of persistent concern about having another panic attack, worry about the consequences of the panic attacks or a significant behavioural change related to the attacks. In DSM-IV-TR agoraphobia is construed as an attempt to avoid situations in which panic attacks may occur rather than as a separate diagnosable condition. Without a reliable diagnosis of panic disorder, clients with other anxiety disorders can be inappropriately treated with a panic disorder protocol.

In DSM-IV-TR (American Psychiatric Association 2000) at least 4 of a possible 13 symptoms, e.g. sweating, shaking, fear of losing control, are required for a diagnosis of panic disorder; clients with fewer than the 4 symptoms are described as having limited symptom panic attacks. The likelihood is that the panic disorder protocol described in this chapter would also be applicable to many clients with limited symptom panic attacks.

The lifetime prevalence of panic disorder is 1–3% and panic disorder is more common in women than men (Weissman *et al.* 1997). The onset of panic disorder tends to be preceded by stressful life events. For example, Scocco *et al.* (2007) found that 38.2% of a sample of 55 panic disorder clients with or without agoraphobia had suffered the loss of a relative or significant other in the year preceeding the onset of panic disorder. In the

Scocco *et al.* (2007) study 92.7% had experienced a role transition and 74.5% a role dispute in the year before onset of the panic disorder. Interestingly 85.5% of the Scocco *et al.* (2007) sample reported inadequate or no close relationships in the year before the onset of the panic disorder. There may therefore be an added unintentional value of GCBT for panic disorder in that it helps sufferers restore their connectedness.

Panic disorder is associated with an increased rate of attempted suicide, with one study (Gorman and Coplan 1996) finding that it occurred in 20% of people with panic disorder, compared with 12% of people with panic attacks alone, and 6% of those with other psychiatric disorders. This highlights the need for a thorough risk assessment (see *Simply Effective Cognitive Behaviour Therapy*, Scott 2009). Reliable diagnosis involves the accurate identification of any coexisting disorders. Comorbid disorders are common for panic disorder; for example about 40% of panic disorder clients also suffer from depression (Zimmerman *et al.* 2008). It is suggested that such comorbid disorders are best addressed in the adjunctive individual sessions/contacts to the group programme.

CBT protocols do not produce remission for all. Approximately 20–40% of clients with panic disorder are classified as non-responders in randomised controlled trials, but group CBT (GCBT) appears more cost effective than individual CBT (ICBT) (Roberge *et al.* 2008). In a study of GCBT by Schmidt *et al.* (2000), 57% of those undergoing GCBT met recovery criteria by a 12-month follow-up.

The cognitive behavioural model of panic disorder

The original model of panic disorder was developed by Clark (1986) (Fig. 5.1). The panic cycle is initiated by an awareness of a cue that might be either external, e.g. the person finds themselves in a confined space, or internal, e.g. heart racing, and if this is perceived as dangerous then, going clockwise around Figure 5.1, apprehension or fear occurs, which is in return reflected in a variety of bodily sensations (e.g. light-headedness, sweating). If these sensations are interpreted catastrophically, e.g. as a sign of imminent collapse, then the perception of threat is heightened, setting up a vicious circle. The perception of threat and the catastrophic misinterpretation can occur at a non-conscious level as in the case of nocturnal panic attacks.

However, Salkovskis *et al.* (1996) observed that clients suffering from panic attacks appear not to learn from their experience; for example, though fearful of fainting in a panic attack the client does not draw on their experience that they have never fainted in a panic attack. Salkovskis *et al.* (1996) suggested that this failure to learn arises from a sufferer's engagement in safety behaviours, e.g. sitting down when feeling faint; in this way there is no opportunity to disconfirm the negative prediction. Thus, for

Trigger stimulus
(internal or external)

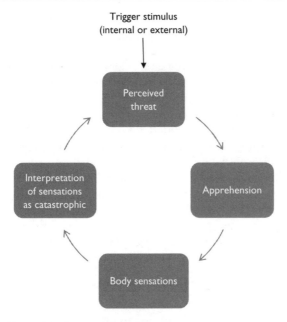

Figure 5.1 Clark's model of panic disorder.

example, the client does not learn that feeling faint in a panic attack does not lead to fainting. The more complete cognitive model therefore involves the inclusion of the reciprocal interaction of safety procedures and the interpretation of sensations as catastrophic (Figure 5.2).

Reiss and McNally (1985) have proposed that sufferers from panic disorder may have a pre-existing set of beliefs about the harmfulness of symptoms, (anxiety sensitivity) that predispose them to panic disorder. They argue that it is this anxiety sensitivity that determines whether a person will experience panic in the wake of bodily sensations. Elevated

Figure 5.2 Extension of Clark's model by Salkovskis.

levels of anxiety sensitivity are hypothesised to emerge from a variety of experiences, e.g. hearing others express fear of such sensations, witnessing the fatal heart attack of a loved one.

Barlow and Cerny (1988) have taken a somewhat different perspective on the development of panic attacks, viewing them as 'false alarms' issued by the body in response to a cue or signal that the client has learnt to associate with danger or threat. The treatment approach of Barlow and his colleagues, Panic Control Treatment (Craske, Barlow and Meadows 2000), focuses on increasing the tolerance of panic symptoms by artificially inducing them – interoceptive exposure. By contrast the Clark and Salkovskis treatment approach focuses on the relinquishing of safety behaviours and more appropriate appraisal of bodily sensations. It seems likely that each of the treatments works by reducing anxiety sensitivity but does so in different ways. The treatment approach taken in this chapter draws on both the Clark (1986) and Barlow (Craske *et al.* 2000) protocols.

Panic disorder and agoraphobia programme

Clients with panic disorder and agoraphobia can present with additional diffficulties in attending a group programme, in that some may wish to be placed near a door, have a door or window open, have ready access to a toilet or immediate access to bottled water or very occasionally a person will only attend with a trusted relative/friend. Whether a client has these special requirements should be canvassed before attending the group so that any necessary arrangements can be made. These 'special requirements' are in many ways the client's 'safety procedures' and the client's perceived 'arm-bands' for 'keeping afloat' in the sessions. In the interest of engaging the client and of the therapeutic alliance, whatever 'arm-bands' are clearly necessary to ensure attendance should be allowed, but they would also be therapeutic targets. These 'special requirements' are a rich opportunity to tackle 'safety procedures' by accessing the 'hot' cognitions that obtain when the client is in situations that may trigger a panic attack. Panic disorder clients often know that their catastrophic cognitions, e.g. my heart racing means I am going to have a heart attack, are untenable when they are not having an attack but believe the catastrophic cognitions during an attack. It is therefore important to help clients challenge their catastrophic cognitions experientially by in-vivo and interoceptive exposure.

Clients who have had a heart attack are probably best excluded from the group programme and should be treated individually excluding interoceptive exposure exercises. Clients who have had a heart attack may understandably scan their bodies more than others for unusual bodily sensations thereby easily mistaking a panic attack for a heart attack. But clients who have had a heart attack are usually offered Cardiac Rehab at which it is explained that any one individual's heart attack usually takes the same form in subsequent attacks and that therefore if their current attack differs markedly from their original attack it is unlikely to be a heart attack. But if there is doubt Hospital Services are happy to re-examine those concerned.

The material to be taught is in the form of a client workbook, the Panic Disorder and Agoraphobia Survival Manual (Appendix I), and the particular sections covered in each session are indicated in the final column of Table 5.1.

The cast of the panic disorder and agoraphobia group is summarised in Table 5.2.

The severity of agoraphobic avoidance can be gauged using the agoraphobia subscale of the Fear Questionnaire (Marks and Mathews 1979), which asks on a scale 0–8, where 8 is always avoid, how much the person avoids: travelling alone or by bus, walking alone in busy streets, going into crowded shops, going alone far from home and in large open spaces. This yields a total score of 0–40 (Section 6 Appendix I, Panic Disorder and Agoraphobia Survival Manual). This information, integrated with interview data, is used to form a judgement about the severity of agoraphobic avoidance, which can range on a continuum from no changes in behaviour because of panic attacks, mild agoraphobic avoidance, moderate agoraphobic avoidance, to severe agoraphobic avoidance where the sufferer/client is totally unable to go out alone. The clients in GCBT for panic disorder usually have varying degrees of agoraphobic avoidance, see Table 5.2. The progress of group members can be charted at each session using the Panic Disorder Severity Scale (Shear et al. 1997) for panic disorder or Fear Questionnaire (Marks and Mathews 1979), both freely available for personal use at www.iapt.nhs.uk. In addition, the Agoraphobic Cognitions Questionnaire (ACQ; Chambless et al. 1984) can be administered to identify and target cognitions that serve to maintain agoraphobia.

Session 1

After the introductions the leader and co-leader distribute the Panic Disorder and Agoraphobia Survival Manual and the leader explains that it is their own private workbook for getting through panic. The session begins with the therapists focusing on the introduction to the Manual and leading a discussion of the common precipitants of panic disorder. This discussion can increase group cohesion as the most common triggers identified are interpersonal (Scocco et al. 2007). Some group members are inevitably more vocal than others and it is important for each group member to be given the space to tell their story, but without pressure to disclose, yet not be allowed to dominate the group. This balancing of individual and group needs is a general group therapeutic skill and is reflected in the inclusion item, item 4 in the General Group Therapeutic Skills Rating Scale

Table 5.1 Panic disorder and agoraphobia programme

	Therapeutic targets	Treatment strategies	Materials – Panic Disorder and Agoraphobia Survival Manual, Appendix 1
Session 1	Fear of fear, anxiety sensitivity, catastrophic labelling of bodily symptoms, hypervigilance for bodily symptoms, monitoring of panic attacks	Psychoeducation – the development and maintenance of panic attacks and agoraphobia	Overview of Manual and Section 5
Session 2	Avoidance of activities and situations	Construction of exposure hierarchy, in-vivo and interoceptive exposure	Sections 6, 7 and 9
Sessions 3–5	'Safety' procedures, avoidance	Daring to gradually wean off 'safety' procedures, troubleshooting cognitive saboteurs to progressing up exposure ladder, continued interoceptive and in-vivo exposure	Sections 1–4
Sessions 6–8	Intolerance of discomfort, feared consequences, key cognitive saboteurs	Interoceptive and in-vivo exposure, challenging 'catastrophic' cognitions, dares as behavioural experiments, downward arrow technique	Sections 4, 8 and 9
Sessions 9 and 10	Relapse prevention	Identifying likely precipitants for panic, distillation and rehearsal of a protocol. Exercise as a possible preventative measure. Regular review of protocol	Section 10

Table 5.2 Panic disorder and agoraphobia group members

Name	Thumbnail sketch
Peter	Redundancy, financial problems, possible repossession of home, mild agoraphobia
Paula	Loss of mum, single parent, child care difficulties, mild agoraphobia
Jasmin	Policewoman, 'betrayal' by partner, moderate agoraphobia
Justin	Teacher, 'impossible targets', no agoraphobia
Greg	Worked in IT, now forced to work at call centre, moderate agoraphobia
Martha	Wife of soldier serving in Afghanistan, severe agoraphobia

(GGTSRS), Appendix D. As the co-leader focused the group's attention on the role of mislabelling bodily sensations in the development of panic disorder the following exchange took place:

JASMIN: But I wake in the night with panic attacks I'm not 'labelling' anything! They freak me out.

CO-LEADER: There are probably a number of non-serious causes of nocturnal panic attacks, they usually occur about 90 minutes into sleep and usually are not in response to dreaming. For some sufferers it may be that they panic at having let their guard down by sleeping. For others sleep apnoea may be involved, which is a slight interruption in breathing. The amygdala, the brain's alarm, is involved in fear reactions and can operate at a non-conscious level, so that a form of 'labelling' can occur in response to any unusual bodily sensation occurring for whatever reason.

JASMIN: The daytime panics I can prepare myself for but not the night time ones.

LEADER: Apart from reducing coffee and alcohol it is difficult to prevent the nocturnal panic attacks but you can change your response when they happen.

JASMIN: I have ended up at A&E with them thinking I was having a heart attack only to be told it was panic, I felt an idiot.

CO-LEADER: You might talk your way through them by noting how long into sleep it is when they occur and remind yourself that it is just your amygdala alarm being oversensitive.

PETER: Can't you just 'switch the alarm off'?

LEADER: No, it's like a neighbour's alarm going off in the night, you usually discover there is no danger, and all you can do is ignore it and let it sort itself out, it is a bit of a pain but no real harm.

MARTHA: My alarm has just gone off just talking about it!

LEADER: We can probably trigger just about everybody's alarm by reading over the paired words in Section 2 of the Manual right now.

In this exchange the therapists are avoiding a didactic presentation of the material in the Survival Manual, rather they are tapping into group members' concerns to illustrate teaching points, i.e. they are ensuring relevance (item 2 of the GGTSRS, Appendix D). At the same time the therapists are ensuring that group members have a ready reference for points made, the Manual, ensuring good presentation skills (item 8 of the GGTSRS, Appendix D). The session continued:

CO-LEADER: How did people feel about reading over the list of words 'breathless suffocate' etc.?

MARTHA: My heart was really beginning to go.

CO-LEADER: What do you make of that?

MARTHA: Well I knew I was safe because you are here.

CO-LEADER: But I didn't make a difference to what was going on in your body, I didn't give you oxygen or an injection.

MARTHA: If I was by myself when I read those words I would probably have gone to pieces.

LEADER: But somehow you have managed the symptoms by telling yourself you are safe.

MARTHA: But it is safe only with people.

CO-LEADER: If you are a policeman or soldier are you safe only when you are with people?

MARTHA: No, my husband is in Afghanistan, he keeps telling me it is his training and experience that keeps him safe.

CO-LEADER: Do you believe him?

MARTHA: Sort of.

CO-LEADER: Maybe you could borrow something of what he says that it is your training and experience of the panic attacks that keeps you safe and not others.

JASMIN: As a policewoman I should be able to buy into that.

In the above dialogue the therapists have kept the material relevant to group members by utilising experiences they would be very familiar with. Further, they have done so in such a way as to draw in a group member to another's experience. Though it was not the leaders' intention to introduce interoceptive exposure at such an early session, they have prepared the ground by seizing an opportunity to flag up that symptoms of panic can be induced, resulting in experiential learning that they do no harm. The session continued:

CO-LEADER: Just as I was suggesting it might be useful for Jasmin to monitor the timing of her nocturnal panic attacks, so too it is useful to get extra information on your panic attacks. In the first column in Table 1 in the Manual you put the situation in which the panic occurred, so that for example Jasmin might have put that her last attack occurred in the night, then in the second column she might say how bad it was. How bad would you say your last one was, Jasmin, where 10 is the worst possible?

JASMIN: About an 8.

CO-LEADER: So we would put an 8 in the second column. The third column is for the catastrophic thoughts, what went through your mind during this last attack, Jasmin.

JASMIN: My first thought was that there must be something wrong with my heart with all the stress I've been through. But then I thought I'll probably end up feeling an idiot again in A&E when I'm told again that there is nothing wrong with my heart. With my luck I'd probably bump into somebody I've locked up.

CO-LEADER: So that could go in the third column. In the fourth column you put what you did, what was that, Jasmin?

JASMIN: Got up, opened the back door into the garden for some fresh air.

CO-LEADER: So that could go in the fourth column of Table 1. In the final column you write whether there was a better way of thinking and playing the panic attack, what would you put there, Jasmin?

JASMIN: *laughing* Don't open the back door on a winter's night, it's freezing!

CO-LEADER: What would have happened if you hadn't opened the back door?

JASMIN: I think I would have felt trapped and needed fresh air.

CO-LEADER: How would staying indoors after the attack have made you trapped?

JASMIN: It wouldn't really really, I suppose I could have switched on the TV.

CO-LEADER: In what way did you 'need' fresh air, you do 'need' food because if you don't have it you starve, in what way do you 'need' fresh air?

JASMIN: I suppose I don't any more than I need an air freshener.

CO-LEADER: So what would you put in the final column, Jasmin?

JASMIN: I'm not trapped and don't need to open the door for fresh air.

In the above dialogue the therapist has continued to use the client's experiences to teach material. Further, the therapist has modelled the use of a downward arrow technique, Section 8 of the Manual, to uncover a group member's core fear of being trapped. This technique is formally introduced later in the programme. The dialogue continues with the provision of a rationale for monitoring the panic attacks:

LEADER: Monitoring the attacks makes you aware that some attacks are worse than others and how often they happen. Without monitoring them it is easy to become demoralised and think just 'these damned panic attacks' but as we go through the programme they happen gradually less often and are less severe and you can see your progress. If there is a panic attack that throws you we can use the details in the panic diary to troubleshoot it.

GREG: It is like ringing an organisation and being told 'your call may be monitored and recorded for training purposes'.

PAULA: If I ring the Department of Social Security once more and hear them saying 'please hold, your call is important to us' and then you get nowhere I will smash the phone!

GREG: That's why I hate working at a call centre.

In this exchange the therapists have fostered group cohesion by allowing space for the interaction of group members and the expression of negative affect. Further, the therapists have been given some feedback that at least some group members have translated what is being taught into the context of their own experiences. But it is necessary to canvass all group members as to whether the panic diary is something that they believe they have the ability to complete and whether they believe it could make a difference. Completion of the panic diary is set as a homework exercise and, as with performance of any task, the group members' sense of self-efficacy (their belief in their ability to perform the task and their belief that it will make a difference) is a crucial determinant of whether the task is completed.

Session 2

This session begins with a review of homework – the completion of the panic diary and reading of the Panic Disorder and Agoraphobia Survival Manual, Appendix I. The session focus is then on construction of an exposure hierarchy and in-vivo exposure exercises. The following exchange took place:

MARTHA: Terrible week, I let my daughter down, I was supposed to go and see her in a Theatre School production on at the Empire Theatre, I went with my friend but panicked outside so many people, I just couldn't go in, I had to get my friend to ask another parent to bring my daughter home, I'm so embarrassed.

LEADER: What did you write down in the third column of the diary, the catastrophic thoughts.

MARTHA: I'm just going to get that weird feeling, like I'm in a bubble others are saying and doing things but I'm not really there, can't work out what is going on. Then in the final column I put I should just have gone in anyway.

LEADER: The weird feeling you describe is what we call derealisation, what is it that is so bad about the derealisation?

MARTHA: I think I'm going crazy.

LEADER: Have you ever gone crazy with this feeling?

MARTHA: No, but I might next time.

LEADER: Derealisation is a normal symptom of anxiety; if you do nothing at all it passes of its own accord. You might need to change the final column of the diary to include 'tell myself derealisation can't make you go crazy' in order to be able to go into such crowded situations.

MARTHA: Hmm that's helpful.

CO-LEADER: It may also be, Martha, that just yet going into a crowded theatre might be too big a step for you, and what we have to do is take baby steps to return to normal life. Looking at Section 7 of the Manual, 'Beginning to dare', it may be, Martha, that going to the theatre accompanied might be a step halfway up the ladder, going by yourself might be top of the ladder and what we need to sort out are what the bottom rungs might be. If we could each spend a couple of minutes sorting out what might be the various rungs of the ladder that would be useful, the leader and I will circulate so you can ask any questions if you are stuck.

The above exchange illustrates the normalisation of unusual bodily sensations. Homework difficulties are a major focus. But the review is conducted not only by reference to previously taught material but with a view to integrating it with the new material to be taught in the session. The interweaving of taught material should be as seamless as possible and not appear as a series of unrelated techniques; this flow is part of the presentation skills (item 8, of the GGTSRS, Appendix D). The first rung of each member's ladder is then targeted for in vivo exposure or interoceptive exposure in the group. The session continued:

LEADER: Over the next 45 minutes, I want to practise getting to the first rung of your ladder; for some this will involve going out and returning with the co-leader and for others it will involve practising some special exercises here. What I would like to do is ask those with the more severe problems in going out, Martha, Greg and Jasmin, to go out with the co-leader and the rest remain with me and we meet back in 45 minutes for a drink and review of how we have got on.

CO-LEADER: Greg and Jasmin, I thought that I would stay outside a crowded shop whilst you go in together for a few minutes, come out, let me know how you have got on and then try going in for a few minutes alone and again meeting me outside. Martha, I thought we might practise you just walking gradually further and further distances from me but with me in sight. After each walk let me know how you are getting on. If that's OK see you all in 45 minutes. *This subgroup leaves.*

LEADER: There is not very much that you avoid, except particular sensations.

JUSTIN: I avoid going to the gym and for a run since the panic attacks.

PETER: I don't avoid being on the taxi rank, I've got to be for work, but I get all worked up when I've been waiting for an hour or two for a fare and I have an attack, I can't just go home because I will be in an even worse financial state.

PAULA: I'm like that in meetings in work, I feel trapped, knowing that sometimes I've just got to get away to pick up my daughter and knowing the boss thinks this is 'unprofessional'.

LEADER: What I would like to do is to teach you not to be afraid of these symptoms in those situations by artificially inducing them, interoceptive exposure, and learning that though they are uncomfortable the sensations don't go anywhere.

Panic disorder groups members can usually be divided roughly into two, those with no or mild agoraphobic avoidance and those with moderate or severe agoraphobic avoidance. It is suggested that their needs, at least initially, are best met by interoceptive and in-vivo exposure respectively. But all members are taught to de-catastrophise. The interoceptive subgroup were first asked to stand, breathe deeply and quickly for a minute, then asked on a scale 0–100 to what extent their symptoms were like the panic attacks they had experienced. Usually a number of different exercises are needed before each subgroup member can report the induction of symptoms at least 60% like their panic attacks. The exercises can include: hold breath for 30 seconds, place head between knees for 30 seconds and raise head quickly, run on spot for a minute, place tongue depressor at back of tongue for 30 seconds and stare continuously at self in mirror for 2 minutes, but this list is not exhaustive. The interoceptive subgroup continued:

PAULA: Placing the tongue depressor on my tongue made me feel I was going to choke and maybe vomit.

LEADER: Is that what you feel at work in meetings?

PAULA: Yes like I'm going to vomit.

JUSTIN: Breathing deeply and quickly didn't seem to have any real effect but might have done if I would have gone on much longer for say 2 minutes.

LEADER: OK give 2 minutes a go now. *after 2 minute pause* How was that?

JUSTIN: No it's much the same.

LEADER: Try running on the spot for a minute.

JUSTIN: OK.

LEADER: *after a pause* How was that?

JUSTIN: I've got that horrible feeling, like I'm walking on pillows, I'll have to sit down.

LEADER: No don't for a while. Peter, how was the breathing for you?

PETER: Didn't make any real difference.

LEADER: Try putting your head between your knees and bringing it up sharply.

PETER: OK.

LEADER: *after a pause* How was that?

PETER: Horrible, it reminded me of my first bad panic attack when I got out of my taxi quickly, I had been on the rank ages waiting for a fare.

LEADER: So it was pretty similar to your panic attack?

PETER: Yes.

LEADER: Justin, I wasn't just being awkward in not letting you sit down, your sitting down after running on the spot would have been a safety behaviour and I wanted to show that nothing bad happens if you give up a safety behaviour. I could have told you that nothing terrible will happen with the sensations you were having but you learn more from the doing.

JUSTIN: That's what we try to get over to student teachers, kids learn more from doing than being lectured.

LEADER: What we have done today is to begin to train your body to tolerate the symptoms you fear, how would you feel doing some daily training with these exercises but in the presence of a relative or friend, just 10–15 minutes a day? *Each of the group members agreed to this and the larger group reconvened.*

CO-LEADER: We've had some success. Martha can go 100 yards by herself and Greg and Jasmin each spent five minutes in a crowded shop by themselves.

MARTHA: Yes but I was in an awful state.

CO-LEADER: OK it might have been 8 on 10, but by the tenth time you have done it that score will likely have come well down.

MARTHA: I guess so, but it is uncomfortable.

CO-LEADER: It is a question of 'no pain no gain', but if we could all daily practise what we have done today in the presence of a friend or relative, we could consolidate our gains and be ready for the next rung of the ladder.

The above dialogue emphasises the role of experiential learning. The leaders have also attempted to build a bridge between the sessions and the client's real world by encouraging members to recruit a relative/friend to act as pseudo therapist in the community to encourage them with their homework.

Sessions 3–5

These sessions begin with a review of homework and the focus then shifts to identifying and planning to relinquish safety behaviours. Finally in-vivo and interoceptive exposure are conducted. The typical session proceeds as follows:

JASMIN: I suppose I climbed another rung of the ladder this week, I went back to work, mind you it is a case of 'needs must' as I was about to go on half pay. It's not too bad because I'm just in the office, not out locking people up and I'm just on days.

LEADER: So you thought that that is a better next step than trying to go back into work just as you did before the panic attacks?

JASMIN: Yes.

GREG: I wish it was like that at the call centre, it is either right back in the middle of it or nothing at all.

LEADER: We do need a 'step by step' or more accurately 'one rung at a time' approach, otherwise you might become demoralised.

GREG: I think I might be better off just advertising in a local free paper and going fixing people's computers. Trouble is if I get stuck in someone's house and I'm having difficulty fixing it I could have a panic attack and make a show of myself.

JASMIN: You could just say 'this is such a difficult problem that I need to take it back to my workshop' or wherever you work from.

CO-LEADER: But that would be a 'safety behaviour', you would feel some relief from getting away but it would make you more fearful of returning to houses.

GREG: I can see that and anyway people are very reluctant to part with their laptops.

JASMIN: Sorry, one more of my crap ideas!

GREG: No, I really appreciate that you are all trying to help me find solutions.

The above exchange illustrates the 'stepping stones' approach to recovery from panic disorder and agoraphobia and the need to identify likely manageable next steps. Further, the dialogue indicates that other group members can act, at least to some degree, as vicarious role models for other group members' problem solving. This modelling can be facilitated by having some group members working together on the same task, e.g. accompanying each other going into a crowded shop. The new material for the session should be introduced if possible in response to group members' experiences since the previous session of implementing their homework. During these sessions in-vivo exposure takes place as well as interoceptive exercises. The session continued:

CO-LEADER: What about today Greg and Jasmin trying to go into a crowded shop by yourselves for a few minutes but alone and just meet outside.

GREG: OK.

JASMIN: OK.

CO-LEADER: What dare do you think you could attempt today, Martha?

MARTHA: I could try walking around the block or maybe getting on a bus.

CO-LEADER: What about trying both but I could go with you on the bus and we could just go a stop?

MARTHA: OK, but you could sit at the back of the bus and I could be at the front.

CO-LEADER: Fine.

LEADER: Justin, Peter and Paula we could look at how you got on with your interoceptive exercises and look at doing some for longer or a different exercise to ensure that you can still induce the panic attacks and can continue with developing a 'radical apathy' for them.

A key feature of the within-session exercises above is that the goals are SMART: **S** – specific, **M** – measurable, **A** – agreed upon, **R** – realistic and relevant and **T** – time-based. In the process of attempting these goals the therapeutic task is to be alert for the operation of catastrophic cognitions. Sometimes the group members will be able to verbalise these cognitions but in other instances the therapist may infer their presence and encourage the group member to consider whether they are salient and if so what would constitute a more realistic appraisal and behaviour. The homeworks set at the end of each session should also be SMART.

Sessions 6–8

These sessions begin with a review of homework and the new material is based around Sections 4, 8 and 9 of the Manual, with a focus on behavioural experiments. In reviewing the between-session homework the following exchange took place:

PAULA: Terrible week had to get to the children's hospital to see my daughter; it was only appendicitis, but going that far by myself was too much.

CO-LEADER: Yes, for homework, you were only planning to go as far as the shopping centre and do your shopping.

PAULA: I know.

LEADER: But did you have a panic attack when you went to the hospital?

PAULA: Funnily not going there, I was too concerned about getting my daughter there, but after they had done the examinations and I was waiting to see the consultant I had one.

LEADER: How bad was it?

PAULA: Well in the panic diary I put 7/10 but thinking about it now I'm sure it was more than that.

CO-LEADER: One of the reasons for recording your panic attacks as near to the time they happened is that you can better tell it how it is; looking back you can magnify the experience, particularly if your mood is low, and then you worry more about the next panic attack. So when you were focusing outside yourself in an emergency situation you were free of panic attacks but when you have got the opportunity to think about your body's reactions you had one?

PAULA: Yes, the stupid thing is that I handle true emergencies fine but they don't give me time to think.

MARTHA: I felt good one day and made the mistake of trying to go to the shopping centre by myself, I got myself in a terrible state when I got inside, felt trapped but just froze and then rushed out to get a taxi.

PETER: Yes, I was on the taxi rank and saw you, you were in a sweat.

MARTHA: I was really grateful for you taking me in for a cup of coffee and calming me down.

CO-LEADER: You are likely to frighten yourself if you try to do a dare that is too big, but sometimes you can be forced to by situations. But even when things go wrong you can learn things from them. What do you think you learnt from your experience Martha?

MARTHA: Not to do too much too quickly.

CO-LEADER: Looking at your panic diary what fuelled your panic attack was a belief that you were 'trapped', was that true?

MARTHA: No, it's crazy, I went out to the taxi rank and back in so I wasn't trapped.

PETER: It's like me in the taxi waiting for a fare sometimes I feel trapped, like I'm going to suffocate, but it is crazy really, this week I've been deliberately holding my breath for as long as I can and telling myself 'go on really suffocate good style' and I have discovered I can't. I had been doing this minutes before seeing Martha.

GREG: We really are the greatest group of underachievers, we can't even produce the catastrophes we imagine!

The above exchange illustrates how the leaders increasingly give other group members the space to act as role models (item 7, Appendix D, GGTSRS] to each other and to perform a therapeutic role. The therapists have also attempted to inoculate clients against failure by emphasising SMART goals and to reframe difficulties as learning opportunities. The session continued:

LEADER: What Peter did in the taxi was an experiment to test out his belief that he could easily suffocate if he stayed in his taxi; putting your fears to the test is a powerful way of moving on. As explained in Section 9 of the Manual an experiment is just the other side of the coin to a dare,

which also stands for 'Don't avoid a realistic experiment'. What realistic experiments might people attempt today?

MARTHA: I suppose I could try what Peter has done.

CO-LEADER: You said suppose, what is it that puts you off?

MARTHA: I might make a show of myself?

CO-LEADER: What would be so bad about that?

MARTHA: I would be mortified?

CO-LEADER: What would be so bad about that?

MARTHA: It would be uncomfortable.

CO-LEADER: Were you uncomfortable when you gave birth to your daughter?

MARTHA: Of course.

CO-LEADER: Would you persuade someone not to go through childbirth
because of the discomfort, embarrassment?

MARTHA: No.

CO-LEADER: What is the difference?

MARTHA: I just have to remind myself that any discomfort is to a good
purpose.

CO-LEADER: If something is putting you off doing a dare just repeatedly ask
yourself 'what is so bad about that?' The downward arrow technique in
Section 8 helps unearth the true obstacle to your dare, and then you
can come up with an antidote to it as Martha has just done.

This exchange illustrates the utility of the downward arrow technique in
removing obstacles to a behavioural experiment. It also emphasises a
bottom-up approach to the teaching of material from the Manual, going
from the group members' experience to demonstrate the relevance of new
material rather than a top-down approach of relying on the authority and
knowledge of the group leaders in declaring what is important. The
bottom-up approach also recognises that group members can be more
credible sources of persuasion than the leaders and become particularly
potent sources as the group progresses. Importantly, however, the leaders
have used Socratic dialogue to help group members discover antidotes to
their catastrophic cognitions. It is possible to further enable group members
to adopt Socratic dialogue themselves by introducing a thought record (see
the MOOD chart described in the previous chapter), but this is rarely
necessary for panic disorder clients, except of course in any accompanying
individual session targeting a comorbid disorder such as depression.

Sessions 9 and 10

The final session should be conducted a month or so after the penultimate
session to allow group members an extended opportunity to practise their
new approach to managing their fear. As such there is greater scope for
group members to encounter difficulties that in turn can be problem solved

in the final session, thereby consolidating learning. At the penultimate session, as well as continuing in-vivo and interoceptive exposure, for homework, members are invited to re-read the Manual and personalise it for revision in the final session. Between these final sessions there should be a full diagnostic assessment using the Cognitive Behaviour Therapy Pocketbook, Appendix A and re-administration of the psychometric tests.

Chapter 6

Post-traumatic stress disorder

Trauma is ubiquitous. Switch on the news any day and one is almost guaranteed to hear about an extreme trauma – as I write (June 2010) it is a week after the terrible shootings in Cumbria in which 12 people were killed. The responses to such trauma are very varied and may include PTSD, depression and alcohol abuse or any combination of these disorders or sub-syndromal level of these conditions. Some traumas, such as traffic accidents, may only make the local news but they are common with 189,000 occurring in the UK in 2006 (Department of Transport 2008).

One in twenty men and one in ten women suffer from post-traumatic stress disorder (PTSD) at some point in their life (Kessler *et al*. 1995). The good news is that the majority of people with PTSD recover; in a study of road traffic accident victims (Blanchard and Hickling 1997) only a third were still suffering from PTSD at 12 months post-trauma.

Whilst individuals are affected by trauma they are not alone in their trauma response; this opens up the possibility of a cost-effective intervention using groups. Further, as social support is the biggest single predictor of recovery post-trauma (Brewin *et al*. 2000), a group intervention may be a particularly effective treatment. In a study of individual CBT for PTSD by Thrasher *et al*. (2010), despite the multitude of demographic and trauma-related variables examined, only perceived social support was related to outcome. The authors speculated that social support might be especially important to help patients manage the demands of treatment, e.g. temporary increases in distress, homework. Other group members are particularly well placed to provide such support and may augment or compensate for support offered by significant others in the client's life.

There are, however, a number of problems about GCBT for PTSD: (i) reluctance of clients to engage – just over half of the people invited to consider attending a group chose not to opt in (Thompson *et al*. 2009), thus making a strong case for the addition of individual pre-group motivational interviewing; (ii) risk of re-traumatisation – hearing of another's trauma, particularly if it is similar to one's own, may act as a distressing reminder, and the wish to avoid such reminders may be a factor in the reluctance to engage in a group; and (iii) presence of additional disorders – nearly three-quarters of those with PTSD suffer from at least one additional disorder (Zimmerman *et al.* 2008); severe comorbidity may prevent the use of the primarily psychoeducational environment of the group.

Clients can be screened for PTSD using the First Step Questionnaire/7 Minute Mental Health Screen; positive screens can be examined further using the Cognitive Behaviour Therapy Pocketbook (Appendix A), with questions that directly access each of the symptoms in the DSM-IV-TR (American Psychiatric Association 2000) criteria sets for disorders. Whilst DSM-IV stipulates that at least one intrusion, three avoidance and two disordered arousal symptoms are required for a diagnosis of PTSD, from a clinical point of view it is not unreasonable to include in a group clients with a sub-syndromal level of the condition, i.e. who fall short by a symptom in either the avoidance or disordered arousal category but not both. The Impact of Event Scale – Revised (Weiss and Marmar 1997) is a useful measure of the severity of PTSD and is freely available on the IAPT website, www.iapt.nhs.uk. This should be complemented by a measure of the cognitions that serve to maintain PTSD such as the Posttraumatic Cognitions Inventory (PTCI; Foa *et al.* 1999).

Trauma-focused individual interventions for PTSD are the most effective (Ehlers *et al.* 2010). But that is not to say that other non-specific interventions are not also effective. Smits and Hofmann (2009) found that 34% responded to such treatments. Whilst the mechanism of action in non-specific treatments remains to be elucidated, it is not improbable that the active ingredients include increasing trust and a lessening of isolation, precisely those aspects that a group modality implicitly tackles. There is, however, a paucity of research on GCBT for PTSD; groups have generally been homogeneous, e.g. road traffic accident victims (Thompson *et al.* 2009), and have needed substantial modification from the individual format to achieve an effectiveness comparable to that of the individual modality (Beck and Coffey 2005). Usually, however, clinicians will encounter clients suffering from PTSD in response to a range of trauma and in the interest of relevance a protocol for a heterogeneous group is therefore outlined. But complete heterogeneity is impossible; for example, it would be inappropriate to have an adult survivor of childhood sexual abuse in a mixed sex group.

There are two primary mechanisms of change thought to underlie efficacious treatment of PTSD: (a) improvement occurs through emotional processing of the trauma memory by way of repeated exposure (Foa and Jaycox 1999) and/or (b) improvement occurs because the meaning of the event changes (Ehlers and Clark 2000). An exposure treatment is particularly problematic in a group context, with a risk of re-traumatising other group members. It is recommended therefore that the exposure component of treatment, such as discussing a written account of the trauma, should be largely addressed in initial individual face-to-face/telephone/e-mail contact that runs alongside the group programme. Interestingly Resick *et al.* (2008) have sought to determine the active ingredients in CBT for PTSD. Their study involved comparing three interventions: standard cognitive processing therapy (which involves both cognitive restructuring and exposure [via written accounts]), a cognitive therapy only condition and an exposure only condition (written accounts). In all three treatments clients improved substantially; however, the cognitive therapy only condition reported greater improvement in PTSD than the exposure only condition. The study focus was female victims of interpersonal violence and the results may not generalise to other populations. The results of the Resick *et al.* (2008) study are nevertheless consistent with the GCBT for PTSD programme described in this chapter, with a primary focus on cognitive restructuring in the groups while the subsidiary emphasis on exposure is located primarily in the individual contacts with group members, minimising the risks of re-traumatisation and possible defaulting.

The cognitive behavioural model of PTSD

CBT represents the clinical application of a cognitive mediational model to the client's difficulties. The Ancient Greeks were aware of the essence of the model, in the first century AD, when the Stoic philosopher Epictetus said 'People are disturbed not so much by events as by the way with which they view them'. In modern terms, the 'disturbance' is the response (R), the 'events' are the stimulus (S) and the 'views' the thoughts. By the second half of the twentieth century the behavioural, S-R model, was largely super-seded by an S-O-R model, where 'O' is the organism (Lazarus 1999). Whilst the 'O' organism is often equated with thoughts it was intended to be much broader, embracing attentional processes, motivation and beliefs about self and world as well as neurophysiology.

In terms of the S-O-R model, PTSD can be regarded as a particular stress response which by definition is triggered by a specific stressor (extreme trauma) in some individuals (organisms). Thus there is no inevitability that an extreme trauma will produce PTSD in all people. Those aspects of the 'organism' that play a mediational role in the genesis of PTSD are summarised in Table 6.1.

From a biological perspective PTSD involves primarily the following anatomical sites: amygdala, hippocampus, anterior cingulate and dorso-lateral prefrontal cortex. The amygdala and hippocampus together form a threat-evaluation system:

1   The amygdala, the brain's alarm, plays a major role in the fear response. Functional magnetic resonance imaging (fMRI) and positron emission tomography (PET) scanning have consistently shown that exposure to trauma-related stimuli provokes greater activation of the

Table 6.1 Mediators of PTSD – biological and psychological

1　Amygdala – brain's alarm (LeDoux 1998)
2　Hippocampus – locator of experiences in context (LeDoux 1998)
3　Anterior cingulate and dorsolateral prefrontal cortex – control-demand system (LeDoux 1998)
4　Attentional processes (Wells 2004)
5　Perceived social support (Brewin *et al.* 2000)
6　Maladaptive PTSD schemas (Clark and Beck 2010)
7　Negative appraisal of intrusions and arousal (Wells and Sembi 2004; Clark and Ehlers 2004)
8　Avoidance (safety seeking behaviour) (Wells and Sembi 2004; Clark and Ehlers 2004)
9　Rumination (Wells and Sembi 2004)

　　amygdala. The amygdala is also a seat of emotional memory and works on a perceptual matching rather than in terms of logic (LeDoux 1998). Thus a victim of a serious road traffic accident with PTSD might react strongly to the sound of screeching brakes outside of his home, even though he 'knows' he is safe inside his home.

2　The hippocampus is responsible for putting events into context and draws on a store of long-term memories. Thus a PTSD client might remind themselves of their general knowledge that being in the house poses no threat.

Following trauma the danger is that the amygdala hijacks the threat evaluation system and the hippocampus is not able to inhibit the amygdala's overreaction, with a consequent ongoing sense of vulnerability and threat. Thus PTSD may be seen as involving a maladaptive functioning of the threat-evaluation system.

However it is not only the threat-evaluation system that is pertinent to PTSD; there is also a control-demand system consisting of the anterior cingulate and the dorsolateral prefrontal cortex. The control-demand system can in principle override the threat-evaluation system to accept challenges despite fear. The maladaptive interplay of these anatomical sites is explained simply in the self-help book *Moving On After Trauma* (Scott 2008) and in Appendix J, the PTSD Survival Manual, giving group members a credible story of their difficulties and an understanding of what the treatment strategies are trying to correct.

The cognitive alterations in PTSD include (Moore (2009):

1　Reduced performance on measures of verbal memory; this seems related to problems in encoding (i.e. making information stick in the first place), making memory aids in the group session, such as a Survival Manual, role play, particularly important.

2　Biased attention to trauma-relevant stimuli, e.g. a client with PTSD following a car accident will vividly remember 'near-misses' but have little recall of 'courteous drivers'. Wells (2004) has proposed that vulnerability to disorder and the persistence of disorder are linked to the activation of a 'cognitive attentional syndrome' that consists of worry/rumination, attentional strategies of threat monitoring and coping behaviours that fail to restructure maladaptive beliefs. Further, Wells and Sembi (2004) have suggested that cultivating 'detached mindfulness' reduces rumination and helps PTSD clients to better manage re-experiencing symptoms and facilitates a natural adaptation.

3   The development of negative trauma-related appraisals (e.g. of the world as dangerous, others as untrustworthy, oneself as incompetent). Clark and Beck (2010) have suggested that there are five core maladaptive schemas that characterise PTSD: (i) beliefs about the self, e.g. 'I have been defiled; I have lost all dignity and respect as a human being. I am just an object'; (ii) beliefs about others, e.g. 'no one really understands or cares about me'; (iii) beliefs about the world and future, e.g. 'in the future bad things are likely to happen to me again'; (iv) beliefs about the trauma, e.g. 'I should not have frozen in the attack'; and (v) beliefs about the post-traumatic stress disorder, e.g. 'I will never get better as long as I keep thinking about the trauma'. The correction of an exaggeratedly negative view of the trauma and its consequences is a major feature of the programme outlined in this chapter. This is consistant with the proposed change in the DSM-IV criteria for PTSD (American Psychiatric Association – www.dsm5.org) to include 'Persistent and exaggerated negative expectations about one's self, others or the world' and 'Persistent distorted blame of self or others about the cause or consequence of the traumatic event(s)'.

4   An overgeneral memory, e.g. the client with PTSD may recall 'good holidays' rather than the details of a particular holiday that was good. Depressed clients also exhibit an overgeneral memory and given the high levels of comorbidity between PTSD and depression, overgeneral memory is an important therapeutic target.

5   Overintegration of trauma memories into one's personal identity is predictive of PTSD. In this chapter the focus is on the trauma as one chapter in the group members' autobiography, with the chapters before as much a part of identity as the trauma and the to-be-constructed chapters.

6   A deficit in conceptual processing; perceptual processing of the traumatic memory alone does not aid recovery but does so if it occurs alongside increased conceptual processing, or processing of the event's meaning. Clark and Ehlers (2004) have suggested three major goals of treatment: (i) reduce re-experiencing by elaboration of the trauma memory and discrimination of triggers; (ii) modify excessively negative appraisals; and (iii) drop dysfunctional behavioural and cognitive strategies.

The above cognitive abnormalities in PTSD (Moore 2009) are a prime therapeutic target. But PTSD is not a purely intrapsychic phenomenon, indeed feelings of being distant and cut off from others is one of the diagnostic symptoms for PTSD as is increased irritability; both these symptoms can have a profound effect on relationships. Whilst flashbacks/ nightmares and to a lesser extent avoidance are often regarded as the cardinal symptoms of PTSD, the biggest predictor of recovery is perceived social support (Brewin *et al.* 2000). A group intervention is particularly well placed to enhance the perception of social support.

PTSD programme

The PTSD programme outline is shown below in Table 6.2. The material to be taught is in the form of a client workbook, the PTSD Survival Manual (Appendix J), and the particular sections covered in each session are indicated in the final column of Table 6.2. The Manual serves as a stepping stone, familiarising clients with many of the concepts and narratives elaborated further in the self-help book *Moving On After Trauma* (Scott 2008). Group members are asked to complete reading this book in the first four weeks of the programme.

The full cast of the PTSD group is summarised in Table 6.3.

Sessions 1 and 2 – individual

At the end of the first session group members are asked, as a homework exercise, to write about the incident and its effects. It is suggested that they have each tried to blank the memory but that has not worked (the orangutan in the Survival Manual) and it appears to have resulted in them 'picking/daydreaming' about it whenever they are not busy, resulting in distress. An alternative strategy is not to 'blank' the memory but to learn to switch attention from it, postponing the concerns to be sorted out on paper at a time and place of the client's choosing. A client's progress in so doing should be reviewed in a telephone call between the first and second session, at which the client should be invited to read out what they have written, which usually takes just a few minutes. During this call clients are also made aware of an exposure rationale for their writing along the lines of the more they deliberately confront the memory, the more they habituate to it. Thus clients are invited to carry on writing but to go into as much graphic detail as possible and hand what they have written to the therapists. Reasons for not completing this homework, e.g. 'it makes it real if I write, when it is just in my head I can pretend it never happened', should be noted but left to be addressed in the group. It is, however, extremely important that clients' accounts are not read out in the group, so as to avoid the re-traumatisation of clients. Again at the end of the second group session

Table 6.2 PTSD programme

	Therapeutic targets	Treatment strategies	Materials – PTSD Survival Manual, Appendix J
Sessions 1 and 2: Group	1. Beliefs about PTSD	Normalisation of symptoms – utilisation of *Moving On After Trauma*	Introduction Sections 1, 2 and 3
	2. Cognitive and behavioural avoidance	Advantages and disadvantages short and long term of avoidance	
	3. 'No one can understand what I've been through'	Realistic portrayal of discomfort to be expected Underlining similarities of trauma and responses	
	4. Managing reminders	The menu of options for handling reminders	
	5. Behavioural avoidance Fear of anxiety	Beginning the journey of a return to normality by gradual 'dares'	
Sessions 1 and 2: Individual	6. Processing of traumatic memory	Written or verbal account of trauma and its effects – elaboration of the memory	
	7. Motivation Group issues	Motivational interviewing	
Sessions 3–5	8. Rumination Cognitive avoidance Disturbed sleep/ nightmares	Addressing the traumatic memory at a specific time and place	Sections 4, 5 and 6
	9. Discrimination of triggers	Using similarities and differences – play 'Spot the differences'	
	10. Irritability, emotional avoidance – 'control freak'	Traffic light routine Managing 'seething' over the trauma and its effects, coping strategies	
	11. Persistent and exaggerated negative expectations about oneself, others or the world and persistent distorted blame of self or others about the cause or consequence of the traumatic event – core maladaptive schemas in PTSD	Use of MOOD chart to modify observed thinking and underlying assumption. Use of magnifying glass analogy to illustrate exaggeratedly negative view of self, others and world	

continues overleaf

Table 6.2 continued

	Therapeutic targets	Treatment strategies	Materials – PTSD Survival Manual, Appendix J
Sessions 6 and 7	11 continued. Core maladaptive schemas in PTSD	Use of MOOD chart to modify observed thinking and underlying assumptions	Sections 4, 5, 6 and 7
	12. Cognitive avoidance Behavioural avoidance Hypervigilance for danger	Attention control and detached mindfulness Continuing to 'dare'	
	13. Impaired relationships	Beginning to invest in people	
Sessions 8–10	14. Low mood Pain/disability View of self, world and future	Mood management strategies Cognitive restructuring, the importance of a broad investment portfolio	Sections 1–7
	15. Relapse prevention	Budgeting for unpleasant reminders and distilling a protocol. Constructing a PTSD Survival Manual	Sections 1–8

Table 6.3 PTSD group members

Name	Thumbnail sketch
Don	PTSD after being hit by a police car chasing a stolen car, pain and disability from the accident
David	PTSD after coming off a motorcycle, unable to work since
Martin	PTSD after losing most of his right hand in an accident at work, marriage strained
Cathy	PTSD from an explosion at work
Niamh	PTSD from witnessing a shooting
Neil	PTSD after being assaulted outside a night club
Maxine	PTSD following physical abuse by ex-husband

members are invited to write about the incident daily, if possible, in detail and not to 'pick' at this memory at other times. Again a client's progress should be reviewed in a telephone call between the second and third session, with the client reading out what they have written. The therapist should be alert for particular features of the account that the client finds very upsetting, i.e. 'hotspots', and ask questions about it in the style of the TV detective Columbo: 'Does that mean that you were much more upset by playing horror videos of what could have happened than a reality video of what did? Are you into horror videos?' Equally the therapist should focus on any omissions from the account. During the call the therapist is trying to gauge whether the client has been actively processing the traumatic memory; without some upset at some point in the written account it will be doubtful whether such processing has occurred and the likelihood is that the client has engaged in cognitive and emotional avoidance. Clients should be encouraged to hand in at the third session the most comprehensive written account of the trauma that they can manage but with the assurance that the contents will not be divulged. Writing about the trauma can be set as a homework again at the end of Sessions 3–5 for those willing to do so.

The other foci in the first and second individual sessions is on motivation. Because the homework has a specific focus on their trauma, there is inevitably an increase in distress, and compliance with homework is often partial. The therapist has to determine whether the client understands the rationale for the homework or whether they have attempted it more out of obedience to the therapist; if it is the latter homework is likely to be incomplete. The client should be invited to verbalise why such a homework was set, encouraging a central processing of the rationale rather than peripheral processing based on an authority figure. In line with motivational interviewing, deciding not to engage with the traumatic material should be canvassed as a 'realistic' choice with advantages and disadvantages short and long term, with the therapist merely facilitating this elaboration rather than advocating a stance. Whilst clients undergoing motivational enhancement (Murphy *et al.* 2009) have shown more improvement in problem recognition, attended more PTSD programme sessions, had lower PTSD programme attrition rates and reported higher levels of working alliance, treatment engagement and satisfaction, they showed no greater increase in readiness to change than those given psychoeducation, suggesting that the effects may not be specific to motivational interviewing.

The individual sessions are also important for picking up issues that can be easily missed in the group, as the following exchange by telephone illustrates:

THERAPIST: How are you finding the group?
NIAMH: *long pause.*
THERAPIST: Are you still there?
NIAMH: Yes, yes.
THERAPIST: Are you OK?
NIAMH: I was thinking of not coming.
THERAPIST: Why is that?
NIAMH: I've had enough of Don spouting, he was going on and on about if the police wouldn't have been speeding, he wouldn't have been hit by them. Then he went on and on that just talking about things in a group wasn't going to make any difference.

THERAPIST: I thought you were quiet in the group.

NIAMH: *angrily* I didn't get a chance, I couldn't even see you and the other therapist, because Don sitting next to me was leaning forward blocking my view of you!

THERAPIST: I am really sorry, we should have included everybody in the session and not got hooked by the most vocal. I think that at the next session one of us will sit next to Don and the leader and I will sit opposite each other in the group.

NIAMH: I think I'm angry at Don because the police have been absolutely lovely to me since I saw the shooting.

THERAPIST: I think it would be great for the group to hear two sides of the story with regards to the police.

NIAMH: OK I'll give it a try.

Following the above telephone conversation the therapist discussed the matter with the group leader, who reflected that in terms of the General Group Therapeutic Skills Rating Scale, Appendix D, in Session 2 they had performed badly on item 4, Inclusion, but also on item 9, Addressing group issues, in that neither had picked up the detrimental effect on other group members of allowing one group member to dominate. It was agreed that the leader would sit next to Don and the co-leader opposite and should Don begin to dominate, a break would be called for in the session. The leader and co-leader reflected further on the wisdom of having included Don in the group and looking at his file they discovered that they had not actually asked him to complete the SAPAS, Appendix G, at assessment, as he had talked so much that the co-leader had not had the time. The leader conjectured that Don probably would have scored more than 5 on this personality screen and would have been excluded but there were never-theless organisational pressures to include all, which needed to be resisted on clinical grounds! The leader telephoned Don as previously arranged to ask him how he was getting on with the group and Don apologised for being so negative as his pain had been particularly bad at the second group session, to which the leader replied that he might benefit from reading the pain chapter in *Moving On After Trauma* (Scott 2008) and that issues arising from it could be discussed further by telephone or e-mail but that at the next session he must make sure that everyone got a turn in the group.

Sessions 1 and 2 – group

The first session gets under way with the provision of coffee and tea, introductions and the distribution of the PTSD Survival Manual, Appendix J. The leader explains the usual ground rules about confidentiality but also stresses that the support and encouragement members give each other can have a major effect on their ability to benefit from the group. The leader explains that a trauma group has a particular benefit in that each member knows that others have been through a similar experience. However, the very similarity of traumatic experiences can also be a problem; others will not want to know the graphic details of a trauma because it may rekindle their own and they fear being overwhelmed. Consequently the graphic details are addressed in homework exercises and in individual contact with the therapists but the interpretation members make of the personal significance of the trauma for themselves and their personal world is an appropriate subject for the group session.

The leader and co-leader take it in turn to take the group through the introduction (explaining the symptoms of PTSD) and sections 1–3 of the Manual ('Normal reaction to an abnormal situation', 'Resetting the alarm' and 'Better ways of handling the traumatic memory'), paraphrasing the material, making reference to it but interacting with group members rather than reading it, in keeping with item 8, Therapist presentation skills, in the General Group Therapeutic Skills Rating Scale, Appendix D. At the end of both the introduction and Section 1 the therapists invite comments on the material presented. In the presentation of Section 2 of the PTSD Survival Manual group members are invited to write down what 'dares' they might tackle for homework and to volunteer what they have written to the group. The following exchange ensued:

NEIL: Just coming here is a dare, it is only the other side of the city centre from where I was beaten up.

CO-LEADER: It is great that you have already made a start on the dares, in a way you have conducted an experiment to test out whether it really is that dangerous to go near the scene of the incident. What do you think the results of that experiment have been?

NEIL: I'm still in one piece, but there were a couple of dodgy characters about on the church steps down the road.

CO-LEADER: How many?

NEIL: About three.

CO-LEADER: How many people did you pass on your way here?

NEIL: I don't know, about twenty I suppose.

CO-LEADER: So about 20 minus 3, 17 weren't a threat.

NEIL: But I don't notice them.

CO-LEADER: Maybe when planning your dares, count the number of people who are not a threat?

NEIL: To get the balance?

CO-LEADER: Yes.

In the above exchange the therapists are not restricting themselves to a didactic presentation of material but are using a group member's experience (item 2, Relevance, Appendix D) to illustrate that 'dares' are possible and constitute a behavioural experiment. Further, the therapist uses the material to illustrate how attentional bias in PTSD serves to maintain PTSD and suggests a corrective strategy that might be employed for homework, but does so without formally using abstractions such as 'attentional bias'.

After paraphrasing Section 3 of the Survival Manual, 'Better ways of handling the traumatic memory' the co-leader invited discussion and the following dialogue ensued:

MARTIN: I wish I could write about how I lost my right hand, I was right handed!

LEADER: Could you perhaps dictate what happened and its effects to your wife and get her to write it down?

MARTIN: I don't like to tell her everything it's not fair. She is fed up with me getting annoyed over stupid things.

DAVID: I've not worked since I came off the motorbike, my grip isn't good enough to do my work as a joiner, I put my hands out to protect myself as I came off. But I've been experimenting with voice recognition software, Dragon Naturally Speaking 10, and it's good enough these days. I could loan it to you.

MARTIN: I've got a laptop but I'm useless on computers.

DAVID: If you want to bring it in or I could take it to yours if it's not too far.

MARTIN: Thanks I appreciate that, but knowing that I'm having to dictate it rather than write would just wind me up more.

LEADER: There is always something about writing/dictating about the trauma that makes you a bit worse before getting better.

DON: There's me thinking things couldn't get worse!

LEADER: But I did say that they then get better.

CO-LEADER: Focusing on things getting worse, rather than on matters improving in the long term, is a bit like Neil earlier focusing on the three suspicious characters, ignoring the seventeen who were OK. In PTSD there is a tendency to zoom in on the negative; if you stand back and see the whole picture it is easier.

The above exchange indicates the difficulties involved in getting group members to confront the traumatic memory; the strategies have to be adapted (item 3, Appendix D) to each group member's needs. Further, the therapists have allowed group members to act as supports to each other and as role models (item 7, Appendix D). Finally the role of attentional biases operating in PTSD is further underlined.

Sessions 3–5

The new material introduced in these sessions is based on Sections 4 ('Safety first?'), 5 ('Taking a photograph of the trauma and its consequences from different angles') and 6 ('PTSD and negativity'), of the Survival Manual. The target in these sessions are the core maladaptive schemas elaborated by Clark and Beck (2010). However, each of the sessions begins with a review of homework; at the start of Session 3 the following exchange took place:

LEADER: How did people get on with writing about their trauma and its effects?

DON: I did it but just bullet points, made sleep difficult, because I kept going over it.

MAXINE: I just couldn't face writing about it.

LEADER: Did you spend much time since the last session going over and over what happened to you?

MAXINE: Yes.

LEADER: How did that make you feel?

MAXINE: Awful.

LEADER: Part of the idea of writing is not to 'pick' at what happened because it makes you feel awful. But to have a special time for writing it off.

MAXINE: How can I write it off, my husband is dead because of me!

LEADER: One of the items we were going to cover in the Survival Manual is the 'responsibility pie' in Section 5 and in view of what Maxine has just said we might go to this now. There's an example given of a bus driver feeling very guilty over the death of an elderly pedestrian who stepped in front of the bus he was driving. Going clockwise around the pie and giving out slices to others, it turned out there was only a small slice for the driver. What slice might you give your husband of the responsibility pie?

MAXINE: God forgive me he was a ******.

LEADER: So how big a slice would you give him?

MAXINE: All of it!

LEADER: So how much does that leave for you?

MAXINE: I see what you mean, but I cut the final knot.

In this exchange the therapists have embarked on problem solving with regard to homework non-compliance – a major issue as such non-compliance is a predictor of a poor outcome. Despite intense negative emotion being expressed by a group member, the therapists have stayed with the client's concern (item 2, Relevance, Appendix D) and shown flexibility in bringing forward material to be taught and in a way that manifests good presentation skills (item 8, Therapist presentation skills, Appendix D). The key targets in clients' accounts of their trauma ('hot spots') are those that evoke the most emotion and often these are the aspects they are most reluctant to write about or verbalise. The exchange continued:

CO-LEADER: Cut the final knot?

MAXINE: I can't remember whether I tried to resuscitate him or not or just slapped his face and I couldn't find the phone for a while to ring 999, then I misdialled.

CO-LEADER: Maybe you can't remember because you were disorientated, can you blame yourself for being disorientated?

MAXINE: I'd not thought of being disorientated.

DON: I was disorientated when the police hit me, didn't know what had happened.

NIAMH: Maybe they were on the way to Maxine's?

DON: Hmm.

LEADER: Maxine, was there anything as deliberate as you 'cutting the final knot'?

MAXINE: He was drunk again, I was defending myself, he fell back and banged the back of his head and that was it.

LEADER: What we were going to discuss in Section 5 of the Manual is taking a photograph of situations from different angles and we have just done that with Maxine; the one that she has been carrying around is of 'deliberately cutting something', the alternative one we have suggested is of 'spinning around disorientated', very different pictures. You can use the MOOD chart to come up with alternative ways of thinking of upsets.

The sessions finish with the setting of homeworks which should include tasks relevant to all the material taught to date. At the end of the third session the following dialogue took place:

CO-LEADER: Neil what could you see yourself daring to do before the next session?

NEIL: I could go to a quiet pub in the countryside?

CO-LEADER: What about trying town in the daytime?

NEIL: I don't know about that.

CO-LEADER: Would you try to persuade (see Section 4 of the Survival Manual, 'Safety first?') other group members not to go to town of a daytime?

NEIL: No.

CO-LEADER: Why not?

NEIL: They would laugh at me.

CO-LEADER: But if you really thought it was dangerous for them wouldn't you try to persuade them?

NEIL: I suppose so.

CO-LEADER: Maybe you don't believe it is that dangerous?

NEIL: It's probably not for everybody else, just for me.

CO-LEADER: How come?

NEIL: My assailants might recognise me?

CO-LEADER: What are the chances of them being there in the daytime?

NEIL: Not great.

CO-LEADER: Given that they had been drinking, are they likely to recognise you?

NEIL: Probably not, I'm just a wimp.

LEADER: In Section 6 of the Manual we were looking at what you take your trauma to mean about yourself, Neil sees himself as a wimp, they are your first thoughts, the first 'O' on the MOOD chart; what might be better second thoughts, the second 'O'?

DAVID: I think you are just gradually getting your confidence back, Neil, you are going to a country pub now, it's like in the Manual, one small step at a time.

CO-LEADER: Perhaps, Neil, you might find it useful to use the similarities and differences in Section 5. Your fear is that being back at the scene of the assault will 'transport' you back to the feelings at the time of the incident. But you could go there and spell out the similarity, such as the same area and a long list of differences, e.g. it is daylight, I am not in the club, the assailants were probably 'night people'. Armed with this strategy would the dare be possible?

NEIL: It is a possibility.

The above exchange illustrates how material to be taught is integrated into the fabric of group members' experiences. Further space is given to other group members to act as credible sources of persuasion. The fifth session began with a review of homework:

NEIL: I finally went near were I was assaulted but of a daytime, But it wasn't the same, they have pedestrianised it now and I didn't get as upset as I thought.

LEADER: Sounds like you put the emphasis on how much it was different?

NEIL: I guess I have.

CATHY: I still can't bring myself to go to the city centre when it is busy.

CO-LEADER: How come?

CATHY: It reminds me of hearing people screaming from inside the factory when I had got outside, I thought they were dead.

CO-LEADER: Did they die?

CATHY: No, but one of them had a heart attack.

CO-LEADER: Could you do what Neil has done, let yourself hear the bustle of the busy shopping centre but tell yourself that though the noise has some similarity it is different in say they are not screaming, it is a Saturday afternoon, they are looking for Christmas presents etc.

CATHY: I could do, but it is the thought of them dead.

CO-LEADER: Maybe swap the horror video for a reality video, nobody died, maybe the Christmas shopping could give one person a heart attack!

In the above exchange reminders of trauma are reframed not only cognitively by cognitive restructuring but also behaviourally by exposure to feared situations.

Sessions 6 and 7

Throughout the programme group members are encouraged to share their homeworks with significant others and to discuss their readings of *Moving On after Trauma*. Such strategies are part of the beginning of an investment in others. In Sessions 6 and 7 the investment in others is increased by encouraging group members to gradually spend more time with others and group members are taken through Section 7 of the Survival Manual. The investment in relationships is mirrored by recommending an investment in activities that give a sense of achievement and pleasure; these may include previous hobbies or pastimes or new investments if previous ones are not possible. The rationale used is 'no investment, no return'. However, group members are encouraged to engage in these investments in a graded fashion and to not expect too much too soon.

The use of metaphor, such as 'investment', is an important part of helping group members understand what has happened to them and provides a framework for understanding current difficulties. For example, by using the metaphor of the 'dodgy alarm', group members can easily understand progress as shifting the alarm anticlockwise and a setback as shifting it slightly clockwise and are inoculated against failure by the suggestion that eventual success is always two steps forward and one back. Such use of metaphor, in pictorial form, is part of a therapist's presentation skills (item 9, Appendix D).

Each of these sessions begins with a review of homework, dares, MOOD charts, written accounts of the trauma. In so doing the focus is on modifying the exaggeratedly negative view of the trauma and its consequences. At the start of Session 7 one of the group members reported back on their homework as follows:

DON: I was just getting my confidence back driving and I was arguing with my teenage daughter as I was reversing my car in the supermarket car park and I hit another car, no one was in it at the time. The driver of the other car, a lady, was very understanding and pointed that I had hardly grazed the bumper, but I got in a right state, hardly driven since.
LEADER: Before being hit by the police car how would such an incident have affected you?

DON: I would have been a bit annoyed at myself, but it wouldn't have bothered me for days.

LEADER: It is as if PTSD sufferers acquire a 'magnifying glass', magnifying any hassle or shortcoming of themselves or others. What have you taken the hassle of the bump to mean?

DON: I guess what really got to me was that it showed it is much too dangerous to drive.

LEADER: You could come up with objective thinking such as 'it was only a very minor bump' but this really misses the point, the problem is that you took this incident as evidence for your post-trauma prejudice against the world, 'it is much too dangerous to drive'.

DON: Dealing with the bigger issue of my prejudice than how serious it was?

LEADER: Sometimes the thought that is really causing problems isn't the most apparent one, the stronger your emotional reaction the more likely it is that some 'nerve' concerning your negative view of self, others or the world has been tapped into.

In this exchange once again metaphor (the 'magnifying glass') is used to convey complex material such as the operation of core maladaptive schemas, without the need to use possibly confusing technical terms. The therapists have also explained that the more heightened the emotional arousal the more likely the source of the disturbance lies in an exaggeratedly negative view of self, others or the world. Further, relapses are used not only to make new material explicit but also to keep it relevant (item 2, Appendix D, General Group Therapeutic Skills Rating Scale) to current concerns.

Sessions 8–10

The last three sessions involve a review of all that has been taught. Group members are encouraged to go through the Survival Manual and underline/annotate what they have found useful and what they have found problematic. During the last group sessions, difficulties with material are problem solved and the Survival Manual is personalised as a relapse prevention aid. The final session should take place a few weeks after the penultimate session, allowing group members more space to try out their new-found skills and providing an opportunity for further refinement of the skills.

Chapter 7

Social phobia

Social phobia is a common disorder, with between 3% and 13% (American Psychiatric Association 2000) of the population suffering from it at some point, and it is the second most common anxiety disorder. However, whilst over a quarter (27.8%) of psychiatric outpatients meet diagnostic criteria for social phobia, only 1.1% give it as the main reason for seeking treatment (Zimmerman et al. 2008). But social phobia does run a chronic course, with 63% still suffering from the original episode even after 12 years of follow-up (Bruce et al. 2005) and with social phobia occurring before alcohol dependence in 80% of comorbid cases (Schneier et al. 2010). Social phobia is a risk factor for subsequent depression and substance abuse (Stein and Stein 2008). Thus despite the low rate of treatment seeking with social phobia it is a major mental health problem. Further, the rate of treatment seeking is even lower when social phoba is comorbid with alcohol abuse or dependence (Schneier et al. 2010).

Social phobia is defined in DSM-IV-TR (American Psychiatric Association 2000) as 'A marked and persistent fear of one or more social and performance situations in which the person is exposed to unfamiliar people or to possible scrutiny by others. The individual fears that he or she will act in a way (or show anxiety symptoms) that will be humiliating or embarrassing.' The concerns of individuals suffering from social phobia are rarely confined to one domain and more typically embrace a number of the following domains: being introduced, meeting people in authority, using the telephone, having visitors to the house, being watched doing something, being teased, eating at home with an acquaintance, eating at home with family, writing in front of others and public speaking (Amies et al. 1983).

Clients can be screened for social phobia using the 7 Minute Mental Health Screen – Revised (Appendix B) and positive screens further examined using the social phobia questions in the CBT Pocketbook (Appendix A). Social phobia can be viewed as on a continuum with shyness and both can be subsumed under the umbrella term social anxiety. The severity of social phobia should be assessed using the Social Phobia Inventory (SPIN; Connor et al. 2000), whilst the cognitions serving to maintain social phobia can be assessed using the Social Cognitions Questionnaire (SCQ; Wells *et al*. 1993). It is suggested that these measures are completed in the 24 hours before each session so that progress of group members can be charted (Appendix F).

Cognitive behaviour therapy for social phobia has proved more effective than either the antidepressant fluoxetine and self-exposure to social situations or a pill placebo plus self-exposure (Clark *et al*. 2003) and in a later study Clark *et al*. (2006) reported a recovery rate of 84% for their individual cognitive therapy, but these clients were initially at most mildly depressed (with a pre-treatment Beck Depression Inventory Score (Beck *et al*. 1979) of 12.40 and standard deviation of 8.65). More generally for 30–40% of clients treatment does not work (Stein and Stein 2008), with over a third of clients (35.3%) dropping out of GCBT (Blanco *et al*. 2010). It may be that the Clark *et al*. (2006) protocol is particularly potent and/or that it was delivered by nationally recognised experts.

The development of social phobia

Social phobia is primarily a disorder of early onset, with 80% of sufferers developing the disorder by age 20. This has led to a search for developmental triggers. Attention has focused upon (a) behavioural inhibition in children, i.e. fear and withdrawal in situations that are novel and unfamiliar, as this has been found to predict the later development of social phobia (Hirshfeld-Becker *et al*. 2008); (b) early interpersonal trauma – about half of sufferers state that the start of their social fears was marked by an uncomfortable social situation, such as teasing (Stemberger *et al*. 1995), and when clients with social phobia were asked (Hackmann *et al*. 2000) to bring to mind the recurrent images they frequently experienced during anxiety-provoking social situations 81% recalled an event that had happened no more than a year following onset of the disorder; and (c) 'self-silencing' – Cuming and Rapee (2010) have suggested that if a child is led to believe that they can only relate to others by a 'selflessness', removing their thoughts and feelings, then this may be a stepping stone to social phobia. These authors found that social anxiety was associated with a paucity of disclosure in both romantic relationships and close friendships in females, but not males. Behavioural inhibition, early interpersonal trauma and 'self-silencing' may be independent paths to social phobia but probably the most common scenario for most affected individuals will be that some combination of these factors operates.

Wells' model of the maintenance of social phobia

The Wells model (1997) of social phobia proposes that when the social phobic anticipates or enters a social situation their negative automatic thoughts are of social 'meltdown'. The content of this 'meltdown' might involve variously, blushing, stammering, sweating, being incoherent or boring. The core of the model is the social phobic's perception of (a) what others remain focused on when they look at him/her and (b) the global negative inferences of others constructed on the basis of the social phobics' 'deficits'. Social phobics develop 'safety' behaviours to help them cope with these situations, e.g. avoiding eye contact, avoiding asking questions. But unfortunately for them such behaviours rarely work, e.g. others persist with communicating despite the avoidance, increasing the social phobic's sense of threat and accompanying distressing bodily symptoms, leading to a sense that 'meltdown' is imminent, often leading to escape. The social phobic's 'post-mortem' on the social encounter often results in a renewed commitment to avoid such situations. Because the feedback in most social situations is ambiguous it is difficult for the social phobic to collect information that contradicts how they see others seeing them. The key features of the Wells (1997) model are summarised in Figure 7.1.

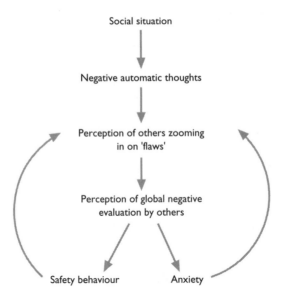

Figure 7.1 Model of social phobia (Wells 1997).

Figure 7.1 indicates a number of points of entry for breaking the vicious circle of social anxiety, relinquishing safety behaviours, insisting that the client's perception of global negative evaluation by others should be evidence-based, challenging the client's view that others operate with a 'zoom' lens, making a global negative evaluation of them. Rapee and Heimberg (1997) have put forward a very similar model to that of Wells (1997), the core of their model being the social phobic's assumption that others have overly high expectations of them. Schmidt *et al.* (2009) have suggested that social anxiety sufferers pay special attention (i.e. have an attentional bias) towards negative social cues, such as certain facial expressions, interpreting them as indicating a negative evaluation. These authors trained clients to disengage from negative social cues using attention training, with 72% no longer meeting diagnostic criteria for social phobia at the end of treatment compared to 11% in a control condition.

Social phobia programme

Some clients with social phobia have a particular problem talking with members of the opposite sex and it is useful therefore to have a group of mixed sexes and two therapists of different gender. The social phobia programme outlined in Table 7.1 is a synthesis of those of Wells (1997) and Clark *et al.* (2006) and an integration of the treatment implications of the findings of Hackmann *et al.* (2000), Schmidt *et al.* (2009) and Cuming and Rapee (2010).

The cast of the social phobia group programme is shown in Table 7.2.

Sessions 1 and 2

For clients with social phobia a group of strangers represents their worst nightmare come true. It is therefore extremely important that they are not coerced into attendance and that the appropriate motivational interviewing procedures detailed in Chapter 2 are followed. This would involve after-session contact (by telephone) with each group member following the initial sessions. The primary aims of the first two sessions are to socialise clients to the CBT model of social phobia and to enhance their sense of self-efficacy, i.e. by adopting a different set of beliefs and behaviours in social situations they could manage them better.

The first session begins with the leader welcoming the group members and congratulating them on their courage in attending when a group of strangers is probably their worst fear. In the following exchange the therapists recognise the probable ambivalent feelings of members:

LEADER: I guess many of you would want to position yourself nearest to the exit or planned to arrive exactly on time so there was no opportunity for small talk. You probably think I can already recognise who has become uncomfortable but I can't, honestly.

CO-LEADER: Nor me and I'm much brighter than the leader!

LEADER: *laughing* Just ignore the co-leader, only here to make up the number.

CO-LEADER: I'll do the peasant's task of handing out the Social Phobia Survival Manual.

Table 7.1 Social phobia programme

	Therapeutic targets	*Treatment strategies*	*Materials – Social Phobia Survival Manual, Appendix K*
Sessions 1 and 2	'I'm an oddity' Beliefs that maintain social anxiety	Distillation of working model of each member's disorder. Questioning of typical thoughts (on 'second thoughts'). Survey to determine what makes people 'acceptable'	Introduction and Sections 1 and 2
Session 3	'Inside' view of self. Expectation of high standards	Contrasting 'inside' view of self with 'outside' view of others using video feedback. Exposure to feared situations. Survey to determine standards of others.	Sections 3 and 4
Sessions 4 and 5	Safety behaviours. Information processing biases	Contrasting anxiety experienced using safety behaviours with those when not using. Vigilance for all or nothing thinking, personalisation, mind-reading and mental filter	Section 5
Sessions 6 and 7	Non-disclosure of personal information	Modelling and role-play of self-disclosure	Section 6
Session 8	Anticipatory anxiety and post-event rumination. Past humiliations	Cognitive restructuring and re-scripting	Section 7
Sessions 9 and 10	Anticipatory anxiety and post-event rumination. Relapse prevention	Moderating worry and disengagement from it. Role play of anticipated difficult situation, ensuring adherence to Survival Manual to prevent full-blown relapse	Section 8. Recap Survival Manual

Table 7.2 The members of the social phobia group

Group member	Thumbnail sketch
Tom	A science undergraduate finding it impossible to relate to fellow students, regarded as a 'swot' at school, parents' marriage acrimonious
Sian	Bullied at school, unemployed, embarrassed at blushing and stammering, terrified of interviews
Helen	An accounts clerk, disappointed passed over for promotion despite achieving formal qualifications, relationship with boyfriend strained, problems shaking
Anne	Very isolated, parents both died, finding social groups overwhelming and frustrating, conscious of humiliation at school
Gus	Manager terrified of making presentations, drinking more than he believes he should

At this point a group member Helen arrives late. The co-leader ushers her to a seat and offers her a cup of tea which she declines, dropping her bag on the floor as she sits down. The leader continues.

LEADER: In this session we were planning to go through the first two sections of the Manual. Before we go through it, just write down what you thought of our illustrious co-leader here when he made the comments about being 'bright' and a 'peasant'. Just take a moment to write down what you thought of him when he said those things, don't worry you won't have to declare it.

After a pause . . .

LEADER: Would anyone dare to say what they wrote down, *silence* Would anyone dare to put up their hand if they felt positive or neutral about what the co-leader said, *all hands go up.* Now if my esteemed co-leader suffered from social phobia he would just think you are all trying to be nice and he wouldn't believe it. So that in social phobia things are set up so you can't win. What I would like to do now is put my dear co-leader on the spot and ask him to collect in what you have written, don't put your name on it, so we can keep them anonymous OK, and we will mix them up anyhow and read them out.

CO-LEADER: *after collecting the written comments reads them out* First 'a bit nervous but trying to put us at ease', second 'got a sense of humour', third 'a little big headed but very pleasant, nice the way he offered the lady a cup of tea', fourth 'he's ok', fifth 'edgy but who am I to talk' and six 'could have some laughs'. If I suffered from social phobia I would have got it wrong, thinking people are just saying positive or neutral things but they don't really mean it. The person with social phobia is shown in Figure 2 of the Survival Manual (Appendix K); they feel they are at the centre and everybody else is around focused on them, critical.

What this little experiment showed was that in fact people have a mix of reactions, some neutral and some positive.

LEADER: What I thought was interesting was that people were positive or neutral despite some thinking you were a 'bit edgy or nervous.' Any comments on this?

In the above exchange the therapists have avoided presenting the introductory material from the Social Phobia Survival Manual, Appendix K, in a didactic manner and have striven instead to illustrate it involving the 'here and now' experiences of group members, facilitating an active learning, which is likely to be more enduring. As such the therapists have made the material relevant (item 2 of the of the GGTSRS, Appendix D) and inclusive (item 4 of the GGTSRS, Appendix D). Further, the therapists have assiduously avoided putting the spotlight on any one group member at this stage, in the interests of forging a therapeutic alliance and in implicitly negating reservations about attending the group. The dialogue continued:

GUS: I suppose people can be OK about you even though you are nervy, but it doesn't get you promoted.

CO-LEADER: But you are a manager?

GUS: Only a first line manager.

HELEN: I've been passed over for promotion too.

SIAN: I can't even get a job, I blush too much.

CO-LEADER: Social phobia can certainly get in the way of people's ambitions and removing this obstacle is one of the goals of the group sessions. Though to be fair it comes at a price of learning to tolerate some emotional discomfort. If we try to eliminate all emotional discomfort it just makes matters worse.

ANNE: I'd rather be just relaxed.

LEADER: But is it realistic to be 'just relaxed' with a group of strangers? Maybe for homework as well as reading the first two sections of the Manual do a survey and ask as many people as you can, would you expect to be 'just relaxed' with a group of strangers.

In the above exchange the therapists have highlighted that one of the common costs of social phobia is underachievement and have utilised this to increase motivation to attend the group and tackle the condition. The therapists are also conscious that anxiety sensitivity is an issue across the anxiety disorders and have flagged up the antidote – learning to tolerate some symptoms of anxiety as an inevitable counterpart to living.

The focus in the second session is on beliefs that maintain anxiety. The ground is prepared for this material by the leader demonstrating that there is such latitude in 'normal' behaviour that oftentimes socially 'inappropriate' behaviour is not noticed. The session began:

LEADER: Did anyone notice any unusual behaviour at the last session? *Silence*. Nothing at all?

HELEN: Me dropping my bag?

CO-LEADER: Before Helen just mentioned it was anyone thinking of her dropping her handbag?

TOM: No.

ANNE: No. but I did think at the time that is the sort of thing I do.

CO-LEADER: So now you can begin being just you and no one really remembers.

ANNE: Maybe.

LEADER: I will give a clue, it was about me.

GUS: You took charge.

LEADER: No, what I did every couple of minutes was scratch under one of my armpits and there was more!

TOM: The mind boggles!

LEADER: I pulled one or other ear lobe every few minutes. No one noticed. I was really just like Figure 3 in the Manual, people noticed me in passing but nobody could be bothered scrutinising me, they weren't zooming in on me. But this is just what many with social phobia expect of others. Indeed this is the first of the beliefs in social anxiety that I would like to discuss.

The leader then led a discussion of this set of social anxiety beliefs about self and others' evaluation of them. This was then followed by the co-leader explaining that social phobia is maintained not only by social anxiety beliefs but also by safety behaviours, i.e. overt or covert behaviours designed to prevent the worst outcomes in social encounters. Finally the discussions were summarised in Table 7.3 to make it dear to each member in what way their particular difficulties are a specific example of the cognitive model of social phobia. Table 7.3 encapsulates the essence of a case formulation of each client's difficulties.

Group members are introduced to a framework for challenging anxious cognitions using Table 1, in Appendix K (reproduced as Table 7.4 here for convenience).

At the concurrent individual contacts, scheduled over the first three sessions, the therapists addressed not only motivation to attend the group but also any comorbid disorders; for example, one of the group was abusing alcohol and motivational interviewing was conducted for this.

Session 3

The key learning objective in the third session is to teach group members to question whether their view of themselves in social interactions is consistent

Table 7.3 The nucleus of a case formulation of each group member's difficulties

Group member	Typical thought	Negative evaluation by others	Safety behaviours
Tom	I'm an oddity	They will think I'm weird if I am not careful	Don't give any personal information away
Sian	I'm boring and I will blush if they talk to me	They will think I am stupid for blushing	Just go to the gathering for an hour
Helen	My voice will quaver and I won't know what to say	They will just disregard me	See if I can make an excuse for not going
Anne	I will make a fool of myself, my mind will go blank, they will see my hands shaking	They will think I am a fraud for having the position I've got	See if I can get someone else to do the presentation
Gus	I can't do small talk, I'll freeze	They will think I am unsociable, aloof	Organise to serve the drinks and get the food out

Table 7.4 On second thoughts

Social situation that made me anxious	
What I thought	
What I did	
What I did afterwards	
What would be a better way of thinking and behaving that I could try out next time, in a similar situation?	

with those of others. But before teaching new material homework was reviewed:

LEADER: How did people get on using 'second thoughts' in the Manual (Table 7.4)?

HELEN: I tried to use it over getting coffee in work, I was desperate for a drink, went to a new machine that had been installed only to discover that it emptied the contents into a flimsy plastic cup. I thought oh no I'll spill it if I pick it up because of my shaking, I looked around and there were other people in the queue behind me, I just died. I made some excuse that I had just forgotten something and left the full cup of coffee in the machine, they must have thought I was an idiot, then I started blushing.

LEADER: So how did you use the form?

HELEN: Well I put all that down in the first four rows of the form but then I was struggling to come up with a new way of thinking and behaving; eventually I thought there's no need to panic I can always empty part of the contents into a nearby bin, just say 'it's too full' if others are around and they probably will not think anything about it.

LEADER: So it is actually the dramatic safety behaviours that attract attention and not that there's a slight difficulty?

HELEN: Yes, I just lose it when others are watching.

CO-LEADER: What makes you shake in the first place?

HELEN: Well I've always had a slight hand tremor, Mum had one as well, but when I was teased at school about it I became more conscious of it.

CO-LEADER: Shaking is made worse by tensing your hand. Try alternately tensing and relaxing your hand as you hold something; this is in effect a relaxation exercise and you might find it easier.

HELEN: That sounds an idea.

LEADER: How does your mum get on with people?

HELEN: Fine, lots of friends.

LEADER: So her hand tremor hasn't put people off?

HELEN: No.

LEADER: Why should your hand tremor put other people off?

HELEN: Not thought of it like that.

The above exchange indicates the type of childhood problems that can lead to social phobia and the way in which safety behaviours create the very problems they are designed to avoid. The dialogue also models for the group that rather than trying to blank perceived social catastrophes it is useful to replay them in detail to come up with a better way of handling them. The exchange continued:

CO-LEADER: You might want to try out this new way of approaching the cup of coffee by getting a drink now or at the end of the session.

HELEN: I think I'll try one at the end if that's OK.

CO-LEADER: That's great, it's all about very gradually daring yourself to do what you have been avoiding and seeing does anything really terrible happen.

GUS: Hmm maybe I could just dare myself to ask if I could have a cup of coffee now as I was late.

CO-LEADER: Asking for what you really want is a dare, great.

HELEN: OK, Gus, I'll go and get you one!

ANNE: I should really volunteer as well, but as you've already offered, Helen!

GUS: Good to have so many slaves.

CO-LEADER: Watch it, Gus, Helen just might deliberately spill it in your lap!
HELEN: *laughing* There's an idea.

This dialogue illustrates one of the advantages of the group format, that other group members are encouraged by the dares ('behavioural experiments') of others. Further, the group is a theatre/stepping stone for trying out new coping strategies, allowing refinement in a safe place, before real world application.

The new focus in Session 3 is on the gap between the view of the self that others have and clients' own view of themselves, suggesting that the latter may be exaggeratedly negative. The session continued:

LEADER: If you hear your voice played back on a tape recorder, do you often think that doesn't sound like me, or is that just me?
SIAN: I sound more confident than I am.
TOM: I think I haven't got an accent but when I hear myself on tape I notice it.
LEADER: I find my voice is much deeper than I think it is. So there is often a gap between how we see ourselves and how other people see us. Why do you think that might be?
SIAN: They don't see what goes on inside.
CO-LEADER: We tend to construct what we think others see from what our concerns are at the time, so that if we are concerned about stammering we will likely think that is what others are noticing. So we can be surprised by someone saying a talk we gave went well when we felt as nervous as hell.
GUS: That happens to me in work, I absolutely hate presentations but people say they are fine, I think they are just trying to be nice.
TOM: Me too, I just die.
LEADER: What I would like to do is use some video to look at the difference between the 'inside' view and the 'outside' view. I've got some material on this digital pen; it will take a few minutes for me to get it up on the laptop. Just take a 5-minute coffee break and chat amongst yourselves. *After 5–10 minutes the leader reconvenes the group* I want you now to do a slow motion action replay of what you thought or the images you had when I said just chat amongst yourselves for a couple of minutes, what were your thoughts/images of what would come across to others, e.g. I thought I would go really red or others are going to notice my hand shaking, and write this on the second row of Table 7.4, then on the third row write down what you did, maybe poured coffee for everyone or went to the toilet, chatted to a particular person. The fourth row we all know I asked you all to sit down. Now don't do the fifth row of Table 7.4 just yet; unless anyone objects I want to play a clip of those few minutes of the session, [*the session was recorded using a*

digital pen camera (about £50), which is shaped like a pen with a sound range of about 15 feet and was positioned on a shelf, it has a USB port to plug directly into a laptop] before the coffee break *[at the outset of the programme all group members had agreed that group sessions would be recorded for training purposes for the therapists and group members only]* and I want you to make a note of how you and others came across but as if you were observing people including yourself that you are reasonably well disposed to. *The leader played back the 15 minutes of the session before the coffee break.*

CO-LEADER: Sian what did you make of what you saw of yourself.

SIAN: I was OK.

CO-LEADER: No stammering or blushing.

SIAN: No, but I think my voice quavered a bit.

CO-LEADER: Did anyone else make a note of that?

OTHER GROUP MEMBERS: *a chorus of no's*

CO-LEADER: How did, how you came over on the video, the 'outside' view, compare with what you may have written down as the 'inside' view as you were going for the coffee break?

SIAN: It's not the same, came over much better.

CO-LEADER: How did the 'outside' view and the 'inside' view square for others? *after a group discussion the co-leader summarised the findings* So there is a gap between the 'inside' view and the 'outside' and the 'inside' is a lot worse.

LEADER: I'd like to pick up on how the type of post-mortem you do on a social encounter helps to keep your anxiety going; for example, in Sian's case, looking back she picked up her 'voice quavering', though no one else spotted this, and I guess Sian used this to justify her feelings of anxiety. This is what we call a 'justifying cognition' and this thought might make Sian anxious about the next social situation. It is as if after a social encounter the person with social phobia has a butterfly net and sets out to capture a butterfly to justify the 'butterflies' they get in their social encounters; what we want to encourage is putting down your butterfly net after social encounters. Having seen the playback and noted your thoughts and behaviours surrounding the coffee break, complete the bottom line of Table 7.4 about playing it differently next time.

In the above exchange the therapists have used the group as a laboratory to illustrate the main teaching point, that there is a discrepancy between clients' 'inside' view of themselves constructed from their private sensations and the 'outside' view visible to others. The therapists have also been careful to guard against the social phobic's typically hypercritical examination of themselves by asking them to take the stance of a well-disposed observer about themselves. Finally the therapists have highlighted that social phobia can be maintained by justifying post-mortem cognitions that use internal experiences during social encounters as an evidence base. The session continued:

LEADER: Looking at the bottom line of Table 7.4 how would people do things differently next time?

SIAN: I won't spend longer than I need to in the toilet, I should just mix.

TOM: It looks as if you can't really tell people's problems on video, beforehand everybody is thinking they are really bad but others are OK, which is weird.

GUS: *looking at the leader* So what you are saying is the 'weird' is in how we look at ourselves?

LEADER: I'm puzzled by how can it be that everybody thinks they perform particularly badly and everybody else is OK? If this is the case can it be that others really have high standards about what is expected?

In this exchange the leader is using Socratic dialogue to help group members discover the core problem in social phobia, the construction of self largely from internal sensations rather than from any current environmental feedback. Group members are led to consider that perhaps after all other people do not have high expectations of social performance. Further, group members are themselves becoming teachers, advocating the need to overcome avoidance. A further advantage of replaying the video of the earlier part of the session is that it reinforces the teaching that had taken place. For homework group members were asked to gradually stay longer in social situations in which they experienced difficulty and to begin to encounter those they were avoiding and to complete Table 7.4.

Sessions 4 and 5

The focus in these two sessions is on the dropping of safety behaviours but the sessions begin as always with review of the previous session's homework and the troubleshooting of difficulties. At the start of Session 4 group members were asked to recall how anxious they felt in the extra coffee break at the last session and to rate their anxiety on a scale of 0–10. It was explained that social situations that are without an agenda – 'just chat amongst yourselves' – are particularly stressful for those with social phobia because there are no clear rules; they are ambiguous, creating an uncertainty which many find intolerable. The therapists then asked group members to list any safety behaviours that they used, such as staying longer in the toilet to avoid conversation. The leader then opened the discussion and focused on including (item 4, Inclusion, in the GGTSRS, Appendix D) Anne, who had been fairly quiet at the last session:

ANNE: I don't know that I do anything special, just look down, hope no one will see me and mumble if someone talks to me, hoping that then they will go away quickly.

LEADER: The safety behaviours often seem nothing special because you are so used to them but look what happens if I used Anne's safety behaviours. *The leader and co-leader then proceed to the following role play*

CO-LEADER: Are you going on holiday this year?

LEADER: *eyes fixed on floor, mumbling* Don't know, might do.

CO-LEADER: Oh.

LEADER: You see these safety behaviours of Anne's are very good for stopping other people in their tracks but not too hot on making a good relationship.

ANNE: Don't I know.

LEADER: What I would like to try, Anne, is you dropping these safety behaviours and really concentrate just on what the co-leader says, let everything else hovering in the background just take care of itself. Decide not to focus on your internal sensations but largely externally on what the other person is saying.

CO-LEADER: Are you going on holiday this year?

ANNE: *looking at the floor* I might go to Devon, I have got friends there.

CO-LEADER: Whereabouts exactly?

ANNE: Ilfracombe.

LEADER: That's great, Anne, you were making conversation, telling a bit about yourself, just try a bit more eye contact. Have a go again.

CO-LEADER: Are you going on holiday this year?

ANNE: *making eye contact* Yes to Ilfracombe.

CO-LEADER: What's it like there?

ANNE: Lovely beaches in the area.

CO-LEADER: Are going by yourself?

ANNE: Yes I will meet up with some old friends.

LEADER: Excellent, was that easier than when you chatted in the coffee break last time?

ANNE: Quite a lot easier.

LEADER: What I would like to do now is have a coffee break but as you chat amongst yourselves focus on the other person, largely forget about your own emotions/sensations, let them take care of themselves. But there is bound to be some awareness of your own sensations, rather like being engrossed in reading something but you are looking after a toddler and you cast a glance now and again to see what they are up to.

In the above dialogue the therapist has given the client first positive feedback on their performance before making specific comments about how performance can be improved. The role play also serves to model effective social interaction and an opportunity is given to practise the necessary skills in the protected environment of the session coffee break. After the group reconvened the following dialogue ensued:

LEADER: On a scale 0–10, write down how anxious you got during the coffee break. How does your score compare with your score at the coffee break last time?

TOM: I was less anxious, just talking to Gus focusing on his job, asking him how easy it was to get time off to come to the sessions, took my mind off myself and it was easier, though I still stuttered a little.

CO-LEADER: So it was easier when you dropped safety behaviours?

TOM: Yes, last week I stood looking into my coffee cup hoping nobody would notice me.

CO-LEADER: What do you take it to mean if someone talking to you stutters slightly?

GUS: I thought it was great Tom made the effort; I could tell he found it difficult but I respected him more because of it.

TOM: I'm going to blush now.

ANNE: Go for it, Tom, I do it all the time.

CO-LEADER: So it's OK for Tom to blush, Anne, but not for you, have I got that right?

ANNE: But when I do it the whole world knows, I go so red.

CO-LEADER: What as red as that box?

ANNE: Well not quite.

CO-LEADER: Is it as pink as on that magazine?

ANNE: Probably.

CO-LEADER: Would you mind if we tested out how pink or red your blushes are? You could have a couple of minutes conversation with the leader, I could record it using this digital camcorder; it has a built-in microphone and plugs into a laptop so we can see afterwards how beetroot you are.

ANNE: OK, but I didn't actually say I go beetroot but it is bad.

In the above exchange the therapists have been concerned to go beyond other group members' assurances that anyone of them is being negatively evaluated, important though this is, to present objective evidence using video of the 'outside' view of themselves, juxtapose it with the 'inside' view and resolve any contradictions. After the role play the leader plays it back on the laptop:

LEADER: How red do you think your complexion is, Anne?

ANNE: Well it is not really red but my neck and face have gone pink.

CO-LEADER: So if your face and neck have gone pink what is so bad about that?

ANNE: It shouldn't.

CO-LEADER: Who says so?

ANNE: I do.

CO-LEADER: I suppose because other kids mocked you about it.

TOM: I think it's nice when you go pink, it shows you are alive.

ANNE: Thanks, Tom.

TOM: But it is not what a bloke should do and stutter as well.

GUS: I'm tempted to say who is bothered? But I am bothered when I do those things giving a presentation.

CO-LEADER: Are you absolutely sure they are negative in a presentation.

GUS: Maybe they are not as catastrophic as all that.

In the above exchange, video feedback and cognitive disputation have been used in tandem to challenge the imagined negative portrayal of self. But clients with social phobia are hyperalert for any signs of threat; even neutral signs such as a blank expression on the part of their listener can evoke anxiety. Using in-session video role play, group members can be trained to continue to focus on the other (either on conveying a message to them or listening), despite blank expressions or even grimaces in their interaction, and taught not to be distracted by their own increased anxiety. This is complemented by modifying the attributions clients typically make about such expressions and creating a more realistic story (theory of mind) about what is going on in the other person's mind. The session continues with the leader drawing the group's attention to the role played by information processing biases in social phobia:

LEADER: If you could all look at the second part of Section 5 in the Manual, you can see that the four bullet points refer to information processing biases that cause problems in social phobia: personalisation, e.g. the other person doesn't seem interested in what I have said so it must be my fault; mind-reading, e.g. they have got a blank expression so they must be critical of me; all or nothing thinking, e.g. I'm not performing just the way I want so it must be awful; and mental filter, e.g. they will just notice my going red. Do these biases ring any bells?

HELEN: I do all or nothing thinking with the bosses in work, I get in such a state feeling I've got to explain it properly, one of them doesn't let you finish your sentences and is looking out of the window or goes over to his fax machine in the middle, I am a lather of sweat before I go and see him.

CO-LEADER: Is he like that with other people?

HELEN: Yes, except when the big boss comes in, then he's all smiles, all over them, it makes me sick.

CO-LEADER: Does it work trying to explain things perfectly to him?

HELEN: No.

CO-LEADER: Why bother? Just maybe to cover your back put what you want to say in a written memo after that you can give/send afterwards.

LEADER: Maybe I could role play being this boss and you try and tell me something; we could video it, then play it back and see what you think.

HELEN: OK *when the 5-minute role play was played back she made the following comments* I got really irritated when you began 'playing a piano' with your fingers as I was explaining what we have to do for the end of the tax year, my mind went blank I was so angry, I just had to stop.

CO-LEADER: Looking at the video can you see that anger?

HELEN: No, I just came to a stop.

CO-LEADER: So that there was nothing wrong in your performance other than you forgot to carry on focusing outside of yourself on the task.

HELEN: I see what you mean.

LEADER: Could we do the role play again but where this time you keep task oriented when the feedback is or seems negative.

HELEN: OK *after which there was another 5-minute role play but this time the leader interrupted her by saying 'let me just check my fax machine'; on reviewing this video the leader commented as follows:*

LEADER: It is great that you didn't allow yourself to be distracted by my going to check the fax machine.

HELEN: I had to swallow hard then.

LEADER: But on the video I couldn't see you swallow hard.

HELEN: No.

LEADER: It's OK to be aware of an increase in negativity of the background emotion, as in this case the boss was being 'ignorant', but it is still about keeping task focused socially. You can note the increase in negativity of background emotion and decide afterwards what you might do about it.

GUS: You can't easily do anything when it is your boss.

CO-LEADER: No, but each time you see him you could imagine him sitting constipated on the toilet, straining, going red!

HELEN: *laughter* I certainly could but he might be wondering what I am laughing about.

LEADER: Maybe by the time you meet him to talk it will be just a slight smile, that because he is so busy looking out of the window he will not even notice.

In the above dialogue the therapists have used role play and video feedback to teach group members how not to get hijacked by internal sensations, particularly when they are heightened by real or imaginary negative feedback from the environment. Further, in highlighting the role that information processing biases play in the construction of the 'inside' view of self, the stage is set for a more accurate reconstruction of social self that incorporates actual data from the environment. In order to ensure maximum involvement of group members, difficult situations encountered by members, such as visits to the family home by relatives and strangers, meeting strangers and informal gatherings, are role played, videoed, with feedback given on performance, and enacted again, with as many scenarios and group members as time permits.

Sessions 6 and 7

The new material introduced in these two sessions targets the tendency of clients with social phobia not to disclose personal information. This is highlighted by reference to Figure 4 in the Social Phobia Survival Manual, Appendix K. But before getting underway with this material the sessions begin with a review of the previous session's homework, which involved exposure to feared situations. Group members reported back as follows:

ANNE: I did go to my cousin's wedding. I felt I've got to keep some links with my family, but when I saw the seating arrangements at the reception, they were all couples except me, so I was uptight before I sat down, then the guys are talking about football and cars, I wanted to scream.

CO-LEADER: What did the other women in the group say or do?

ANNE: One of them spoke of how she only managed to get a suitable dress for the wedding at the last minute, another was saying that she wasn't sure she could eat at the moment because of morning sickness. They were boring.

CO-LEADER: Probably most conversations are boring in terms of the topic, like talking about the weather they are just a way of recognising others, so you follow them through just out of recognition.

TOM: I think that is my problem, I expect me or them to have something interesting to say.

CO-LEADER: You can put a lot of pressure on yourself expecting to have something interesting to say.

TOM: Hmm. Perhaps Anne and I expect it all to be like an interesting lecture.

CO-LEADER: Perhaps, Tom, you and Anne could practise as if you were seated at the same table, we could video it and see what you think.

In the above exchange the therapists are reframing the meaning of everyday conversation, whilst space is given to group members to identify core problems and to suggest that they are not alone with these difficulties. The session continued:

TOM: OK.

ANNE: OK.

Inspection of the videoed role play of Anne and Tom conversing revealed no major problems and both group members felt that they did not appear particularly odd. The following feedback ensued:

LEADER: How come you performed so well?

ANNE: I was just concentrating on asking Tom questions.

TOM: And I was just concentrating on asking Anne questions but I was running out of them in the end.

ANNE: So was I.

LEADER: It flows much better then when you are concentrating outside of yourself. *Tom and Anne nodded their assent* But what was interesting is that neither of you volunteered anything about yourself even though you answered the other's questions.

SIAN: I never tell anything about me,

HELEN: Me too, I am happy asking questions for a bit about others but you run dry. For my homework I have been trying to have lunch with colleagues but after a bit I just want to escape.

LEADER: This brings us on to today's topic about letting others know something about you, if we could read through the second part of Section 5 of the Social Phobia Survival Manual.

After reading through the section the following discussion took place:

HELEN: My ex used to say I was like a closed book and he would say that he didn't know whether he had upset me or not. I used to make him mad if we went to any gathering, I'd insist he stayed by my side so I would have someone to talk to. I'd get cross with him if he wandered off abandoning me. Even when we were with people I'd give him daggers for giving personal information such as what we paid for a new three piece suite and I'd get really uncomfortable when he would express his political beliefs strongly, afterwards I would give him a hard time.

LEADER: That restricted self-expression often goes back a long time.

HELEN: I think it stems from when I was a teenager and disagreed with my parents' views and was told there is the door if you take that sort of attitude.

SIAN: I think mine goes back to being bullied at school because I said once that I wasn't that interested in boys, I just got homophobic ridicule constantly, you learn to shut up.

CO-LEADER: The danger is, that as an adult, others feel anxious around you because they don't know what they are dealing with and as in Figure 4 you might pick up their anxiety and want to escape. You get some relief from escaping and it then gets a pattern and no one gets to know you and you then feel isolated.

SIAN: I think I end relationships to stop them getting to know me.

CO-LEADER: What would be so bad about them getting to know you?

SIAN: I've got nothing to offer.

CO-LEADER: Why not let them be the judge of that?

SIAN: It will only end in tears.

HELEN: How do you know?

SIAN: I suppose I don't.

LEADER: Maybe Sian and Helen could chat but letting a bit about themselves out and we could video it. OK, Sian and Helen? *nods of assent*

SIAN: I wish I had your job.

HELEN: With a boss like mine? You might get a job now with your new confidence.

SIAN: I'm OK here but it's difficult out there.

HELEN: At least it's a first step.

SIAN: Once they know I'm gay that is it.

HELEN: Would they all hang, draw and quarter you?

SIAN: No.

HELEN: Give them a chance, not everybody is the same. I used to get called 'Nelly the Elephant' at school. Looking back I was only a bit overweight but one kid who was not very good at spelling, spread around that it was my real name because it was like Helen spelt backwards and it stuck, and I got a bit obsessed about my weight.

After viewing the video of this conversation the dialogue continued:

HELEN: Never told anyone other than my mum about this, it still hurts.

SIAN: It was such a relief just to say it and you are all just there for me. *tears*

GUS: Sian's bravery makes me think that the least I can do is to tell one of my colleagues about problems doing presentations instead of making ridiculous excuses.

LEADER: Maybe at the next session, Gus, you could give us a presentation on dealing with difficult bosses; we could video it and give you feedback.

GUS: OK.

For homework after Session 6 group members are asked to read Section 6 of the Social Phobia Manual, approach feared situations and practise disclosing personal information. Session 7 begins with a review of this homework, in-session role play of situations that were difficult and feedback for improved performance. Finally in Session 7 the beliefs that maintain social anxiety, reviewed in Section 1, are revisited and the importance of continuing to challenge them underlined.

Session 8

The new material introduced in this session draws upon Section 7 of the Social Phobia Manual and involves a re-scripting of past humiliations with the knowledge of an adult. But this ought not to be a purely cerebral exercise; group members should be invited to role play themselves at the time of the humiliation and the therapists take the role of comforter. In this way the therapists are modelling the process of self-soothing. Roles can then be swapped, with the therapist playing the role of the distressed child/adolescent and the client the 'soother', and feedback given on how to better self-soothe. Such role plays can evoke strong feelings about the inability/unwillingness/perceived unapproachability of adults at the time to provide the necessary soothing and the culpability of those adults may need to be reassessed. Care has to be taken to remind the group members of their oftentimes naivety at the time of the humiliation so that they do not resort to excessive self-blame.

The eighth session begins with a review of homework and it had been agreed at the previous session that one of the members would make a presentation at this session, which would be videoed. After playing back the video, the following discussion ensued:

LEADER: That was good, Gus, I liked your advice of documenting everything when dealing with a difficult boss so you have got some evidence and I liked your humour pinched from the last session of imagining the boss sitting constipated on the toilet. What did others think?

HELEN: You'd be much easier to deal with than my boss, but keeping looking at your notes made me feel you were very unsure.

GUS: I think I am going to forget things and get muddled up, so I write the whole thing out with headings.

CO-LEADER: Maybe just dare yourself to write down a few bullet points and only glance at them. Maybe take a minute or two to jot down a couple of ideas about places we could go on holiday in the UK and then do a presentation just with this?

GUS: OK.

CO-LEADER: We can just take a break for 2 minutes whilst Gus gathers his thoughts *after which Gus gave a brief presentation which was videoed and replayed and the session continued*

LEADER: OK, what did people think of that?

HELEN: It was much better, more relaxed.

GUS: Thanks, Helen, really appreciate that.

LEADER: How did people find that brief break, with no distraction not even coffee?

TOM: I was much less bothered by it than I would have been at the beginning of the programme; I didn't feel under pressure to say something smart.

In the above exchange once again the group has been used as a laboratory for refining social skills and group members are playing a clear therapeutic role, offering not only emotional support but specific suggestions for improving social skills. The therapists are also using the session to gauge group members' progress in handling intolerance of uncertainty in the ambiguous situation of a brief break in the session.

After reviewing the material in Section 7 the leader suggested that because of the obvious rapport between two group members one of them re-enact their feelings of humiliation as a child and the other act as the comforting adult. The session proceeded:

HELEN: It's embarrassing to be me as a 13-year-old.
CO-LEADER: Just try it as best you can.
GUS: I always hated Drama in school.
CO-LEADER: It's a good match, you're equally embarrassed!
HELEN: Right here goes, it's just not fair, they call me Nelly the elephant and say here comes 'frumpy'.
GUS: They are just jealous, having a go at you because you are quiet.
HELEN: I don't like them and I don't want to go to school.
GUS: Are there some nice kids in school?
HELEN: Yes.
GUS: Why don't you ask them if they ever get called names?
HELEN: I could do, but it is not the same.
GUS: Why?
HELEN: I don't know, stop asking me all these questions.
GUS: *Out of role* I am blank now.
HELEN: *Out of role* It was great, I was a stroppy cow as a teenager.
GUS: Not now!
HELEN: No.
CO-LEADER: Could you see yourself telling the teenage you what Gus said if this memory comes to mind when you are getting anxious?
HELEN: I think I could, I only wish my dad hadn't always been too busy to be bothered listening to what upset me. I think I feel angry with him and his macho behaviour.

It is possible to advise a client troubled by flashbacks of humiliation, to soothe the younger version of themselves (then) with what they know now without doing a role play but the latter probably provides more comprehensive access to the emotions that were around at the time. In addition, experiencing the provision of soothing from another adds to the memorability of that soothing, making it more likely it will be utilised. The role play involved a very limited re-parenting. Further role plays between other group members are then conducted.

Sessions 9 and 10

In the last two sessions of the programme, after reviewing homework, the focus is on Section 8 of the Manual, which deals with anticipatory anxiety, catastrophising about social encounters and post-event rumination. This section draws on work done at earlier sessions and thereby provides an opportunity to consolidate previous learning. Group members are prepared for independent functioning outside the group by inviting them to brainstorm situations that may crop up that they anticipate would be challenging and then to problem solve their response using the material taught in the programme. Responses are visualised before the anticipated challenging situations are role played with feedback. In Session 9 the following exchange took place:

LEADER: A major difficulty for people with social phobia is that their problem is not just the meeting of people but the worrying beforehand and the agonising afterwards; together they are often almost as bad as the actual contact. If we could take a few minutes just to read through Section 9 of the Manual. *After a pause the leader continued* Any comments on what we have just read?

SIAN: I still want a job but I'm terrified of interviews, I worry such a lot that I'm a nervous wreck before I even get there, then afterwards I either think I have rambled or said too little.

CO-LEADER: It's a bit like Gus at the previous session; he had prepared his talk so much, writing every bit down, that it got in the way, then when he had written just a couple of things down he was much better. It may be that all you need to do is jot a few things down to explain how you are suited to the particular job. What job would that be?

SIAN: Admin Officer.

CO-LEADER: Maybe we could role play it, I could be interviewing you and you are being interviewed by me and, say, Helen because she works in an office environment; if we just grab a coffee whilst we collect our thoughts.

SIAN: *laughing* I can't even hold this cup I'm so nervous and this isn't the real thing!

HELEN: So you left school with 5 GCSEs?

SIAN: Hmm I didn't do much at school.

CO-LEADER: Why was that?

SIAN: I was bullied.

CO-LEADER: Can't you stand up for yourself?

SIAN: I couldn't then, I can now.

HELEN: Well I think you did well getting 5 GCSEs when you were bullied. What makes you think you could do this job?

SIAN: I'm into organising, always making lists and working to them.

CO-LEADER: OK if we step out of role I think you did great your letting a bit of personal information out about yourself, so other people can feel they know what they are dealing with and you were firm when there was a bit of a put-down without being offensive.

HELEN: *Laughing* You've got the job!

LEADER: We've talked a lot in the sessions about concentrating on who you are talking to, working out what is their story. In this example the likelihood is that the interviewers would only call for interview those who could in principle do the job, so they are not really that bothered about qualifications etc., they are really trying to work out could I see myself being able to work with this person, which is really what Helen did.

SIAN: It puts a whole new angle on it, I just have to get to interview first.

GUS: Maybe there is some Access course you could do to help, perhaps ask at the Job Centre.

SIAN: OK.

LEADER: I think that if this was a real life interview, Sian, there may have been a danger of your afterwards doing a post-mortem on the interview, where you used a mental filter and focused on your hand shaking, if you were offered a drink at the start of the interview.

SIAN: I would just have gone over and over being asked about my qualifications and felt low.

LEADER: It is trying to see the bigger picture, where other people are coming from, their 'outside' view of you, rather than being ruled by the 'inside' view. What I would like people to do for homework is go through the whole of the Manual, underline parts that seem really important to you and add in any extra bits you have picked up in the sessions that seem particularly important. The idea is that you can then make sure you stick to the Manual after the group is ended and if in difficulties you can do a repair job using the Manual.

Social phobia is quintessentially an interpersonal problem and group treatment is therefore the natural vehicle for treatment, albeit that historically GCBT for social phobia whilst effective has been less effective than individual CBT. It may be, however, that by incorporating video feedback (and the dropping of safety behaviours) into treatment and addressing past humiliations, GCBT can become as effective as individual CBT. The optimal time per group member that needs to be spent on these new developments in GCBT remains to be determined.

Chapter 8

Obsessive compulsive disorder

Obsessive compulsive disorder (OCD) is rare compared to the other disorders considered in this volume, affecting just 1.1% of the UK population (Torres *et al.* 2006), but approximately two-thirds are severely functionally impaired, not engaging in occupational or social life. Sufferers from OCD alone are the exception (18.8%) rather than the rule, 81.2% suffering at least one additional disorder (Zimmerman *et al.* 2008). The multi-psychiatric disorder screening devices, the 7 Minute Mental Health Screes and the self-report version, the First Step Questionnaire, have both been revised to better screen for OCD and incorporate the NICE (2006) recommended five-symptom screen, the Zohar–Fineberg Obsessive Compulsive Screen (Fineberg *et al.* 2003), as well as asking the client whether this is something that they want help with. The Zohar–Fineberg Obsessive Compulsive Screen correctly identified (sensitivity) 94.4% of those with OCD and 85.1% (specificity) of those without OCD in a study of outpatients attending a dermatology clinic. Positive screens can be evaluated further using the Cognitive Behaviour Therapy Pocketbook, Appendix A.

GCBT for OCD is particularly challenging. In a study of GCBT for OCD, O'Connor *et al.* (2005) found that 38% of clients refused treatment in a group format, suggesting that a client's readiness for an OCD group is an important issue. Meyer *et al.* (2010) added two individual sessions of motivational interviewing and thought mapping (a process akin to problem solving) before GCBT for OCD, and in a comparison with GCBT alone found the former superior. By the end of GCBT plus two individual sessions, 58.3% of clients were in full remission and this proportion rose to 66.8% at follow-up, whereas in the GCBT alone modality the comparable figures for full remission were 35.6% post-treatment and 44.4% at follow-up. The authors speculated that the main effect of the individual sessions was to enhance compliance with homework.

In addition to the strategies suggested in Chapter 2, saboteurs of engagement in GCBT for OCD can be highlighted by having the client complete the Personal Significance Scale, reproduced in Appendix N (PSS;

Rachman 2003) and noting in particular affirmative responses to the items shown in Table 8.1.

Table 8.1 Saboteurs of engagement in GCBT from the Personal Significance Scale

1. Is it important for you to keep these thoughts secret from most or all of the people you know?
2. Would other people condemn or criticise you if they knew about your thoughts?
3. Would other people think that you are a bad, wicked person if they knew about your thoughts?

Whilst attendance at a group would be a particularly powerful way of a client testing out the truth of the appraisals in Table 8.1, these beliefs may also stop them attending in the first place. Such beliefs if endorsed would need to be a particular focus in a pre-group motivational interview/s. One way of weakening the power of these beliefs is to utilise another item on the PSS, 'Would other people think that you are crazy or mentally unstable if they knew about your thoughts?', and to rephrase it slightly to 'Are you absolutely sure that other people, *in a group suffering from what you suffer*, would think you are crazy or mentally unstable if they knew about your thoughts?', 'Would they all think this way or just some of them?', 'Could some be positive, some be neutral and some negative? In so doing the therapist is creating an uncertainty about a negative outcome yet leaving the client to entertain the possibility of a negative outcome and in the tradition of motivational interviewing leaves the client to resolve the dissonance. Use of the PSS should be complemented by administration of the Obsessive Compulsive Inventory (Foa *et al.* 2002), a measure of the severity of OCD, which is freely available for personal use at www.iapt.nhs.uk.

NICE (2006) recommended GCBT for mild OCD only, but without offering a justification. It is suggested that a more fruitful approach is, for the most part, to let the client decide on their readiness for a group rather than prejudge the issue.

GCBT for OCD, whilst effective, often appears somewhat less effective than individual CBT (Cabedo *et al.* 2010), albeit that independent of format only 50% of sufferers recover (Whittal *et al.* 2008). Whittal *et al.* (2005), reflecting on the McLean *et al.* (2001) study of GCBT, commented that there was insufficient time for therapists using CBT to adequately identify and challenge each participant's idiosyncratic cognitive distortions, so that GCBT may result in under-treatment compared to individual CBT. It may, however, be possible to circumvent this difficulty by having all group members complete the PSS (Appendix N) for each session, thereby highlighting the salient appraisals and providing a format for systematically addressing these appraisals between sessions. If an integral part of the reappraisal is daring to act contrary to the initial appraisal, this may in effect constitute an exposure and response prevention and may have as positive results as the latter in group format (McLean *et al.* 2001).

There are two types of knowledge: declarative, e.g. 'there are dark clouds in the sky, it will rain shortly', and procedural, which is automated, e.g. 'the knowledge I had as to how to sit down at my computer just now' (Wells (2000). OCD beliefs are not just declarative, e.g. 'touching this door knob means I might get contaminated', but also procedural, e.g. 'hesitating at a door to let someone else open it first'. Behavioural experiments or dares target procedural knowledge and arguably a GCBT programme that focuses on this source of knowledge as well as targeting the declarative aspects of OCD is likely to be particularly potent.

In an open trial of group metacognitive therapy for OCD (Rees and van Koesveld 2008), seven of the eight participants in the group recovered by the 3-month follow-up. Interestingly there were no dropouts, suggesting that this may be a very acceptable form of group treatment (in individual CBT the dropout rate is typically 10% and somewhat higher, 18%, for exposure and response prevention; Abramowitz *et al.* 2005). Simons, Schneider and Herpertz-Dahlman (2006) have combined metacognitive therapy and CBT in their treatment of children and adolescents and the GCBT programme described in this chapter is a similar fusion intended for adults.

A cognitive behavioural model of obsessive compulsive disorder

The cognitive behavioural model of OCD presented here is an appraisal model and an amalgam of the work of Rachman (2003), who in turn has drawn on the work of Salkovskis *et al.* (2000) and Wells (1997). The cognitive-behavioural model of OCD is presented in Figure 8.1.

The model posits that OCD sufferers and non-sufferers do not differ in their intrusions but differ only in their appraisal of their intrusions (Salkovskis and Harrison 1984). Rachman (2003) suggests that OCD sufferers make a serious misinterpretation of their intrusions. These misinterpretations involve (Wells 1997) an overestimation of the danger posed by the intrusion, e.g. 'thinking I could throw the baby down the stairs means I am likely to' and/or exaggerating the significance of the thought/image, e.g. 'having a sexual image of Christ means I am wicked/damned'. The serious misinterpretations then lead to a destabilisation/lowering of mood 'safety' behaviours, e.g. avoiding the top of the stairs or praying harder to stop the blasphemous images. A compulsion may be a repetitive observable behaviour or covert, e.g. trying to replace a 'bad thought' with a 'good thought'. The compulsive behaviour is either an exaggeration of a normal behaviour, e.g. repeated handwashing to avoid contamination, or bears no relationship to the feared scenario, e.g. switching kettle on and off three times to prevent

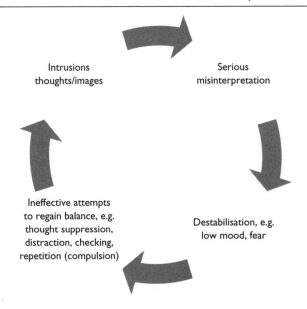

Figure 8.1 The cognitive behavioural model of the maintenance of OCD.

death of grandmother. The covert safety behaviours are ineffective. For example, attempts to stop thoughts/images have been found to have a rebound effect (Wegner *et al.* 1987), causing the individual to ruminate about their intrusions. Similarly overt safety behaviours, such as seeking reassurance, may temporarily reduce fear and remove the troublesome thought, but ultimately there is never enough reassurance and the mere act of seeking reassurance acts as a reminder of the troublesome thoughts. Further, the compulsive behaviour is maintained (Salkovskis and Harrison 1984) because the OCD sufferer never has the opportunity to learn that not engaging in the ritual does not have dire consequences. The obsessional level of concerns results in a hypervigilance (or what Wells [1997] has described as a cognitive attentional syndrome) for signs of danger, e.g. a person obsessed about getting AIDS might be alert for stains, agonising about whether they might be semen leading to the contracting of AIDS. There are two aspects to the 'worry': a positive belief, e.g. that the worry will produce a feeling of certainty that they had not contracted AIDS by touching a stain, and a negative belief, e.g. 'all this worrying is going to make me ill'. Others are then contacted to provide reassurance that what is feared is ungrounded but the effects are short-lived e.g. 'was my friend really listening when I asked about the stain?', and the doubts return, leading to a further fuelling of the intrusions. The intrusions of a person with pure obsessions tend to be in the opposite direction to the domain the person values, e.g. a caring nurse with obsessive imagery of harming people with a knife. Between 20% and 30% of OCD sufferers suffer from pure obsessions, i.e. without any overt compulsive behaviour (Stein *et al.* 1997).

The metacognitive approach

The word 'obsession' is derived from the Latin *obsidere*, meaning 'to besiege', and clients with OCD are besieged by intrusive thoughts/images, at the mercy of a power that is perceived as using all or some of the rules of thumb heuristics (Wells 1997) in Table 8.2.

Table 8.2 Rules of thumb prominent in OCD

1. Determining whether particular events will happen or have happened on the basis of the vividness of the imagery or the extremity of the thought (thought event fusion; TEF); i.e. there is a direct causal relationship between the two, such as a person with vivid intrusive imagery of having lost something regularly checking their bag or turning around to check behind them as they are walking.
2. Judging thoughts/images almost as harshly as actions (thought action fusion (TAF), moral TAF), e.g. the person castigates themselves for imagining an inappropriate sexual exhibition almost as much as if they had performed it; or using the existence of the thought/image as sufficient evidence that the feared content of the thought/image is likely to come to pass (probability TAF), e.g. the person besieged by an image of shooting family members seeks reassurance that they are not going to shoot relatives.
3. Judging wholesomeness on their proximity to an object (thought object fusion (TOF)), e.g. an adult survivor of childhood sexual abuse hearing the name of their abuser feels dirty and has to repeatedly wash.

The rules of thumb in Table 8.2 are not the exclusive property of clients suffering from OCD, most people including therapists will from time to time use one or more of them. To illustrate this the reader is invited to write down something really horrible happening to a loved one, e.g. ' I hope X loses an arm in a really bad car accident'. The author confesses that he cannot bring himself to write this (thought event fusion)! The essence of the metacognitive approach to OCD is to substitute a general bypassing of the above rules of thumb and create a better relationship between the client and their intrusive images/thoughts.

The cognitive approach

The cognitive approach to OCD focuses on the content of obsessions rather than focusing on the client's heuristics for making inferences about their mental life. Just as Beck's cognitive theory of emotional disorders suggests that the different disorders are distinguished by their different cognitive content (Alford and Beck 1997), so it is proposed that the different cognitive vulnerabilities underlie distinct symptom presentations of OCD

(Laposa and Rector 2009). OCD subtypes have been grouped into the following categories: contamination/cleaning, symmetry/order, pure obsessions, harming/doubting/checking, hoarding and contamination/washing symptoms but where the locus of the fear relates to the harming of others through the spread of contamination – 'harming contamination'. Shafran (1997) showed that inflated responsibility beliefs were especially related to harming/doubting/checking. Laposa and Rector's (2009) study suggests that directly addressing responsibility beliefs may be particularly salient for those with harming-contamination concerns.

The Obsessive Compulsive Cognitions Working Group (2005) has addressed the issue of the content of appraisals pertinent to OCD and identified the cognitive domains shown in Table 8.3 as likely to be important in the development and maintenance of OCD.

Table 8.3 Obsessive compulsive cognitions

1. Inflated responsibility
2. Overimportance of thoughts
3. Excessive concern about the importance of controlling one's thoughts
4. Overestimation of threat
5. Intolerance of uncertainty
6. Perfectionism

The domains listed in Table 8.3 have been embodied in the Obsessive Beliefs Questionnaire (Obsessive Compulsive Cognitions Working Group 2005). In Table 8.3 inflated responsibility refers to excessive responsibility for safety or harm coming to others. However, Salkovskis *et al.* (2008) has suggested that it is rather the sense of responsibility for collecting an overwhelming body of evidence that the feared outcome will not occur, i.e. the Elevated Evidence requirement, as opposed to utilising the more common gut reaction of 'it just feels right' in making a decision, that plays a pivotal role in the maintenance of OCD.

Obsessive compulsive disorder programme

An obsessive compulsive disorder programme is outlined below and partly draws on Rachman's work (2003) and developments in the application of Wells' (1997) metacognitive approach to GCBT (Rees and van Koesveld 2008). Further, Whittal *et al.* (2010), in a comparison of CBT and stress management training (SMT) for OCD, found that the latter was almost as effective as the former even though there was no direct focus on the obsessions. One possible explanation offered by Whittal *et al.* (2010) is that obsessions and mood reciprocally interact and that therefore teaching sufferers to better manage their stresses will result in less obsessive rumination and more readiness to approach situations they avoid, resulting in disconfirmation of their obsessive beliefs. But the SMT in the Whittal *et al.* (2010) study was unlike many stress management programmes (that have hitherto proved ineffective with OCD) in that it had a module focusing on interpersonal stress – dealing with criticism, providing negative feedback when necessary, resolving conflicts and assertiveness, which may have accounted for its potency. Taking these findings into account the OCD programme outlined in this chapter also details management of mood and interpersonal stresses. The focus is on promoting interaction with others based on genuineness rather than fear of their opinions or attitudes – the group modality particularly lends itself to this.

At the start clients are introduced to the self-help material, Appendix L, which is discussed and referred to throughout the programme.

The cast of an OCD group is shown in Table 8.5.

Sessions 1–3

Tea and coffee were provided before the start of all the OCD sessions. The leader and co-leader noted, over the first three sessions, that though Joe always arrived early enough for refreshment he never took a drink. Further, Marlene always arrived late for the sessions, apologising profusely and with a 'tut-tutting' from Eric. The therapists also noticed that Joe on being introduced to other group members never shook hands. Joe had been given the Depression Survival Manual at the pre-group individual assessment because of his coexisting depression and it was agreed that the co-leader would telephone him between sessions to discuss his progress with it as well as any ambivalences about attending the OCD group. Similarly, Marlene was recommended to read those aspects of the self-help book *Moving On After Trauma* (Scott 2008) that related to her childhood sexual abuse and the leader (a female) would give her a ring between sessions to see how she was getting on with this material.

The first session began with the distribution of the OCD Survival Manual, Appendix L, and members were asked to complete the Personal Significance Scale, Appendix N. Marlene arrived just as everyone had completed the PSS and the co-leader handed one to her and suggested she might complete it at the end of the session. However, Marlene could not resist a glance at it and muttered 'I'm a weirdo'; this brought laughter from the group, particularly as the first section to be considered in the OCD Survival Manual was 'And I thought I was weird'. Thus from the outset the group experience was implicitly normalising clients' experiences of intrusive thoughts/images.

The leader said that she and the co-leader would like to cover the first four sections of the OCD Survival Manual, Appendix L, and began by

Table 8.4 The obsessive compulsive disorder programme

	Therapeutic targets	Treatment strategies	Materials: OCD Survival Manual, Appendix L
Sessions 1–3	1. Model of mental life, serious misinterpretation of intrusions – thought action fusion (TAF), thought event fusion (TEF), thought object fusion (TOF)	Develop more appropriate model; detached mindfulness about intrusions	Sections 1: 'And I thought I was weird', 2: OCD – a serious misinterpretation of mental life, 3: OCD – playing by different rules
	2. Inappropriate goal state, e.g. absolute certainty, perfect cleanliness	Distilling achievable goals, not knowing what you know	
	3. Appraisals of intrusions	Encourage perception of reasonable degree of control by postponement strategies. Use of bOCD chart and completion of Personal Significance Scale	Section 4: Developing a different story about your mental life
	4. Neutralising images, thoughts, behaviours (compulsions)	Behavioural experiments – Dare: Don't Avoid a Realistic Experiment	Section 6: Daring to postpone 'safety' behaviour
Session 4	5. Overestimation of danger/intolerance of uncertainty	Distillation of realistic probabilities. The necessity of tolerating uncertainty	Sections 1–4 and 6
	6. Cognitive and behavioural avoidance	Demonstration of the harmlessness of thoughts. Discussion of 'why don't you warn others of these dangers?'	
Session 5	7. Excessive responsibility, low mood	Responsibility pie, therapist contracts to remove responsibility, MOOD chart, memory aids	Section 5: Managing your mood
Session 6	8. Unassertive communication	Communication guidelines	Section 7: Managing relationships

continues overleaf

Table 8.4 continued

	Therapeutic targets	Treatment strategies	Materials: OCD Survival Manual, Appendix L
Sessions 7 and 8	9. Unrealistic appraisals	Leader playing devil's advocate of personal significance of intrusions, co-leader challenging the leader's 'appraisals', assisted by group members	Section 8: The thought police – revision
Sessions 9 and 10	10. Relapse prevention	Personalising the OCD Survival Manual	Sections 1–8

Table 8.5 OCD group members

Name	Thumbnail sketch
Joe	A librarian, obsessed that he might contract AIDS from stains, OCD developed after a protracted viral illness, mild depression
Eric	A policeman repeatedly checking: paperwork, that he has locked cars/doors; marriage strained by his wife's affair
Marlene	Cleans incessantly, worse since her divorce three years ago, concerned about harming others, sexually abused as a child
Gary	An accountant, disturbed by images of exposing himself and incest, worse since redundancies
Hannah	A student, repeated washing since attempted rape, extreme concern over wellbeing of family
Alex	Unemployed since injury at work, become a 'control freak', aligning jars, materials on coffee table etc., moderate depression
Greg	Blasphemous images of screaming obscenities in church and hoarding, panic attacks

focusing on normalisation (see Table 8.4). The leader asked whether anybody would dare to volunteer all thoughts/images that had passed through their mind in the past 30 minutes and there were no takers. It was suggested that for homework they ask as many people as possible if they would dare to reveal all thoughts/images that had gone through their mind in the previous 30 minutes, keep a record of how many people they asked and how many were prepared to disclose all, then report back at the next session and the group could discuss the results. The session began:

ERIC: I could ask my colleagues, but I wouldn't believe them, they would probably just wind me up!

LEADER: Maybe we should exclude policemen and maybe prisoners, just go for those that you think of as having a reasonable chance of being honest.

ERIC: So no policemen or politicians!

In these early exchanges the group leader has already touched upon the first domain of the General Group Therapeutic Skills Rating Scale (Appendix D), agenda and homework. The session continued:

MARLENE: I don't know that what is on my OCD TV is the same as what is on normal people's TV?

LEADER: I think it starts off the same programme, but then the OCD sufferer gets in a state with it, starts fiddling with the settings, using the remote control and ends up viewing something that looks very odd to others. Treatment is very much about learning not to fiddle with the remote control.

ERIC: The kids hide the remote control in our house, left to them you would never find anything.

In this exchange the therapists have avoided pressurising Marlene to disclose her disturbing thoughts and images, to have done so would have threatened the therapeutic alliance. However, the leader has acknowledged her domain of concern. The concerns are dealt with by suggesting that her difficulties are like those of other group members in that they catastrophically misinterpret what they 'see'. Finally there is a hint of disclosure from another group member, Eric, of his perfectionism. The exchange has been kept relevant (item 2 of the GGTSRS, Appendix D) to members' concerns.

The leader then went on to explain the OCD model (Figure 3, Appendix L), using the example given of a client besieged by thoughts of shooting the rest of his family, which initiated the following discussion:

ERIC: But people do shoot the rest of their family or all the kids in school, the Columbine High School massacre.

CO-LEADER: The difference in OCD is that the behaviour the person fears is the total opposite of what they are like as a person, so the OCD client with a fear of shooting has been very warm and loving to his family, it is as if the mind balances out the extremes.

GREG: Yes, that makes sense.

LEADER: Eric would know probably better than me, but when people are violent they have almost always been that way and see nothing wrong in it?

ERIC: Yes little *****s.

LEADER: So that is very different to the OCD person. The other big difference is that OCD sufferers do not plan harm, offenders do, e.g. 'I will shoot X at about midnight, take his body down the dock and drop it in, nobody will be about'.

ERIC: Too many crime thrillers!

CO-LEADER: It is plans that lead to actions not thoughts/images, the thoughts/images, what we call intrusions, can be of anything.

GARY: That's reassuring.

LEADER: Often OCD suffers will not talk about the intrusions to others or a professional, because they feel it makes it 'real', more likely to happen. Section 3 of Appendix L is about this, the odd rules OCD sufferers play by, e.g. if I talk about the horrible thing it will make it happen. But can talking about something make something happen?

GARY: I suppose I could talk about winning the lottery but it isn't going to make it happen unfortunately.

LEADER: In OCD sufferers often join the thought and the event together, thought event fusion, like two magnets and we have to separate them.

ERIC: If you planned to rig the machine, that would be like 'loitering with intent' and you could be charged.

CO-LEADER: Planning is the missing link in OCD between the intrusions and the 'horrible' behaviour.

GARY: But isn't thinking something almost as bad as doing it?

LEADER: That is what we call a moral thought action fusion; again it is like two magnets together, having a thought for example 'I wish the boss was dead' and believing that this is as bad as seeking someone out with a samurai sword and arranging his decapitation.

ERIC: Think we might arrest someone who did that.

LEADER: What no arrest for wanting the boss dead?

ERIC: No, in my station there isn't anyone who doesn't want the boss dead, asked me to cancel my rest days last week because I was taking time off to come for therapy!

Throughout this first session no group member was put under any pressure to disclose intrusions. The focus was on the normalisation of intrusions and the pivotal role that the appraisal of intrusions plays in the maintenance of OCD. The intent of the therapists was to cover the first four sections of the OCD Survival Manual, but as sometimes happens the amount of group discussion if relevant can lead to a need to revise the agenda and Section 4 of the OCD Manual was left to the second session. For homework group members were asked to (a) read the OCD Survival Manual, paying particular attention to the first three sections, (b) survey others as to whether they would disclose their intrusions, and (c) complete the Personal Significance Scale in the 24 hours before the next session. At the end of the session the co-leader handed Gary the Panic Disorder Survival Manual and arranged to ring him to see how he was getting on with it.

At the beginning of the second and third sessions copies of the completed PSS scales were collected. The second session began with a review of homework; in the event nobody had found anyone who was prepared to divulge all that had passed through their mind in the previous 30 minutes. These findings were then discussed:

LEADER: What does it mean that nobody was prepared to confess all?

ERIC: Maybe everyone we know is depraved? (*Laughter*)

CO-LEADER: Are you less or more depraved than them?

ERIC: Hmm, that would be telling!

LEADER: Draw a ladder, on the top of the ladder put the most 'depraved' of the people you talked to about confessing all and on the bottom rung the most 'saintly' (*pause for a minute to hand out pen and paper and to let members complete the task*), then decide how far up the ladder you would put the others you talked to (*again pause for a minute or two*). Finally put yourself on the ladder.

CO-LEADER: What was it about the person you put at the bottom of the ladder that made you think of them as 'saintly'?

GREG: Jean my wife always does for others, she is totally unselfish and unassuming.

CO-LEADER: What if you could inject intrusions and Jean was injected with thoughts/images of shooting the whole family?

GREG: Wouldn't be too happy about it!

CO-LEADER: Would she be a less saintly person?

GREG: No, but she would be a more troubled person.

LEADER: You don't really know other people in the group or the therapists, but draw another ladder and put on the bottom the most saintly of us and at the top the most depraved and then put everyone else on the ladder. Now think for a moment about injecting thoughts/images that might trouble you into just one other person in the group, mentally select the person, now inject, give it a while to take effect. Now ask yourself would you move this person up or down the ladder because they have these intrusions?

MARLENE: I'm inclined to move them up the ladder to more depraved but I know that is stupid.

LEADER: What makes you think it is stupid?

MARLENE: It is really what people do that counts, I injected them into Eric because he tut-tutted again when I came late today, but he is no worse a person if he had my thoughts.

ERIC: Gee thanks Marlene! What have I been injected with?

CO-LEADER: No need to tell Marlene.

GREG: But surely, injections apart, you are responsible for the thoughts/ images you have?

LEADER: Is it possible to choose good without also considering what would be involved in choosing bad? Rather like in an unfamiliar restaurant going through the whole menu before settling on something that would be 'good' to eat.

GREG: So you would always have to consider the bad?

LEADER: Yes.

GARY: It's the staying with the bad that's the problem?

LEADER: Strangely the staying with the bad is to do with trying to block or neutralise it. I could say to everyone now don't think about black polar bears, (*pause*) how many of you are thinking of black polar bears?

HANNAH: Me, I still like to cuddle my bear, but he is brown!

The above exchange reiterates the normalising of intrusions. It also questions the personal significance that should be addressed to intrusions by first of all asking group members whether they would use them as a yardstick for assessing others and then questioning why they should use them as a yardstick for evaluating themselves. Finally the maintaining role of neutralising behaviours is underlined. Importantly the leaders protect clients against disclosure unless it has become their expressed wish to disclose. The therapists are also showing good presentation skills (item 9 of the GGTSRS, Appendix D), utilising written material available to the group members, engaging the group in activity (not just lecturing) and synchronising with each other in the exposition of material.

At the second session group members were introduced to a strategy for having second thoughts about their catastrophic misinterpretations of intrusions (Section 4 of Appendix L). The bOCD table and an example are reproduced here for convenience (Table 8.6).

After the leader took the group through the above example of the use of the beat OCD (bOCD) form, the following discussion ensued:

MARLENE: Were you thinking of me when you wrote this? I was late again because I was busy cleaning, realised I was late, rushed out, now I don't know whether I did switch the cooker off.

LEADER: But 10 minutes ago you were OK about having left the house.

MARLENE: Yes.

ERIC (*looking at the leader*): You are doing great, she was OK before and now she is in a state!

LEADER: To show further how to use the form I want to stay with Marlene's upset and see if we can tackle it using the form; this will be a second example. In the first column we might put that Marlene is besieged by thoughts that she hasn't switched the cooker off. And what are your thoughts about this?

MARLENE: I'm a stupid idiot for not being able to remember, if I hadn't got obsessed with cleaning and running late I would be able to remember.

LEADER: OK that would go in the second column. In the third column it suggests considering alternative thoughts; what would be a different way of looking at it?

HANNAH: I can't remember switching my cooker off this morning.

ALEX: Nor can I.

CO-LEADER: Do you want to ring the Fire Brigade, Marlene, get them to visit your home, Hannah's and Alex's?

Table 8.6 bOCD

bOCD is a mnemonic for remembering how to shrink disturbing thoughts about images/ thoughts to size. In the first column, detail the thought/images that may have **b**esieged you today and indicate, if you can, what may have triggered them. The **O** of OCD here stands for **o**bserve your thoughts about your thoughts/images and record these in the second column. The **C** of OCD here stands for **c**onsider alternative thoughts to your thoughts about your images/thoughts and, if you can, record these in the third column. The **D** of OCD here stands for **d**aring to begin to act as if the thoughts in the third column are true.

I am **besieged** by these images/ thoughts	**O**bserve your thinking about these, images/ thoughts:	**C**onsider alternative thoughts, ones that others may have about these *same* images/ thoughts. Also **C**onsider why you would not try to persuade others of the truth of your thoughts about the besieging army of images/ thoughts:	**D**are to act, however briefly, as if the thoughts in column 3 (C) are true, and see what happens. Record the 'dare' and the consequences.
I don't remember switching the cooker off, the house could burn down, the kiddies next door could die in the fire	This means there is danger. I should go home and check	I'll probably be OK, even if I can't remember having switched the cooker off, it is unlikely to end in catastrophe. Just because I have thoughts about it doesn't mean it's going to happen – thought event fusion. There would be no point in trying to persuade my boss that I needed to go home from work just because I couldn't remember having switched the cooker off, he would look at me as if I was daft. I wouldn't try to persuade my mum to stop whatever she is doing and go home if she couldn't remember having switched the fire off, why is it OK for her and not me?	This time I will dare myself not to go home but I will ring my mum to go around and check, at least it is a start. Rang my mum who said 'do you think I've got nothing better to do', but she went round and later rang me to say everything was OK. I felt down that I had obviously inconvenienced her.

MARLENE: A bit of me wants to but no.

LEADER: The third column suggests that one way of coming up with second thoughts about your catastrophic misinterpretation of your intrusions is to ask would I try to persuade others that what I fear is true. So that if you wouldn't try to persuade the Fire Brigade to visit your three homes do you really believe that not being able to remember something means you have not done it?

MARLENE: I see what you mean, so I would write in the third column 'not being able to remember having done something doesn't mean I have not done it, this is normal'.

LEADER: Yes, but it doesn't stop there. You have got to put your new way of thinking into action, so the final column on the form is a dare and it might be, say, stay back at the end of the session for the cup of coffee, don't rush back to check that the house hasn't burnt down.

ERIC: I must admit I find it very difficult not to check.

CO-LEADER: Rather than try to stop checking altogether, as a stepping stone have a day when you postpone all checking by 15 minutes and another day do your usual checking and see if there is any worse outcome by postponing.

ERIC: A day on and a day off, hmm interesting.

In the above exchange the leader has focused on what is relevant (item 2 of the GGTSRS, Appendix D) to a group member, rather than continue an abstract explanation of Table 8.6. Further, the leader is not side-tracked from this endeavour by another group member's charge that she has caused some discomfort for another member. The leader has proceeded much as a dentist would, whilst committed to minimising pain aware that some discomfort is inherent in the therapeutic process. This persistence has paid off as the discussion has also become relevant to the member who had taken issue with the leader. The exchange is governed by the knowledge that clients are more likely to learn from a focus on 'hot' cognitions than abstractions, however eloquent. Further discomfort is also inherent in the 'dares' that are part of the final column of Table 8.6. For homework it was suggested that group members complete the bOCD.

At the start of Session 3 the bOCD forms were collected, but Alex handed in a blank form and Marlene had not been able to separate what she was 'besieged' by, column 1, from column 2, her appraisal of the intrusion. Rather than single people out, and desirous of making material relevant to all group members, the leader adapted (item 3 of the GGTSRS, Appendix D) materials by introducing 'the tortoise' in Figure 8.2, as an aid to the completion of the bOCD.

It was explained that the four columns in Figure 8.2 correspond to the four headings in Table 8.6. In order to illustrate the use of the tortoise the following exchange took place:

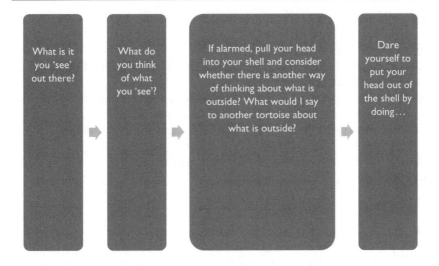

Figure 8.2 The tortoise.

LEADER: Just to show how the tortoise operates, Alex was there some situation you saw since last session that got to you?

ALEX: Yes, my wife had been for the weekly shop and put everything away.

LEADER: So in the first column we could put that what you saw was shopping items put away the way your wife does. What did you think of what you saw?

ALEX: It's terrible, it's not right, it will cause an argument if I go and rearrange things.

LEADER: OK we could put that in the second column. You were clearly alarmed by this, so we could imagine you as a tortoise pulling your head into your shell and having a think. What alternative ways could you think?

ALEX: I suppose I could say it doesn't really matter, but it does.

CO-LEADER: Why does it matter?

ALEX: I've got to feel that it has been done right?

CO-LEADER: Why?

ALEX: I just have to.

CO-LEADER: Is it useful to have a goal of feeling that it has been done right?

ALEX: No, it ****** me off.

CO-LEADER: Perhaps in the third column you might write, 'it is not useful to pursue a goal of feeling you have done things right'. You might also ask yourself whether you would try and persuade a brother or a friend or other members of this group that they must take charge of the shopping items and arrange them properly. If it is so right that things should be done the right way, why don't you persuade others of this?

ALEX: Hmm I don't think I will bother trying to persuade other group members.

LEADER: Why not, if it is so right?

ALEX: Right, I suppose for the final column, the dare, I could put some of the small jars behind the big jars.

CO-LEADER: Because it is a dare you will feel uncomfortable but you can't beat OCD without some discomfort and so for starters you might leave the jars mixed up just for say 15 minutes and see does anything terrible happen.

MARLENE: The tortoise makes it much clearer for me.

ALEX: Certainly helps me.

In the above exchange what is taught is moulded to fit each group member. This exchange also highlights the way in which sufferers from OCD pursue inappropriate goal states such as doing things perfectly or seeking absolute certainty. For homework group members were asked to complete the bOCD or use the tortoise if they found it more helpful.

In a post-mortem after the third session the therapists reviewed group members' progress by looking for any shifts in their appraisals of intrusions on the PSS. The PSS also indicates the extent of the group members' belief in the need for behavioural avoidance (item 21 on the PSS) and their belief in the need to neutralise their intrusions (item 23 on the PSS). In this way further treatment targets were highlighted. Usefully the PSS also asks group members what triggered their thoughts, thereby suggesting other potential targets for intervention. Importantly the final question on the PSS asks why these thoughts keep coming back, and over the first three sessions there should hopefully be an increased awareness that their 'safety' behaviours are contributing to the persistence of the intrusions.

Session 4

One of the foci in Session 4 is on the overestimation of danger. It can be suggested that an inflated view of danger arises, usually, from expecting a series of improbable events to happen. The longer the 'causal' pathway, the greater the opportunities to reappraise stepping stones en route to the feared catastrophe. The example of contamination could be used and it could be suggested that the stepping stones shown in Figure 8.3 would be needed.

Each stepping stone can be put into context by asking 'what are the chances of . . .?' Each stepping stone has to be taken to reach catastrophe and in the example in Figure 8.3 the actual chances of 'others dying' (statistically the cumulative probability) is $1/100 \times 1/10 \times 1/10 \times 1/50$, i.e. 1 in 500,000. Group members can then be asked whether they have ever bet

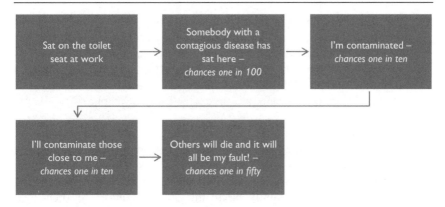

Figure 8.3 Danger stepping stones.

on a horse at these odds?, and then whether their behaviour today should be affected by such an unlikely event, e.g. ordering a yacht today because you are going to win the National Lottery on Saturday. At the fourth session the following exchange ensued:

MARLENE: I've tried telling myself the chances of terrible things happening are almost nil, but it doesn't work.

CO-LEADER: You have to match it with an action that matches your words. So that, for example, if you insist that visitors to your home telephone you after they get to their home, though in your better moments you might think the chances of serious harm coming to them is virtually nil, you will continue to be fearful unless you behave as if they're safe by not requiring them to ring you.

MARLENE: I would be pacing up and down.

CO-LEADER: Not forever, as you kept doing this you would gradually pace less.

ERIC: I suppose that would apply if I stopped myself continually going back to the car to check that it's locked, it is no use my just telling myself it's locked. I even check in the police station car park at work, how crazy can you get?

CO-LEADER: I think it would be useful Marlene and Eric calculating the risks but you would each have to decide on a dare that would be a realistic experiment.

JOE: When it comes to crazy, Eric, I've got the gold medal. I fear touching things and I found the stepping stones idea useful. I've been getting myself in a state at work afraid to touch old books and if I do I will wash and wash. My hands are in such a mess that I have to attend a dermatology clinic next week.

LEADER: So how were you thinking of using the stepping stones, Joe?

JOE: Well if it is an old book more people are likely to have touched it but even for a new book I am looking for stains. I could ask myself the first step, what are the odds that someone with a contagious disease has touched it? At the next step ask myself what are the odds I will have caught it from the book? It has never struck me before that lots of individually unlikely events are necessary for catastrophe.

In the above exchange although the therapists' agenda was to focus on teaching new material, they had to underline the significance of previously taught materials to ensure openness to what was new. Thus the agenda was approached with the necessary flexibility (item 1, GGTSRS, Appendix D). Group members were gradually disclosing their difficulties at their own pace yet sufficiently for other group members to be able to identify with them. The dialogue for Session 4 continued:

MARLENE: Joe, I think that I must have the silver medal when it comes to crazy, I've got to know that bad things are not going to happen, probabilities are no good for me!

JOE: But can you 'know' anything, I don't know that my mum who is in her eighties and in good health hasn't had a heart attack this morning!

MARLENE: You shouldn't say things like that!

JOE: Why not?

MARLENE: You just shouldn't.

CO-LEADER: Why is that?

MARLENE: You could make it happen.

ERIC: Sorry, Joe, maybe the gold medal is Marlene's, I am struggling for bronze.

GARY: I can see what Marlene is saying, what is in your mind might spill over.

LEADER: Let's look at this spilling over. Each think for a couple of minutes about an injury you want me to have (*pause*) OK who will confess what they thought?

ERIC: I wanted you to fall off your chair, because you always swing back on it.

LEADER: Sorry to disappoint you, Eric, maybe you didn't think hard enough.

MARLENE: I kept thinking I want you to have a heart attack but then started thinking I shouldn't be thinking that, now I am agitated.

LEADER: OK, Marlene, so you have tried doing two things at once, thinking of me having a heart attack and trying to block it. What about doing a dare, a realistic experiment, see if you can really make me have a heart attack by not blocking the thought, just let the thought 'give him a heart attack' go over and over for a minute or two. I could order the ambulance whilst we are waiting if you like, Marlene!

MARLENE: I don't think you should order an ambulance; OK I will go for it and just think 'give him a heart attack'.

LEADER: *after 2 minute pause* I'm still OK, what does this mean?

GARY: Your thoughts don't make a difference; trouble is I can see that for Marlene, but not me.

CO-LEADER: Would you have ordered an ambulance if you had done it, Gary?

GARY: Well no.

CO-LEADER: One way of seeing that your thoughts about your intrusions are out of focus is that you will not try to persuade others of the truth of your photograph of your intrusions. For example, if you are worried about stains and you have not bothered to persuade others of the great harm that comes from them you might ask yourself 'do I really believe that stains are harmful?

MARLENE: I would just start thinking that I should be warning others and I would have another problem.

LEADER: One of the topics we were going to consider in the next session is an inflated sense of responsibility in OCD. Marlene, I'm going to write out a contract here in which I take full responsibility for anyone coming to any harm because you decided not to warn them about the dangers of stains before the next session. Is that ok?

MARLENE: I'm relieved you're taking responsibility.

LEADER: Oh by the way, Marlene, how did it feel when you didn't try to block the thought 'give him a heart attack'?

MARLENE: It was easier.

LEADER: For homework, I would like everyone to just let trains of thought/images come into your station and depart at their convenience. Use the bOCD form to get a proper perspective on them and complete the PSS scale before the next session. If there are repetitive behaviours you are engaging in such as handwashing, try postponing such activities for 15 minutes and see does anything terrible happen, it's a dare Don't Avoid a Realistic Experiment.

GARY: What if there appears to be a rail strike and I have got a train that is not moving?

LEADER: Just sit it out, calmly get on with other things; eventually the trains start moving.

In the above exchange the therapists have addressed thought event fusion experimentally, as well as focusing on important domains of concern in OCD (overestimation of danger, and intolerance of uncertainty), and have also touched upon inflated responsibility, the prime focus of the next session. At the same time the therapists have reiterated the new metacognitive model of the significance of intrusions.

Towards the end of the session the leader asked members how they had felt about the day's session and there were the following responses:

MARLENE: What struck me is that other people's OCD seems even weirder but much easier to tackle, I mean I would happily touch the books in Joe's library all day.

JOE: And I have no problem leaving the house in a mess before I come out.

ERIC: *laughing* Maybe we could part exchange our OCDs and we would then have no problem sorting them out.

CO-LEADER: That's an idea, maybe knowing that some other OCD sufferers would quite happily dare to do what you are avoiding, might tempt you to be a little daring yourself: 'can't be that bad if even Marlene/Joe would have a go at this'.

The approach above has not been didactic; other group members have been given the space to act as therapists, acting as more credible sources of persuasion (item 7, GGTSRS, Appendix D).

Session 5

This session as with all sessions began with a review of homework and the clients reported back:

ERIC: I'm pleased with myself, I'm managing to delay checking I have locked the car for 15 minutes, but it is a lot easier to do at work than at home.

JOE: I'm still just the same, I've just got to get stuck into doing things like Eric.

One of the particular virtues of GCBT is that group members can be encouraged by the successes of others. The therapists' agenda for this session was upon inflated responsibility and management of mood. The latter is based around Section 5 of Appendix L. Rather than provide didactic instruction on the pivotal role that inflated responsibility plays in the development and maintenance of OCD, the therapists use the experiences of a group member to make the teaching more relevant (item 2, GGTSRS, Appendix D):

LEADER: Eric. What is it about not checking you've locked the car in work that makes it easier than at home?

ERIC: There's more people around at work, they have all got to make the station secure.

CO-LEADER: So when you think responsibility is divided your OCD is easier.

ERIC: Yes I guess so.

LEADER: The main new topic to be covered today is the part a sense of responsibility plays in OCD. Marlene, did you do much warning of people about stains?

MARLENE: I did look at them more, but I wasn't bothered by them.

LEADER: How did you come not to be bothered?

MARLENE: Hmm, can I say?

CO-LEADER: Go on, we are all curious!

MARLENE: *looking at leader* Well I thought it is all our stupid fault if anything happens, you have a heart attack or someone is contaminated.

LEADER: So you can just carry on like most people do if it is someone else's fault or responsibility?

MARLENE: Yes.

LEADER: What if there is no one else about or involved?

MARLENE: I am stuck then. It's like getting here this morning, I was only on time became I left the house with my 6-year-old daughter and dropped her off at my mother-in-law's.

ERIC: How can that make you on time!

MARLENE: If I would have been by myself I would have kept going back to the front door to check that it was locked.

LEADER: So even though your daughter makes no objective difference to security, you can do the more normal thing when she is there?

MARLENE: Right, it does sound crazy, doesn't it?

LEADER: It sounds as though, you say to yourself, 'if I can come up with any way to divide responsibility even if it is bizarre I must'.

ERIC: God almighty, I'm like Marlene! If I get out of the car at home with my wife I hardly check I have locked it, but if I am by myself the checking can go on for hours.

LEADER: It is a matter of daring yourself to be left with responsibility and testing out whether anything bad does happen if you check only once.

CO-LEADER: You can make the once you check memorable by saying something really strange like 'red octopus' and then when you are tempted to go back to check the door or car door you remember 'red octopus' and it's a reminder that there is really no need to check.

ERIC: Sounds good.

MARLENE: Yes.

In this exchange the therapists have suggested that for those group members for whom inflated responsibility is an issue that they 'deflate' it by testing out whether there are dire consequences from acting normally when solely responsible. The therapists then located this strategy within the framework of Table 8.6 and Figure 8.2:

CO-LEADER: This dare is really the final columns of Table 8.6 and Figure 8.2. The first column would be 'Besieged by thoughts I have got to go back, something terrible will happen if I don't and it will all be my fault'. Then in the second column you might put 'This means I must check until I feel certain'. In the third column you might put what?

HANNAH: Checking once is enough, that is what I need to do with my relatives.

In this extract the therapists are integrating newly taught material with earlier material. The focus of the session then moved on to mood management, and the attention of group members was drawn to Section 5 of the OCD Survival Manual, Appendix L.

LEADER: OCD behaviours are usually worse when your mood is low for whatever reason and the example given in the Manual is of coming back from holiday, a bit low because you are back to the everyday and you have thoughts about doing the washing that has built up, and the very word 'washing' strikes a raw nerve and you are starting to get in a state. This is described in the first two columns of the MOOD chart, in the third column you put your objective thinking, e.g. 'everyone has to wash after a holiday', and the final column is again a dare; in this case you might decide 'just get on and do it, if I start getting plagued by intrusions about it I will use the bOCD form'.

HANNAH: When I get low I sometimes cut myself, it releases the tension I feel better. I think sometimes I do this so I won't wash repeatedly.

CO-LEADER: You could use the MOOD chart for that. In the first column you might put, say, mood dipped, not been able to get hold of grandparents on the phone, in the second column the observed thinking might be:

HANNAH: Something bad has happened to them, I should have known. I can't stand this.

CO-LEADER: What would the objective thinking be?

HANNAH: Don't know.

GREG: How old are your grandparents, Hannah?

HANNAH: Both 85.

GREG: It is probably a fair bet something bad will happen to them in the next ten years but today?

CO-LEADER: So to get to the objective thinking you could look at the probability of something bad happening today, but what would it be that you can't stand?

HANNAH: I suppose I've got to know that they are safe.

CO-LEADER: So we are back to an intolerance of uncertainty.

HANNAH: My objective thinking would then be probably nothing really bad has happened today, I've got to put up with the uncertainty, I can stand the uncertainty.

CO-LEADER: So what would go in the final column?

HANNAH: Just ring them once more and leave it at that.

CO-LEADER: That could be part of it but what about daring yourself not to cut or handwash, for at least 15 minutes, so that you can begin to prove to yourself that you can stand the uncertainty.

HANNAH: OK, I suppose I've got to get it into my head that I'm not exceptional having to deal with real dangers while others play games with imagined fears.

LEADER: Would you mind if we put a notice up at each session that says: *'I'm not exceptional having to deal with real dangers whilst others play games with imagined fears'*?

HANNAH: That's fine.

JOE: I've really got to take that on board.

MARLENE: I'm a bit confused about when you use the MOOD chart and when you use the bOCD chart?

LEADER: The MOOD chart is for any general upsets and the bOCD is for when you feel plagued by particular regular thoughts/images which are the opposite of what is important to you.

In this exchange the therapists are once again having to underline the importance of earlier taught material so that sessions are a synthesis of new material and a revision of old material. The session continued:

GREG: I can see that what bothers you is the opposite of what is important to you, I just want to scream horrible things in church.

ERIC: You see I'd have no problems with that.

MARLENE: I don't think you would have any problems shouting obscenities anywhere!

ERIC: True, but how often, Greg, have you shouted these things out in church?

GREG: I haven't.

ERIC: Well looking at your form I wouldn't bet on you doing it.

GREG: But what if I did?

ERIC: It's like me saying what if I was pregnant?

LEADER: It's really a question of just ignoring the gremlin/devil/child having a temper tantrum that is in your mind, but if you are in a bad mood it is harder to have enough apathy for these intrusions.

GREG: It reminds me of the philosopher/theologian C.S Lewis who wrote about a 'devil' called Screwtape and now I can see the message was not to try and blank it but to play it subtly.

CO-LEADER: Sounds good.

In this exchange the therapists are going with the grain of the assumptive world of group members, acknowledging that the psychological problems are not those assumptive worlds per se but the particular angle the client has taken within that perspective. Not to go with the assumptive world would violate inclusion (item 4, GGTSRS, Appendix D). In instances where it appears that it is the client's frame of reference that causes their problems it is important to enquire how other members of their reference group have managed to avoid developing OCD and whether the client can borrow the perspective of a 'respected' member of their ideological group. Other members of the OCD client's religious group are likely much more credible sources of persuasion than the therapists or indeed other members of the therapeutic group. The exchange continues:

LEADER: I guess, Greg, C.S. Lewis as a philosopher might suggest testing out your belief that it is horrible thoughts that lead to actions, by spending say 15 minutes a day having all your most horrible thoughts and seeing whether they do lead to the actions you fear or whether it is only plans that lead to actions.

GREG: OK I'll give it a try, maybe thinking of C.S. Lewis looking on.

LEADER: Great.

In the above exchange the therapists have ensured that treatment is culturally/religiously sensitive. This can particularly be a problem if the therapists are opposed to the ideology and they are probably best seeking guidance as to how to proceed from a colleague from at least the same background. The same advice may apply, though less forcibly, if the therapists are simply ignorant of the client's tradition.

Session 6

This session began as do all sessions with a review of homework and a troubleshooting of any difficulties, but often there are materials in the presented homework that can be used as a springboard to illustrate the new material that is to be taught in the session. In Session 6 the focus is on unassertive communication. Using the homeworks in this way ensures the therapists are addressing material that is relevant to the group members (item 2, GGTSRS, Appendix D). The following dialogue ensued, when the co-leader glanced at the MOOD charts that had been completed at the start of the session:

CO-LEADER: Bit of a problem on the home front, Gary?

GARY: Yes my wife was getting fed up over the finances, it's a real problem since I was made redundant. She was talking to me about it but then she said I wasn't listening and I said I was.

CO-LEADER: Were you?

GARY: Sort of.

CO-LEADER: How do you mean?

GARY: Well I was looking at the picture frame behind her and tracing my eye around it, then when she got angry I would have to stop and go back to the beginning again. I think she knew something was going on but I could hear her.

ALEX: That's like me when my wife is talking. If we are in the kitchen I will count the tiles and if she gets ratty I will have to start again. Mine has got worse since becoming unemployed.

CO-LEADER: But you weren't able to come up with any objective thinking, Gary?

GARY: No she got so angry I just thought I've lost my job, my marriage is next, then the kids.

LEADER: What I would like to introduce the group to today are some communication guidelines (Section 7, OCD Survival Manual, Appendix L) that can help prevent a deterioration of relationships. Thinking about these might help you come up with objective thinking about what is going wrong in your relationships and how you can rectify it. If you could all take a few minutes to read through Section 7 and we could discuss it. *a pause*

MARLENE: I can never keep to one subject.

ERIC: I am always mind-reading, drives my wife mad, she tells me to stop being the ***** detective.

LEADER: I don't think anyone obeys them all the time, a bit like the Highway Code, but you have got to know they are there and at least try to obey it most of the time if you don't want an accident. Maybe we could apply it to Gary and Alex's difficulties about 'not listening'. Perhaps we could role play it, Gary, you be your wife and I'll be you or Alex for that matter. Then the rest of the group keep an eye on which if any parts of the 'Highway Code' I break.

GARY: OK.

LEADER: I know I've been a pain to live with since not working, but I am listening when you talk but I get distracted by counting things and it makes it hard to tune in. I am like an old radio that needs tuning to the station, sometimes the reception isn't good.

GARY: I don't think you try.

LEADER: I do.

GARY: No you don't.

LEADER: It's you who doesn't listen. Right group what did you make of that?

JOE: You never said anything positive to your wife at the beginning.

LEADER: No I didn't, so I broke the first rule in the code, I didn't get her in the right frame of mind before starting on the problem.

JOE: Instead of getting defensive and saying 'I do' you could have said she was mind-reading, then it got worse you started mind-reading her saying she never really listens.

MARLENE: The way it escalated was just like at home.

LEADER: You can get your partner to read the communication guidelines and agree to both try and obey them but you can also use the guidelines in other contexts such as at work, as in the example in Section 7 of the Manual (Appendix L). There is a chapter on managing relationships in *Moving On After Trauma*, and there is also an example on page 141 of a lady dealing with OCD symptoms who is actually very similar to you, Marlene.

MARLENE: Not another me, I'm not sure the world could cope.

HANNAH: I could do with using the guidelines with my Gran, she keeps going on about what a nice boy my ex was and how we should be getting back together again. She knew his grandmother, but I can't tell her what he did to me, just the mention of his name makes me go and have to wash.

CO-LEADER: We could role play it if you like, Hannah; I could be you and you be gran.

HANNAH: Fine.

In the above exchange the therapists have not relied entirely on a verbal exposition of assertive communication but have endeavoured to teach it as a skill by role play (item 8, GGTSRS, Appendix D). Further, in order to ensure the skill translates to the real world the role plays have focused on materials relevant to group members.

Sessions 7 and 8

In these sessions the catastrophic appraisals of intrusions embodied in the PSS (Appendix N) are put on trial; group members in turn select an appraisal for 'trial'. The group act as jury, the leader takes on board the catastrophic misinterpretation and co-leader prosecuting barrister. Finally group members decide whether to accept the sentence of the catastrophic appraisal or to dare to conduct a realistic experiment to test it out. The catastrophic appraisals from the PSS are summarised in Table 8.7.

In the exchange below the group leader models taking on board the catastrophic appraisal selected by a group member and the co-leader aids the process of a reconsideration of the mis-appraisal. If a group member selects an appraisal very similar to one that has already been put on trial, that group member is invited to 'prosecute' the appraisal. Thus there is a process of first helping group members to be able to identify in another person (the group leader) a similar mis-appraisal to their own, secondly there is a modelling of a reconsideration of the catastrophic appraisal and finally the group member is actively involved in the construction of the reconsideration. In the following extract the therapists invite group members to select one of the 17 appraisals in Table 8.7. for scrutiny:

MARLENE: Number 2, 'These thoughts mean I might lose control and do something awful', is a constant worry.

Table 8.7 Catastrophic appraisals from the PSS

1. These thoughts mean something important about me.
2. These thoughts mean I might lose control and do something awful.
3. These thoughts mean I might go crazy someday.
4. It is important that I keep these thoughts secret from most or all the people I know.
5. These thoughts mean I am a dangerous person.
6. These thoughts mean that I am untrustworthy.
7. Other people would condemn me if they knew about my thoughts.
8. These thoughts mean that I am really a hypocrite.
9. Other people would think I am crazy or mentally unstable if they knew about my thoughts.
10. These thoughts mean that one day I may actually carry out some actions related to these thoughts.
11. These thoughts mean I am a bad, wicked person.
12. I am responsible for these thoughts.
13. It is important that I cancel out or block these thoughts.
14. Other people would think I am a bad, wicked person if they knew my thoughts.
15. I think that I should avoid certain people or places because of these thoughts.
16. These thoughts mean I am weird.
17. I should fight against and resist these thoughts.

GARY: For me too.

GREG: And me too.

LEADER: OK I will imagine you guys have just injected me with this way of looking at my thoughts, I'll speak out loud the sort of thing that I think goes on in the mind of someone with these type of thoughts. The co-leader's task is to try and help me consider an alternative way of looking at these thoughts but he might get stuck and you should all feel free to come in with your pennyworth.

Here the therapist has invited group members to consider alternative interpretations to their catastrophic appraisal but with a reduced level of emotional arousal because the focus is outside of themselves, on helping someone like them. In a state of high emotional arousal the OCD client appears unable to process information that is contrary to their OCD template for processing information (schema). However, having processed a contrary point of view first at a medium level of arousal they can become more able to access it in different emotional states. Whilst the contrary information could be taught purely didactically, it is likely that this would be insufficient to activate the combination (schema) of thoughts/images, emotions (action dispositions), involved in OCD, whereas the role playing indicated is more likely to produce the medium level of arousal necessary for complete processing. Importantly the privacy of group members is protected and they are left in charge of what they disclose. The session continued:

LEADER: I have just seen a knife left on the kitchen table, I wish the family would keep them hidden away like I have asked them to, time and time again, they don't listen, they'd be sorry if I stabbed them. Oh God I shouldn't be thinking that, that is terrible, I'll just do some cleaning to forget about it.

CO-LEADER: Why do you think your family don't really listen to you when you say hide the knives away?

LEADER: They just think I am off my head.

CO-LEADER: But if a masked man came into your house and there was a knife on the kitchen table what would they do?

LEADER: Get to it before the robber.

CO-LEADER: So the difference is that they don't see you as a robber/murderer

LEADER: No.

CO-LEADER: We are all sitting here chatting away. I could put this knife on this coffee table, the others could go out of the room; we could do this to test out whether you really are a murderer.

LEADER: I'd be frightened,

CO-LEADER: The others would be just in the next room, they could be very quick organising an ambulance if I'm stabbed.

LEADER: I'll leave it there.

MARLENE: I see it is about testing out the danger from knives, not hiding them away.

GARY: What about though if the thing you fear acting out is shameful?

LEADER: Right, I have got this fear that I might rip off my clothes and run through the street naked.

ERIC: Oh no, what an awful sight!

LEADER: Well you could imagine a younger me!

CO-LEADER: So how often have you streaked?

LEADER: Never.

CO-LEADER: So your form is that you have never streaked.

LEADER: Yes but have wanted to.

CO-LEADER: How do you know you have wanted to?

LEADER: Well it keeps going over and over in my mind.

CO-LEADER: When you want to do something there is enjoyment, do you have enjoyment when you have these thoughts of streaking?

LEADER: No I'm horrified.

CO-LEADER: So having thoughts/images going over and over is not at all evidence that you want to act on them.

LEADER: Well why do I have them then?

ERIC: Because you are a ******.

CO-LEADER: Thank you, Eric, for your assistance.

HANNAH: *looking at the leader* Maybe your thoughts/images are like the weather, it is pouring down outside right now, but we just get on with things here and eventually the weather changes.

LEADER: It's been a long winter.

CO-LEADER: Why do you think that might be?

GREG: *looking at the leader* I think it might be because you keep running faster and faster to get away from your shadow.

The above role plays are a potent way of ensuring that (a) the pertinent concerns of group members (item 2, GGTSRS, Appendix D) are addressed, (b) all are included (item 4, GGTSRS, Appendix D), (c) other members of the group are used as role models (item 7, GGTSRS, Appendix D) and (d) there is variety in the ways in which material is taught in order to retain interest (item 8, GGTSRS, Appendix D). Further, these goals are achieved without in any way embarrassing group members. Homework is set involving completion of the bOCD chart, MOOD chart and PSS and an underlining of the importance of continued 'dares'.

Sessions 9 and 10

These sessions begin by the therapists inviting the group to engage in further role plays if there is an appraisal in Table 8.7 that they still feel needs putting on trial. The topics covered in the earlier session are also briefly revised. In revising the importance of 'dares' the following exchange took place:

JOE: I'm still not good at dares, let's be honest I won't touch family members or friends.

LEADER: What if I wrote a contract taking full responsibility for any harm that comes to group members between now and the next session if you just shake hands with everyone. We could then compare whether group members have become any more ill than your family and friends. So that if there is no group next week you were right about how dangerous you are to others.

JOE: I'll give it a go, I've got to start.

GREG: I've still made no start on my hoarding, I wish I was more like Marlene.

MARLENE: Oh thanks, Greg.

GREG: I just can't throw stuff out.

MARLENE: Start with a little thing such as a poached egg maker.

GREG: I could but you never know when things might come in handy.

MARLENE: It's like me wanting to be certain, you want to be certain you won't need the poached egg maker.

GREG: I know it sounds stupid.

CO-LEADER: It is about daring to tolerate the uncertainty that something will be needed. Alternatively you could just hoard.

GREG: I can't keep hoarding, I'll get evicted in the end.

ERIC: Go and live at Marlene's for a week, she will sort you out!

GREG: *laughing* I think I'll just start with the poached egg maker, that's if I can find it in my mess!

By this stage in the programme, as the above dialogue reflects, much of the direct therapeutic work is being done by other group members and there is a greater confidence in disclosing personal information. The above exchange once again emphasises the important role that inflated responsibility plays in the maintenance of OCD and the need to tackle it, and further that it can be profitably tackled within the context of a behavioural experiment.

The new focus in the last two sessions is on the distillation of a personalised Survival Manual. The OCD Manual in Appendix L acts as a framework for this but group members are asked to highlight parts that are important for them, and annotate it. The therapists can also suggest additional reading materials such as pages 141 and 142 in *Moving On After Trauma* (Scott 2008), which describes the trials and tribulations of a person with OCD symptoms and suggested coping strategies, and/or contacting OCD Action, support@OCDaction.org.uk, a self-help group for OCD sufferers.

Chapter 9

Generalised anxiety disorder

Clients suffering from generalised anxiety disorder (GAD) are probably the population most amenable to a group intervention amongst sufferers from depression and the anxiety disorders. So much so that White *et al.* (1992) evaluated a purely didactic CBT programme for generalised anxiety disorder in which treatment consisted of groups of 20 or more clients attending six 2-hour 'evening classes' for 'stress control'. Clients were told that no personal problems were to be discussed. Although there was no individual CBT control group, the results of the large group programme were comparable to those found in GAD programmes up to that time and were judged more cost-effective. Interestingly in a comparison of individual and group CBT for GAD, Dugas *et al.* (2003) found that both were equally effective and produced very positive outcomes for approximately two-thirds of clients with GAD. However, Dugas *et al.* (2003) also urged caution as whilst there were no dropouts from individual CBT, 5 out of 48 dropped out of GCBT. In the Dugas *et al.* (2003) study the groups were much smaller, 4–6 clients, than in the White *et al.* (1992) study.

The key feature of generalised anxiety disorder is persistent uncontrollable worry about a wide range of matters. DSM-IV-TR (American Psychiatric Association 2000) requires that this cardinal symptom be present more days than not for the past six months. In addition, the person has to have at least three of the following six symptoms: (1) nervous, anxious, or on edge; (2) easily annoyed or irritable; (3) afraid as if something awful might happen; (4) restless and unable to sit still; (5) unable to stop or control worrying; and (6) trouble relaxing. Over 50% of GAD sufferers report an onset of their difficulties in childhood or adolescence. The course of GAD tends to be chronic but often worse in times of stress.

Clients can be screened for GAD using the 7 Minute Mental Health Screen Audit – Revised, Appendix B, or the self-report version, the First Step Questionnaire – Revised, Appendix C, and positive screens evaluated further using the CBT Pocketbook, Appendix A. The severity of GAD can be gauged using the GAD-7, freely available for personal use at www.iapt.nhs.uk. The cognitions that serve to maintain GAD can be identified and targeted using Anxious Thoughts Inventory (AnTI; Wells 1994). It is suggested that these measures are completed in the 24 hours before the session and progress can be monitored using Appendix F.

A cognitive behavioural model of generalised anxiety disorder

The presence of persistent uncontrollable worry is a necessary condition for the diagnosis of GAD in DSM-IV-TR (American Psychiatric Association 2000) and in the Wells (2008) model of GAD the client's belief in the uncontrollability of worry is accorded a central place. He suggests further that most GAD sufferers believe their worry poses a danger, e.g. 'worrying like this will have me in an early grave'. The Wells (2008) model of GAD is a metacognitive one in that the focus is on perceptions of worry, rather than the content of the worry. In Figure 9.1 a metacognitive model of the development of GAD is presented, based on the Wells (2008) model.

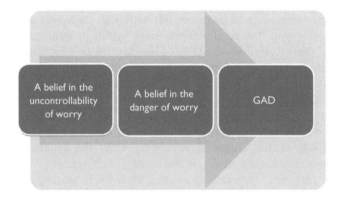

Figure 9.1 A metacognitive model of the development of GAD.

Thus the proximal causes of GAD are a belief in the uncontrollability of GAD and usually, in about 80% of cases, a belief in the danger of worry. However, a distal cause of worry is often positive beliefs about the benefits of worry, e.g. 'worrying makes me cautious, prevents catastrophe'. Though this distal cause may set the scene for GAD, without the evolution of the proximal causes, GAD will not occur. However, once GAD is established this same distal factor helps maintain GAD alongside avoidance, thought control strategies and heightened negative emotional arousal. The factors involved in the maintenance of GAD are shown in Figure 9.2

Avoidance may take the form of, for example, avoiding reading newspapers so as not to learn of harm coming to children, but avoidance is an ineffective coping strategy as the person will inevitably learn of harm from

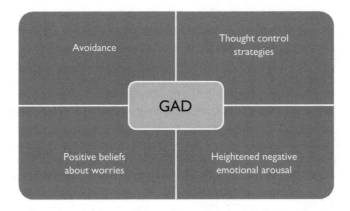

Figure 9.2 A metacognitive model of the maintenance of GAD.

other media. Similarly thought control strategies such as trying to suppress a thought are also ineffective, because of the rebound effect (Wegner *et al.* 1987), e.g. the more one tries not to think of green polar bears the more one thinks of them. In a state of heightened negative emotional arousal, beliefs about the negative consequences of worry are likely to come onstream. GAD clients also have positive beliefs about worry. GAD sufferers are not aware that they hold contradictory views about the merits of worry.

Though it is not shown in Figure 9.2, for simplicity, heightened negative emotional arousal will also directly increase worry itself, by typically lengthening the 'what if . . .' chain itself, e.g. 'what if I don't check on the children in the night, what if one of them dies, what if I am prosecuted, what if I am imprisoned'.

From Figures 9.1 and 9.2 the treatment targets in a metacognitive approach to GAD are the proximal and maintaining factors. Wells (2008) suggests that the GADS-R should be administered at each session to check that appropriate metacognitions are being targeted and belief in them changed. The GAS-R focuses on identifying the frequency of (a) maladaptive coping strategies, e.g. tried to distract myself; (b) avoidance of situations in order to prevent worry, e.g. news items or thoughts of accidents/loss; and (c) maladaptive beliefs about worry, e.g. I could go crazy with worry or worrying keeps me safe. In a comparison of metacognitive therapy (MCT) and applied relaxation (AR), (Wells 2010) found that the rates of recovery for MCT at post-treatment were 80% on measures of worry and trait-anxiety compared with 10% following AR. However, AR is not without benefit; whilst at post-treatment 100% of the MCT group no longer met diagnostic criteria for GAD, 50% of clients in the AR condition no longer met criteria. Arntz (2003) has reported recovery rates of 35% with standard CBT for GAD and 44% with AR.

In traditional CBT for GAD the focus is on the content of the worries, the 'what if . . .' chains, assessing how realistic a negative prediction is and, if one did come to pass, whether it would be truly catastrophic. The cognitive behavioural (problem solving) approach to GAD of Dugas *et al.* (2007) focuses on the content of worries and appears to bring about recovery in about two-thirds of GAD sufferers by a 12-month follow-up. Problem solving consists of the following stages: problem orientation, problem definition, brainstorming a menu of options, considering the advantages and disadvantages of each option, choosing an option, planning implementation of the option, review of effectiveness of chosen solution, if unsuccessful return to menu of options and continued recycling through the stages until successful. Dugas *et al.* (2007) found that intolerance of uncertainty along with negative problem orientation were the major predictors of severity of GAD. Intolerance of uncertainty is the tendency to react negatively to an uncertain event or situation, regardless of the probability of the outcome and any associated consequences. He suggested that whilst GAD sufferers are not deficient in problem solving skills per se, i.e. given an already defined problem they can solve it as well as anyone, they do have a deficit in problem orientation, i.e. they do not see discrete problems, deal in generalities, e.g. 'it's all too much' and consequently do not lock on to problems. Dugas *et al.* (2007) have suggested that GAD sufferers use cognitive avoidance, i.e. they block the answering of anxiogenic questions, e.g. what if I fail this exam? This applies to images as well as thoughts, e.g. 'I replace threatening mental images with things I say to myself in my mind'.

There are similarities between the Wells (2008) approach and that of Dugas *et al.* (2007) in that the deficits in problem orientation to which the latter refers can be understood as maladaptive metacognitive beliefs, beliefs surrounding the processing of information, e.g. 'if there are hassles either I am to blame or someone else is to blame, sorting out the perpetrator is what is necessary'. Maladaptive metacognitive beliefs may also interfere directly with the problem solving process. For example, if a person believes that they have to feel certain to make a choice then they may never get beyond the menu of options open to them for the solving of a particular task. This particular difficulty reflects an intolerance of uncertainty.

The approach to the treatment of GAD taken in this chapter is to first utilise interventions based on the Wells (2008) model and towards the end of the programme focus on strategies derived from the Dugas *et al.* (2007) model. It may be both theoretically and practically confusing to apply both models at the same time and it is recommended that the two approaches are modularised. It may be that the utilisation of two models results in a dilution of any one approach, a case of more being less, but this is an empirical question. The author's clinical experience is that clients do not see a contradiction or confusion in focusing both on the content of worries and on the beliefs they bring to bear in considering worry. The optimal way of sequencing and weighting an emphasis on cognition and metacognition remains to be determined. In the later sessions clients who have not benefited from the MCT or CBT approach can be directed along an AR route, but this is conducted primarily between sessions with individual contact.

Generalised anxiety disorder programme

The GAD programme is summarised in Table 9.1.
The cast of the GAD programme is summarised in Table 9.2.

Staying on course

Sometimes group programmes can suffer possible derailment from unexpected quarters and in these circumstances it is necessary to be clear about the evidence-based protocol that is being followed and to be faithful to it. For example, managers may become aware of the cost savings involved by running an anxiety group and therapists come under pressure to have an open door policy with regard to the group. The therapists have to make it clear that evidence-based group work requires homogeneous groups and that there is not an evidence base for heterogeneous groups. As such, careful screening of clients is required lest groups are sabotaged by the extreme difficulties of a member. (Though a case can be made for a more open group if the group is purely didactic [White *et al.* 1992].) It is also sometimes the case that even with a carefully recruited group, the therapists have to make unexpected adaptations but need to do so within the framework of what is being taught, as the following vignette illustrates.

The therapists had invited a former group member, Jack, to attend the first session of the group to give his testimony. They reasoned that he would be a credible source of persuasion, increasing the motivation of group members to attend. However, as the group assembled it became apparent that Jack and a group member, Wayne, knew each other in passing as they both had children at the same school. The leader took Wayne to one side and asked him what he felt about Jack giving his testimony. Wayne was clearly put out by the encounter and it triggered a worry episode 'what if it gets all around the school, what if it gets around the whole estate, what if I can't talk in the group'. The leader reiterated that a continuation of the two scheduled individual sessions was an option, but that it might be useful to test out whether his fears come to pass rather than assume they are true. Thus the

Table 9.1 GAD programme

	Therapeutic targets	Treatment strategies	Materials – Generalised Anxiety Disorder Survival Manual, Appendix M
Sessions 1–4	1. Beliefs about the uncontrollability of worry	Worry postponement, worry time	Introduction. Sections 1–4
	2. Beliefs about the danger of worry	Planned ignoring of worries	
	3. Avoidance, reassurance seeking	Openness to all triggers of worry episodes, trusting in own judgement	
	4. Thought control strategies	Demonstration of rebound effect of thought suppression	
	5. Positive beliefs about worry	Examination of the evidence and counter-evidence	
Sessions 5–7	6. Maladaptive metacognitive beliefs about problem solving and intolerance of uncertainty	Problem orientation and effective problem solving	Sections 5–13
	7. Task interfering cognitions (TIC). Horror video	Switching to task-oriented cognitions (TOC) TIC/TOC Switching from horror video to reality video	
	8. Perception that demands exceed resources	Working sequentially rather than simultaneously, weaning off excessive responsibility – responsibility pie	
	9. Managing mood	Use of MOOD chart	
	10. Tension	Applied relaxation	
Sessions 8–10	Relapse prevention	Recap of all treatment strategies and distillation of relapse prevention protocol	GAD Survival Manual

Table 9.2 GAD group members

Name	Thumbnail sketch
Wayne	IT specialist, department being outsourced, worry about letting family down
Barony	Teacher overwhelmed by paperwork, exhausting herself, perceives herself performing poorly
Chris	Unemployed graduate, trying to write a novel, carer of mother with Parkinson's disease
Katrina	Support worker, understaffed visiting those with head injuries
Michael	Medical student, poor performance following viral illness, fearful of exams
Marion	Solicitor anxious about work and relationships

therapists had addressed both using group members as role models (item 7, Appendix D) and inclusion (item 4, Appendix D) to a degree even before the first group session got under way. The leader had also used Wayne's hot cognitions about expectations to illustrate a different way of handling them, in so doing making the therapeutic process relevant (item 2, Appendix D).

As the first group session got under way, the leader reiterated the ground rules for the group surrounding attendance, parking, breaks, timekeeping and particularly laboured the issue of confidentiality. Fortunately the 'guest', Jack, used the experience of his chance encounter with Wayne to illustrate how much he had changed by attending the group. He explained that if this had been his first group session he would probably have run out of the door but since the group he stops and thinks before letting his first thoughts race away. Jack said that his second thoughts were 'would Wayne really place an advertisement in the local free newspaper that he had met Jack at an anxiety group'; this in turn evoked laughter from Wayne.

Sessions 1–4

These first sessions follow a metacognitive framework. At the first group session members are introduced to the GAD Survival Manual, Appendix M, and the first four sections are used as the basis for discussion. The session begins with a description of the typical thoughts of GAD sufferers and members are invited to discuss which ones are most pertinent to themselves. Then group members are invited to volunteer their degree of belief in the two key beliefs that drive GAD, the uncontrollability of worry and the danger of worry. The focus then shifts to the worry time strategy that can potentially undermine belief in the uncontrollability of worry. Homework includes the practice of the worry time strategy. It is explained that typical strategies of GAD sufferers such as blocking worrying thoughts result in a rebound effect that increases their frequency. In order to illustrate the 'rebound effect' members are asked to conjure up an image such as a black rabbit and then try to block it and observe the effects of this strategy. Homework thus also involves practising a detached mindfulness about worrisome thoughts rather than the blocking of such thoughts. The detached mindfulness approach is probably best conveyed using the metaphor of planned ignoring employed with a child having a temper tantrum. The parent/carer remains aware of the child sufficiently to prevent them harming themselves; the equivalent of this is assessing whether there is a real and imminent threat to themselves right now. In the absence of a real and present danger that others would concur with, the group member is advised to see the worry as a temper tantrum that will sort itself out if simply ignored and given no feedback (processing). Further, rather like a child's tantrum the worry may initially get worse as it is being ignored but finally because of the lack of reinforcement/effortful processing the worry peters away. By the time of the scheduled worry time most worries have evaporated but if they are still an issue the group member can spend a few minutes sorting out the issue on paper by writing about it for a couple of minutes. Alternatively the person might dictate their concerns into a tape recorder or even finger write their issue if dyslexic. In this way group members learn that there is a time and a place for their concerns, worry is controllable and there is no benefit in picking at worries 24/7.

Most GAD sufferers also have a belief that worry is dangerous and in the first session the therapists explore with group members the feared consequences of worry, as in the following exchange:

MARION: I can't go on getting myself in the state I do.
CO-LEADER: Why not?
MARION: I'll lose my job.
CO-LEADER: Has anyone complained about your work?
MARION: No, but that is only because I work extra hard to make up for my mistakes.
CO-LEADER: In Figure 2 of the GAD Survival Manual there is a picture of how the 'fire' of anxiety is kept going; one of the 'coals' is avoidance, it sounds as if one of your particular 'coals', Marion, is avoiding cruising at your optimal speed, the speed that makes best use of the petrol in the tank.
MARION: I've always gone at a great pace.
CO-LEADER: How do you know that is necessary?
MARION: As a solicitor I don't think I've any evidence that would stand up.

LEADER: Perhaps you could conduct an experiment; on alternate days this week you could cruise and on the other days avoid cruising, exceed the optimal speed and see if there is any difference in productivity.

MARION: OK.

The above dialogue illustrates that though the Manual is the basis of the presentation in the first session, it is not conveyed in a didactic fashion, rather there is a natural movement around its content that follows the flow of the concerns expressed in the group. This ensures that session content is relevant to group members (item 2, Appendix D) but also that the client has an aide-memoire for taught material, i.e. that the therapists exhibit good presentation skills (item 8 Appendix D). Finally the therapist suggests a behavioural experiment to test out a belief in the dangerousness of worry rather than relying on persuading the client in the manner of a barrister. Clients' beliefs are held not just at the level of an idea (declarative knowledge) but also at the level of an associated procedure (procedural knowledge), thus whilst cognitive disputation would tackle declarative knowledge a behavioural experiment is more potent as it operates at both levels. The homeworks set are reviewed at each session and become the focus of group discussion, leading to a deeper understanding of material taught and a refinement of coping strategies. In reviewing homework at the start of the fourth group session the following dialogue ensued:

MARION: I'm getting better at going at a steady pace in work, but I have to constantly remind myself to operate a turnstile and do just one thing at a time and of a weekend, particularly on a Sunday, I worry like mad about work.

LEADER: Why?

MARION: I just do.

LEADER: What is the benefit of worrying all Sunday?

MARION: So I'm prepared.

LEADER: So if you weren't prepared what would happen?

MARION: It would be so disorganised.

LEADER: Have you had a Sunday where you didn't have a chance to do your worrying because you were distracted with other things?

MARION: Yes, a couple of months ago when my mum had a fall and I had to take her to hospital.

LEADER: In the week after your mum's fall did you perform any less well in work than you do normally?

MARION: Not that I can remember.

LEADER: What do you make of that?

MARION: Hmm.

BARONY: I do a similar thing but over the whole weekend. My last Ofsted (teacher monitoring body) report wasn't great, so I fret over the next week, but if I have been away walking with friends for the weekend I'm not so bad.

CO-LEADER: Is your performance in school any better when you have been able to worry 24/7 about it the weekend before?

BARONY: No not at all.

MARION: I see what you mean, believing that worrying helps just gets me in such a state that by Monday morning I'm almost out the game.

BARONY: Me too.

LEADER: It may be particularly important, Marion and Barony, to ensure that you employ the worry time strategy at weekends.

Challenging positive beliefs about worry is important but initially it should be the negative beliefs about worry that are the focus and given priority. In the above exchange the therapists have focused on naturally occurring interruptions to worry to review group members' experiences and consider whether, contrary to their long-held anxiogenic belief, they actually perform better when they have not been worrying. In drawing on members' experiences the therapists have ensured that the teaching is relevant (item 2, Appendix D) and the cohesiveness of the group is enhanced as group members identify with others' experiences.

Sessions 5–7

These sessions follow a traditional CBT approach to GAD, with an emphasis on a problem solving framework. There is some overlap with the metacognitive approach of earlier sessions in that there is a focus on modifying the maladaptive metacognitive beliefs which sabotage (a) engaging in problem solving, e.g. hassles mean others or I are to blame, that is the important thing to address, and (b) the process of problem solving, e.g. I have got to feel certain that my solution is right before trying anything. The material for these sections is based on Sections 5–13. After introducing Section 5 at the beginning of the fifth session the following dialogue ensued:

CHRIS: That's me always making mountains out of molehills.

CO-LEADER: Can you give us an example, Chris.

CHRIS: Well over the weekend I started worrying about what is going to happen to me when my mother dies. We have got the house from a Housing Association because of my mother's Parkinson's disease. I was thinking I will be on the street when she dies.

CO-LEADER: Have they said that your mum is close to death?

CHRIS: Oh no, she is still walking around and can go out if accompanied, she could go on for years and years.

LEADER: What were the effects of this worrying over the weekend?

CHRIS: I couldn't settle to do my writing or sleep properly, then I got low because I started thinking who do I think I am that I will finish a novel and have it published. So I started brooding about that then. If I am not worrying about one thing I am worrying about another.

CO-LEADER: Did you try to use the worry time?

CHRIS: No, I got myself into such a state I just went on a worry binge. Started pestering my uncle and then a friend about whether I would really become homeless, they must be getting sick of me.

The above exchange illustrates how increased negative affect can trigger a worry episode and how reassurance seeking perpetuates the worry. It is therefore useful to teach group members how to nip such 'binges' in the bud by using the MOOD chart, Table 1 in the Survival Manual, Appendix M. The session continued:

MICHAEL: I'm like Barony, I always assume the worst, such as failing my exams.

LEADER: You could put that plan, 'assume the worst', under the microscope. The rules you have for organising your approach to things is what we call a metacognitive belief. So if, for example, your mood dipped because you were already running late to get to the group on time and then remembered that you hadn't fed the cats, you might put that in the first column. Your observed thinking (second column) might be 'it will be terrible if I'm late, here I go again assuming the worst', in the objective thinking column you could address the metacognitive belief and ask yourself 'how useful is it to always assume the worst?' and you could also address the cognitive belief itself with a 'so what if I'm a couple of minutes late, will I be hanged, drawn and quartered?'. Having got yourself in the right frame of mind, you would then move to the fourth column, Do; for example, do what you have to do in order to feed the cat, drive to the group, find a parking space, etc., no longer fuss over the thoughts that initially bothered you, use planned ignoring, and postpone any ongoing thoughts to the worry time.

MICHAEL: I think I'm a constructive pessimist, assume the worst to be prepared.

BARONY: Me too but it doesn't get you anywhere!

KATRINA: When I am going on visits to people with head injuries, I imagine the worst. I'm just a support worker, no real training. I was embarrassed a few days ago: one of the service users had an outburst when another user knocked his coffee over in a café. They soon settled, but I imagined one of them running across the road being killed and it would all be my fault!

MICHAEL: Maybe we should have a club for people to wean themselves off their addiction to horror movies!

CO-LEADER: I think in recognising that you are 'hooked' by them you are halfway along the road to recovery. Then to 'unhook' you can use the MOOD chart.

MICHAEL: I think I take the 'horror movies' on board without really realising I am dong it, then I am in such a state that I can't think straight.

CO-LEADER: That is where carefully monitoring your mood is important and adjusting it as you go along is important, rather like having a person in hospital on a heart monitor and adjusting blood pressure as you go along rather than waiting for a major change before attempting anything. Try the MOOD charts for homework.

In the above exchange the therapists have used a metaphor that is within the life experience of group members to illustrate teaching points, ensuring that what is presented is relevant (item 2, Appendix D). Further, the therapists have illustrated how the MOOD chart framework has an integrative function – it encapsulates a challenging of not only maladaptive cognitions but also maladaptive metacognitions and implicitly directs the client to a detached mindfulness about worrisome thoughts. In the use of the 'horror movie' metaphor there is an implicit acknowledgement that what distresses a GAD sufferer may be as much imagery as thoughts and as with thoughts this may be addressed using a planned ignoring/detached mindfulness.

In these sessions the focus is also on Section 7 of the GAD Manual, problem solving. Problem solving is presented as a particular way or algorithm of dealing with worrisome thoughts, different in kind from both agonising about the thoughts or blanking them. The specifics of problem solving, such as problem definition, brainstorming, choosing a solution, implementing the solution, reviewing the working of the solution, can be the subject matter of a scheduled worry time. Problem orientation may be viewed as a descriptor of a set of adaptive metacognitive beliefs that hassles/ concerns are for everyone inevitable, there is rarely certainty that any one solution is going to work, and they are usually soluble to some degree albeit after a number of options have been exhausted. Implicit within problem orientation is a view that neither the person experiencing the hassles nor others are necessarily to blame. Because problem solving beyond problem orientation does involve effortful processing it is usually best conducted/ postponed to a time when there are few interruptions. However, the problem/worry is often no longer a concern by the allotted time. The thoughts that interfere with problem solving can be described as TICS (task interfering cognitions), whilst the problem solving process involves TOCS (task orientated cognitions) and group members are encouraged to remember the mnemonic TIC/TOC. After introducing Section 7, the following exchange took place:

MICHAEL: I can see myself using TIC/TOC to help when I'm revising for exams. I'll keep thinking I am going to mess them up again or whenever I am revising one thing I think I should be revising another, in the end I can't concentrate.

CO-LEADER: You could see how you revised for exams last time as one option for passing your forthcoming exam but you could also look at other options.

MICHAEL: Last time I was so concerned I gave up playing football and didn't socialise.

MARION: You are likely to just get stale with that.

MICHAEL: Looking back now I probably was.

CO-LEADER: One option might be to keep up the football and to slightly reduce socialising.

MICHAEL: Yes, I might also need to reduce the drinking. Medics are terrible drinkers.

WAYNE: That's not a good advert!

MICHAEL: No.

KATRINA: I like a drink at night, stops my mind racing so I can get off to sleep.

LEADER: Problem is the drink-induced sleep does not give you energy the next day, it just gives you a period of unconsciousness.

WAYNE: Since coming to the group, now when my mind is racing like that I just laugh at it and ask it where is it racing to? Then use the worry time.

The above exchange illustrates how as the group progresses members increasingly become therapists to each other (item 7, Appendix D) and often come up with innovative strategies if the therapists have the flexibility to allow discussion to wander a little off the agenda for the session. The dialogue continued:

MARION: But there are some problems that you can't do anything about, like I need an operation for glaucoma (slowly deteriorating vision), otherwise I go blind in my left eye.

MICHAEL: I can see having the operation is a big hassle but once it is done there is no further deterioration, what's getting to you about it?

MARION: It would be awful not to see my kids.

LEADER: That sounds like a horror video.

MARION: I think I just keep watching it.

CO-LEADER: What is a realistic scenario, Michael?

MICHAEL: Well I'm not even qualified yet, but as far as I'm aware it is very straightforward, though even the simplest procedure like going to the dentist can go wrong.

MARION: Yes I asked the consultant about it; he was very nice, but then I had to go and see my GP.

LEADER: Why?

MARION: Looking at the Manual it's me seeking reassurance again.

LEADER: Did it work?

MARION: No, because here I am again seeking reassurance, maybe the addiction to horror movies is the other side of the same coin as addiction to reassurance.

LEADER: Sounds like it. But the assurances you are given, like Michael's, are never enough for you because you want to feel absolutely certain.

MARION: I don't feel in control if I am not certain.

CO-LEADER: How do you manage to delegate tasks in work?

MARION: I don't, I exhaust myself doing everything properly myself.

CO-LEADER: Is that viable long term?

MARION: No, I have got to begin tolerating some uncertainty both in and out of work.

CO-LEADER: Maybe you ought to practise tolerating uncertainty alongside a realistic video of the statistically most likely sequence of events. If you find yourself staring at the horror video, switch your attention to the channel showing the reality video.

MARION: Sounds good.

The above exchange illustrates that important issues, such as 'making mountains out of molehills', intolerance of uncertainty, appear in many different guises and the root causes of distress require highlighting and targeting.

In these sessions the group's attention is also focused on Section 10 of the Survival Manual, which underlines the importance of exercise and relaxation exercise. Applied relaxation is a credible alternative to standard CBT (Arntz 2003) and the two are not mutually exclusive. In the group programme only the essence of AR is presented and it is suggested that a full implementation of AR (Ost 1987) is reserved for those who have not responded to the MCT or CBT module and that this is conducted by individual contact between sessions. An easily understood rationale for relaxation exercises is to present them as a specific form of exercise. The leaders first canvass the effects of exercise on group members and underline the way in which problems that seemed nearer to the mountain end of the mountain–molehill line beforehand tend to shift to the molehill end afterwards. Three or four periods of exercise a week can be recommended as a way of 'keeping hassles in perspective'. Relaxation exercises are then introduced by asking group members to rate their tension on a scale 0–10, where a 10 would be the most tense ever and 0 totally relaxed. Members are then asked to close their eyes whilst the therapist takes them through a relaxation exercise, at the end of which members re-rate their anxiety, 0–10, and discuss the impact of the exercise. The relaxation exercise is usually best done near the beginning of a session when members are likely to be more tense, giving more opportunity for the exercise to have an impact. The relaxation exercise consists of asking group members to tense and relax each muscle group in turn, noting the difference between tension and relaxation and the muscles becoming warm. A typical script would be 'tense your toes really tight, really tight, hold that tension (5 seconds), now just let the tension go, feel the tension flow out of the tips of your toes, now your calves, tense them really tight, hold that tension (5 seconds), now just let go of the tension in your calves, feel the tension flow out, you calves becoming warm (10 seconds) etc.' and so on through each muscle group including the face. It is suggested that group members may want to practise this procedure several times a day to get into the right frame of mind. This particular exercise (tension and release of muscle groups) is in fact only the first stage of Ost's (1987) AR programme; the further stages are release-only relaxation, cue-controlled relaxation, differential relaxation, rapid relaxation and application training. There are, however, a minority of GAD sufferers who suffer relaxation-induced anxiety, i.e. after the exercise their score worsens rather than improves, and they are best advised to stick to whatever they have already benefited from.

Group members who benefited from the relaxation exercise can also be introduced to rapid relaxation response for use in 'emergency situations', e.g. they have just been told that their boss wants to see them. This strategy involves the taking of a deep breath and breathing out slowly whilst saying slowly a favourite word, e.g. 'ree. . .l. . .a. . .x', whilst at the same time dropping shoulders and jaw. But any full implementation of an AR programme would take place outside of the group in individual contact between sessions and would be reserved for those who have not benefited from MCT or CBT.

Sessions 8–10

These sessions are for review of all the material taught to date and involve revisiting the Survival Manual in the sessions and further group discussion. Group members are invited to annotate the Manual with whatever is particularly pertinent to them. The final session should be a booster session about a month or so after the weekly group sessions, allowing clients more time to practise and refine the Survival Manual. In the group clients should be asked to identify and write down the likely particular triggers for worry episodes, the particular metacognitions they need to be alert for and their antidotes/strategies.

New directions in the treatment of GAD?

The DSM V working group (Andrews *et al.* 2010) have proposed renaming GAD generalised worry disorder, if field trials of new diagnostic criteria are successful. The rebranding of GAD emphasises the centrality of 'worry' to the condition. Andrews *et al.* (2010) are to field test the criteria, shown in Table 9.3, for generalised worry disorder:

Table 9.3 Proposed criteria for generalised worry disorder

A:	The person experiences excessive anxiety and worry (apprehensive expectation):
	(a) about two (or more) domains of activities or events (e.g. domains like family, health, finances, and school/work difficulties)
	(b) which occurs on more days than not
	(c) for 3 months (or more)
B.	The anxiety and worry are associated with one (or more) of the following symptoms:
	(a) restlessness or feeling keyed up or on edge
	(b) muscle tension
C.	The anxiety and worry lead to changes in behaviour shown by one (or more) of the following:
	(a) marked avoidance of potentially negative events or activities
	(b) marked time and effort preparing for possible negative outcomes of events or activities
	(c) marked procrastination in behaviour or decision making due to worries
	(d) repeatedly seeking reassurance due to worries.

Criterion C suggests new foci for the treatment of generalised worry disorder that lend themselves to being easily addressed in a group format. For example, with regard to C(a), group members could be invited to volunteer situations they avoid, e.g. visiting people in hospital, sleeping in the dark, and group norms utilised to help members to tackle those situations they are avoiding. Similarly, with regard to C(b) in Table 9.3, group members could be invited to volunteer situations in which they overprepare, e.g. arriving an hour early for appointments out of a concern that they might get lost or stuck in traffic, and members could be invited to dare each other to prepare less. In the same way, with regard to C(c) in Table 9.3, group members could be asked to dare to buy one or other of the leaders a very small gift but to do so within 10 minutes of entering a department store; indeed this could be a group in-vivo exercise. Finally group members could be asked to desist from asking the leaders whether the 'gift' was 'really' liked. Such strategies might be integrated into the GCBT programme outlined in this chapter (it might be like Christmas for the group leaders) but whether it would make for a more potent treatment remains to be established!

Cognitive Behaviour Therapy Pocketbook – Revised

The CBT Pocketbook is used after first screening clients for possible disorders using the 7 Minute Health Screen Audit – Revised (Appendix B) or the First Step Questionnaire – Revised (Appendix C). The disorders in the Pocketbook are listed in alphabetical order. For each disorder there are questions which directly access each symptom in the DSM-IV-TR criteria. For a symptom to be regarded as present it must produce clinically significant distress or impairment. When there is a need to reassess the client, the same questions can be asked again to check progress.

A conceptualisation of each disorder is presented for sharing with the client. A 'Sat Nav' for that disorder follows, to be used as an aide-memoire during therapy (it is not intended to replace the session-by-session guidelines). The 'Sat Nav' identifies and summarises treatment targets and treatment strategies. Finally usage of the Pocketbook is governed by the mnemonic FACT. The F and A stand for first assess. The third letter of FACT, 'C', stands for conceptualisation. The last letter of FACT, 'T', stands for treatment and under this heading the core cognitive behavioural interventions are summarised in the Sat Nav.

Depression

During the last 2 weeks have you been:

1. Sad, down or depressed most of the day nearly every day?
2. Have you lost interest or do you get less pleasure from the things you used to enjoy?
3. Have you been eating much less or much more?
4. Have you been having problems falling asleep, staying asleep or waking up too early of a morning?
5. Have you been fidgety, restless, unable to sit still or talking or moving more slowly than is normal for you?
6. Have you been tired all the time nearly every day?
7. Have you been bothered by feelings of worthlessness or guilt?
8. Have you had problems taking in what you are reading, watching/ listening to or in making decisions about everyday things?
9. Have you been hurting or making plans for hurting yourself?

If the client answered yes to five or more of the above (at least one of which has to be question 1 or 2) then it is likely that the client is suffering from depression.

Conceptualisations – present a story that makes sense to the client and is consistent with the CBT model. Examples:

(a) 'on strike for better pay and conditions'
(b) 'stopped investing so there can't be a return'
(c) 'you equated your worth with doing . . . how do you know there can't be other routes to a sense of achievement and pleasure?'
(d) 'why would the dice be forever loaded against you?'

Depression Sat Nav

Therapeutic targets	Treatment strategies
1. Depression about depression	Focus on responsibility for working on solutions and not on responsibility for problem
2. Inactivity	Developing a broad investment portfolio, wide-ranging modest investments
3. Negative views of self, personal world and future	Challenging the validity, utility and authority by which these views are held. Use of MOOD chart
4. Information processing biases	Highlighting personal biases and stepping around them using MOOD chart
5. Overvalued roles	Valuing multiple roles, renegotiation of roles in social context
6. Relapse prevention	Personally constructed self-help 'manual', utilising key points from therapy and drawing on self-help books and computer-assisted material

Generalised anxiety disorder

Ask the client if they would regard themselves as a 'worrier', in the sense that they always find something to worry about and if they are not worrying they worry that they are not worrying? If the worry has been excessive or uncontrollable (more days than not) for at least six months and they have three or more of the following symptoms (more days than not):

1. tiring very easily
2. restlessness, keyed up or on edge
3. difficulty concentrating or mind going blank
4. irritability
5. muscle tension
6. difficulty falling or staying asleep

then it is probable that they are suffering from generalised anxiety disorder. (However, a diagnosis of GAD is not given if they are suffering from depression; the latter is regarded as more significant in the diagnostic 'bible' DSM-IV-TR, American Psychiatric Association 2000).)

Conceptualisation – the essence of GAD can be conveyed to clients as follows: 'worry about everything and nothing, worry even if there is nothing to worry about', 'imagination runs riot, what if this, what if that, what if the other'.

Generalised anxiety disorder Sat Nav

Therapeutic targets	Treatment strategies
1. Beliefs about the uncontrollability of worry	Worry postponement, worry time. Planned ignoring of worries
2. Beliefs about the danger of worry	
3. Avoidance, reassurance seeking	Openness to all triggers of worry episodes, trusting in own judgement
4. Thought control strategies	Demonstration of rebound effect of thought suppression
5. Positive beliefs about worry	Examination of the evidence and counter evidence
6. Maladaptive metacognitive beliefs about problem solving and intolerance of uncertainty	Problem orientation and effective problem solving
7. Task interfering cognitions (TIC), horror video	Switching to task oriented cognitions (TOC) TIC/TOC Switching to reality video
8. Perception that demands exceed resources	Working sequentially rather than simultaneously, weaning off excessive responsibility – responsibility pie
9. Managing mood	Use of MOOD chart
10. Tension	Applied relaxation
11. Relapse prevention	Recap of all treatment strategies and distillation of relapse prevention protocol

Obsessive compulsive disorder

Obsessions

1. Are you bothered by thoughts, images or impulses that keep going over in your mind?
2. Do you try to block these thoughts, images or impulses by thinking or doing something?

Provided the client's concerns are not simply excessive worries about everyday problems and provided the client sees these thoughts/images as a product of their own mind, then yes responses to questions 1 and 2 above indicate a likely obsession.

Compulsions

1. Do you feel driven to repeat some behaviour, e.g. checking, washing, counting, or to repeat something in your mind over and over again to try to feel less uncomfortable?
2. If you do not do your special thing do you get very anxious?

Yes responses to these last two questions indicate a probable compulsion.

Note: the client has to be aware that their obsession and compulsion are excessive or irrational and they must also significantly interfere with functioning or cause significant distress.

Conceptualisation – normalise the client's thoughts/ideas/fantasies by likening the mind to a 'railway station', nobody can control what 'train of thought/ image comes in'. Point out that (a) trying to neutralise them by overt behaviours, e.g. repeated handwashing, or covert rituals, e.g. counting to a certain number, 'feeds' the intrusions, (b) pursuing a feeling of certainty is like searching for the 'Holy Grail'; and (c) they take an excessive share of the 'responsibility pie'.

Obsessive compulsive disorder Sat Nav

Therapeutic targets	*Treatment strategies*
1. Model of mental life, serious misinterpretation of intrusions – thought action fusion (TAF), thought object fusion (TOF) and thought event fusion (TEF)	Develop more appropriate model, detached mindfulness about intrusions
2. Inappropriate goal state, e.g. absolute certainty, perfect cleanliness	Distilling achievable goals
3. Appraisal of intrusions	Encourage perception of reasonable degree of control by postponement strategies. Use of bOCD chart and completion of Personal Significance Scale
4. Neutralising images, thoughts, behaviours	Behavioural experiments – Dare Don't Avoid a Realistic Experiment
5. Overestimation of danger/ intolerance of uncertainty	Distillation of realistic probabilities. The necessity of tolerating uncertainty
6. Cognitive and behavioural avoidance	Demonstration of the harmlessness of thoughts. Discussion of 'why don't you warn others of these dangers?'
7. Excessive responsibility, low mood	Responsibility pie, therapist contracts to remove responsibility, MOOD chart, memory aids
8. Unassertive communication	Communication guidelines
9. Unrealistic appraisals	Leader playing devil's advocate of personal significance of intrusions, co-leader challenging the leader's 'appraisals', assisted by group members
10. Relapse prevention	Personalising the OCD Survival Manual

Panic disorder and agoraphobia

1. Do you have times when you feel a sudden rush of intense fear, that comes on, from out of the blue, for no reason at all?
2. Does it take less than ten minutes for the panic attack to reach its worst?
3. During your last bad panic attack did you have four or more of the following:
   i. Heart racing
   ii. Sweating
   iii. Trembling or shaking
   iv. Shortness of breath or smothering
   v. Feeling of choking
   vi. Chest pain
   vii. Nausea
   viii. Dizzy, light-headed, unsteady or faint
   ix. Things around seemed unreal
   x. Fear of losing control
   xi. Afraid you might die
   xii. Numbness or tingling sensations
   xiii. Chills or hot flushes

If the client answered yes to each of the three questions above it is likely that they are suffering from panic disorder.

Some people with panic disorder avoid certain situations for fear of having a panic attack, e.g. going places alone, crowded shops. If this is the case it is then necessary to establish whether this avoidance interferes with their daily routine, job or social activities. If the answer to this is also yes then they are probably suffering from panic disorder with agoraphobic avoidance. The agoraphobic avoidance would be regarded as severe if they are totally unable to go out by themselves, mild if they just can't go great distances by themselves and moderate if how far they can go by themselves is in between.

Conceptualisation
(a) *Advise that panic attacks are fuelled by catastrophic interpretation of unusual but not abnormal bodily sensations. View panic attacks as a 'Big Dipper Ride', ascending the symptoms get worse, tempting to get off near the top, but if the client does not do anything then the symptom comes down the other side within ten minutes.*
(b) *Suggest that using 'safety behaviours' prevents learning that nothing terrible would happen if they did nothing at all in the panic situation.*

Panic disorder Sat Nav

Therapeutic targets	Treatment strategies
1. Fear of fear, anxiety sensitivity, catastrophic labelling of bodily symptoms, hypervigilance for bodily symptoms, monitoring of panic attacks	Psychoeducation
2. Avoidance of activities and situations, anxiety sensitivity	Construction of exposure hierarchy, in-vivo and interoceptive exposure
3. 'Safety' procedures, avoidance	Daring to gradually wean off 'safety' procedures, troubleshooting cognitive saboteurs to continued interoceptive and in vivo exposure
4. Intolerance of discomfort, feared consequences, key cognitive saboteurs	Interoceptive and in-vivo exposure, challenging 'catastrophic' cognitions, dares as behavioural experiments, downward arrow technique
5. Relapse prevention	Identifying likely precipitants for panic, distillation and rehearsal of a protocol. Exercise as a possible preventative measure. Regular review of protocol

Post-traumatic stress disorder

A.

1. Have you ever been involved in a very serious accident, incident or assault that still plays on your mind?

If more that one trauma is reported: which one of these affected you most?

2. How did you react when it happened?

If unclear: Were you afraid or did you feel terrified or helpless?

In order to meet criterion A the person must have both objectively experienced an extreme event A(1) and felt intense fear, helplessness or horror at the time A(2).

B.

i.   Do you have distressing memories or pictures of the incident popping into your mind?
ii.   Do you have distressing nightmares of the incident?
iii. Do you ever feel that you are not just remembering the incident but that you feel like it is happening again and lose some awareness of where you are, what you are doing?
iv.   Do you come across any reminders of the incident that cause you to get very upset?
v.   Do you get any physical symptoms such as breathing heavily, heart racing, sweating when you come across reminders?

In order to meet criterion B at least one of the symptoms in this category must be endorsed.

C.

i.   Do you try to block thoughts/images and avoid conversations about the incident?
ii.   Do you avoid activities, places or people that bring back memories of the incident?
iii. Is there any big gap in your memory of the incident that you don't remember even though it was at a time that you were conscious?
iv.   Have you lost interest in or stopped bothering with things you used to do that you enjoyed?
v.   Have you felt that you are not connecting with others, more than just a bit out of sync?

vi. Do you feel flat, unable to feel warm to people?

vii. Do you have a sense that you are going to die young, by a particular age?

In order to meet criterion C at least three of the symptoms in this category must be endorsed.

D.

i. Are you having difficulty falling or staying asleep?

ii. Have you been having outbursts of anger or snapping?

iii. Do you have trouble concentrating sufficiently to read or watch TV?

iv. Are you on guard a lot of the time, keep checking on things?

v. Are you easily startled, taking more than seconds to calm down?

In order to meet criterion D at least two of the symptoms in this category must be endorsed and these sympyoms must represent a change in functioning from before the trauma.

For a diagnosis of PTSD not only must the client have at least one intrusion, three avoidance and two disordered arousal symptoms but the symptoms must have lasted at least a month and significantly interfered with their working or domestic life.

Conceptualisation – suggest client has developed a 'dodgy alarm' (amygdala) that goes off (a) at any reminder, (b) anything not exactly the way you want it to be and (c) unexpected noises or sudden movements. Client reacts as if in a 'war zone', making communication with others very strained.

Post-traumatic stress disorder Sat Nav

Therapeutic targets	Treatment strategies
1. Beliefs about PTSD	Normalisation of symptoms – utilisation of *Moving On After Trauma*
2. Cognitive and behavioural avoidance	Advantages and disadvantages short and long term of avoidance
3. 'No one can understand what I've been through'	Realistic portrayal of discomfort to be expected. Underlining similarities of trauma and responses
4. Managing reminders	The menu of options for handling reminders
5. Behavioural avoidance Fear of anxiety	Beginning the journey of a return to normality by gradual 'dares'
6. Processing of traumatic memory	Written or verbal account of trauma and its effects – elaboration of the memory
7. Motivation Group issues	Motivational interviewing
8. Rumination Cognitive avoidance Disturbed sleep/nightmares	Addressing the traumatic memory at a specific time and place
9. Discrimination of triggers	Using similarities and differences
10. Irritability, emotional avoidance – 'control freak'	Traffic light routine. Managing 'seething' over the trauma and its effects, coping strategies
11. Persistent and exaggerated negative expectations of oneself, others or the world and persistent distorted blame of self about the cause or consequence of the traumatic event – core maladaptive schemas in PTSD	Use of MOOD chart to modify observed thinking and underlying assumptions Use of magnifying glass analogy to illustrate exaggeratedly negative view of self, others and world
12. Cognitive avoidance Behavioural avoidance Hypervigilance for danger	Attention control and detached mindfulness Continuing to 'dare'

continues

Therapeutic targets	Treatment strategies
13. Impaired relationships	Beginning to invest in people
14. Low mood, pain/disability View of self, world and future	Mood management strategies Cognitive restructuring, the importance of a broad investment portfolio
15. Relapse prevention	Budgeting for unpleasant reminders and distilling a protocol Constructing a PTSD Survival Manual

Social phobia

1. When you are or might be in the spotlight, say in a group of people or eating/writing in front of others, do you immediately get anxious or nervous?
2. Do you think you are much more anxious than other people when the focus is on you?
3. Do you think that you are more afraid of social situations than you should be?
4. Do you avoid social situations out of a fear of embarrassing or humiliating yourself?
5. Do these social anxieties bother you?

If the client answered yes to each of the above five questions it is likely that they are suffering from social phobia..

Conceptualisation – present a formulation that makes sense to the client and is consistent with the CBT model. Examples:

(a) 'It is as if people with social phobia think that they are at the centre of a circle, others are on the edge of the circle looking at them marking them out of 10. If it was really like that no one would do anything, I'd be like a frightened rabbit frozen in car headlights on a country road'.
(b) 'Can you be sure that the story you carry around of how others think about you is correct? Maybe different people have different stories?'
(c) 'Who says you have to be perfect socially, to be acceptable, politicians are never short of words but who trusts them?' When you think of people you like are they really the most socially skilled people?'

Social phobia Sat Nav

Therapeutic targets	Treatment strategies
1. 'I'm an oddity'. Beliefs that maintain social anxiety	Distillation of working model of each member's disorder Questioning of typical thoughts (on 'second thoughts'). Survey to determine what makes people 'acceptable'
2. 'Inside' view of self. Expectation of high standards	Contrasting 'Inside' view of self with 'Outside' view of others using video feedback. Exposure to feared situations. Survey to determine standards of others
3. Safety behaviours. Information processing biases	Contrasting anxiety experienced using safety behaviours with those when not using. Vigilance for all or nothing thinking, personalisation, mind-reading and mental filter
4. Non-disclosure of personal information	Modelling and role play of self-disclosure
5. Anticipatory anxiety and post-event rumination. Past humiliations	Cognitive restructuring and re-scripting
6. Anticipatory anxiety and post-event rumination. Relapse prevention	Moderating worry and disengagement from it. Role play of anticipated difficult situation, ensuring adherence to Survival Manual to prevent full-blown relapse

The 7 Minute Health Screen/Audit – Revised

This screen is an interview format for The First Step Questionnaire – Revised (Appendix C) and provides guidance on interpreting the latter. It covers the common mental disorders and positive findings can be investigated further by turning, where indicated, to the relevant page in the Cognitive Behaviour Therapy Pocketbook (Appendix A). If the focus is on auditing the effects of an intervention, the time frame for questions can be altered, e.g. past 2 weeks.

1. Depression	Yes	No	Don't know
During the past month have you often been bothered by feeling depressed or hopeless?			
During the past month have you often been bothered by little interest or pleasure in doing things?			
Is this something with which you would like help?			

A positive response to at least one symptom question and the help question suggests that detailed enquiry be made, page 182.

2. Panic disorder and agoraphobia	Yes	No	Don't know
Do you have unexpected panic attacks, a sudden rush of intense fear or anxiety?			
Do you avoid situations in which the panic attacks might occur?			
Is this something with which you would like help?			

A positive response to at least one symptom question and the help question suggests that detailed enquiry be made, page 188.

3. Post-traumatic stress disorder	Yes	No	Don't know
In your life, have you ever had any experience that was so frightening, horrible or upsetting that, in the past month, you:			
i. Have had nightmares about it or thought about it when you did not want to?			
ii. Tried hard not to think about it or went out of your way to avoid situations that reminded you of it?			
iii. Were constantly on guard, watchful, or easily startled?			
iv. Felt numb or detached from others, activities, or your surroundings?			
Is this something with which you would like help?			

A positive response to at least three symptom questions and the help question suggests that detailed enquiry be made, page 190.

4. Generalised anxiety disorder	Yes	No	Don't know
Are you a worrier?			
Do you worry about everything?			
Has the worrying been excessive (more days than not) or uncontrollable in the last 6 months (a time frame of the last 2 weeks can be used if the intent is to audit an intervention rather than screen)?			
Is this something with which you would like help?			

A positive response to at least two symptom questions and the help question suggests that detailed enquiry be made, page 184.

5. Social phobia	Yes	No	Don't know
When you are or might be in the spotlight, say in a group of people or eating/writing in front of others, do you immediately get anxious or nervous?			
Do you avoid social situations out of a fear of embarrassing or humiliating yourself?			
Is this something with which you would like help?			

A positive response to at least one symptom question and the help question suggests that detailed enquiry be made, page 194.

6. Obsessive compulsive disorder	Yes	No	Don't know
Do you wash or clean a lot?			
Do you check things a lot?			
Is there any thought that keeps bothering you that you would like to get rid of but can't?			
Do your daily activities take a long time to finish?			
Are you concerned about orderliness or symmetry?			
Is this something with which you would like help?			

A positive response to one or more symptom questions and the help question suggests that detailed enquiry be made, page 186.

7. Bulimia	Yes	No	Don't know
Do you go on binges where you eat very large amounts of food in a short period?			
Do you do anything special, such as vomiting, go on a strict diet to prevent gaining weight from the binge?			
Is this something with which you would like help?			

A positive response to the symptom questions and the help question suggests that detailed enquiry be made.

8. Substance abuse/dependence	Yes	No	Don't know
Have you felt you should cut down on your alcohol/drug?			
Have people got annoyed with you about your drinking/ drug taking?			
Have you felt guilty about your drinking/drug use?			
Do you drink/use drugs before midday?			
Is this something with which you would like help?			

A positive response to at least two of the symptom questions and the help question suggests that detailed enquiry be made.

9. Psychosis	Yes	No	Don't know
Do you ever hear things other people don't hear, or see things they don't see?			
Do you ever feel like someone is spying on you or plotting to hurt you?			
Do you have any ideas that you don't like to talk about because you are afraid other people will think you are crazy?			
Is this something with which you would like help?			

A positive response to at least one of the symptom questions and the help question suggests that detailed enquiry be made.

10. Mania/hypomania	Yes	No	Don't know
Have there been times, lasting at least a few days, when you were unusually high, talking a lot, sleeping little?			
Did others notice that there was something different about you? If you answered 'yes', what did they say?			
Is this something with which you would like help?			

A positive response to at least one of the symptom questions and the help question suggests that detailed enquiry be made.

IMPORTANT NOTE: If, when you inspect the 7 Minute Mental Health Screen/Audit – Revised or the First Step Questionnaire – Revised, the person screened positive for either items 1 (depression), 8 (substance abuse/dependence), 9 (psychosis) or 10 (mania) ask:

Have you been hurting or making plans for hurting yourself?

The First Step Questionnaire – Revised

This questionnaire is a first step in identifying what you might be suffering from and pointing you in the right direction. In answering each question just make your best guess, don't think about your response too much, there are no right or wrong answers.

1.	Yes	No	Don't know
During the past month have you often been bothered by feeling depressed or hopeless?			
During the past month have you often been bothered by little interest or pleasure in doing things?			
Is this something with which you would like help?			

2.	Yes	No	Don't know
Do you have unexpected panic attacks, a sudden rush of intense fear or anxiety?			
Do you avoid situations in which the panic attacks might occur?			
Is this something with which you would like help?			

3.	Yes	No	Don't know
In your life, have you ever had any experience that was so frightening, horrible or upsetting that, in the past month, you:			
i. Have had nightmares about it or thought about it when you did not want to?			
ii. Tried hard not to think about it or went out of your way to avoid situations that reminded you of it?			
iii. Were constantly on guard, watchful, or easily startled?			
iv. Felt numb or detached from others, activities, or your surroundings?			
Is this something with which you would like help?			

4.	Yes	No	Don't know
Are you a worrier?			
Do you worry about everything?			
Has the worrying been excessive (more days than not) or uncontrollable in the last 6 months?			
Is this something with which you would like help?			

5.	Yes	No	Don't know
When you are or might be in the spotlight, say in a group of people or eating/writing in front of others, do you immediately get anxious or nervous?			
Do you avoid social situations out of a fear of embarrassing or humiliating yourself?			
Is this something with which you would like help?			

6.	Yes	No	Don't know
Do you wash or clean a lot?			
Do you check things a lot?			
Is there any thought that keeps bothering you that you would like to get rid of but can't?			
Do your daily activities take a long time to finish?			
Are you concerned about orderliness or symmetry?			
Is this something with which you would like help?			

7.	Yes	No	Don't know
Do you go on binges where you eat very large amounts of food in a short period?			
Do you do anything special, such as vomiting, go on a strict diet to prevent gaining weight from the binge?			
Is this something with which you would like help?			

8.	Yes	No	Don't know
Have you felt you should cut down on your alcohol/drug?			
Have people got annoyed with you about your drinking/ drug taking?			
Have you felt guilty about your drinking/drug use?			
Do you drink/use drugs before midday?			
Is this something with which you would like help?			

9.	Yes	No	Don't know
Do you ever hear things other people don't hear, or see things they don't see?			
Do you ever feel like someone is spying on you or plotting to hurt you?			
Do you have any ideas that you don't like to talk about because you are afraid other people will think you are crazy?			
Is this something with which you would like help?			

10.	Yes	No	Don't know
Have there been times, lasting at least a few days, when you were unusually high, talking a lot, sleeping little?			
Did others notice that there was something different about you? If you answered 'yes', what did they say?			
Is this something with which you would like help?			

General Group Therapeutic Skills Rating Scale

1. REVIEW OF HOMEWORK/AGENDA

0	Therapist did not set an agenda/did not review homework
2	Therapist set an agenda that was vague or did not involve group members/vague reference to previous session's homework
4	Therapist worked with group members to set a mutually satisfactory agenda/ difficulties with previous session's homework were locked onto
6	Therapist set an agenda that was suitable for the available time. Established priorities and tracked the agenda/difficulties with previous session's homework were effectively problem solved

2. RELEVANCE

0	Therapist did not ensure content was relevant to every group member at some point in the session
2	Therapist ensured content was relevant to most members most of the time
4	Therapist ensured content was relevant to all group members most of the time
6	Therapist ensured content was relevant to all group members throughout session

3. ADAPTATION

0	Therapist did not check out group members' understanding of what was being taught
2	Therapist did some checking out of group members' understanding but failed to successfully adapt material for those who had some difficulty
4	Therapist checked out understanding of all group members and was able to suitably adapt material for most of those with difficulties
6	Therapist tailored explanations to the level of understanding of each group member

4. INCLUSION

0	Therapist allowed the most vociferous group members to dominate the group
2	Therapist made attempts to include less vocal members but was not able to give them sufficient space to express themselves verbally and emotionally
4	Therapist ensured all group members had reasonable air time but had some difficulties with some of the less vocal group members
6	Therapist ensured that all group members had sufficient air time to express both their thoughts and feelings, including commentary on the group session as a whole

5. ADDITIONAL DISORDERS

0	Therapist either did not acknowledge a group member's expression of difficulties with a disorder that was not the prime focus of the group or spent such time on these concerns that other members were losing focus, e.g. chatting amongst themselves
2	Therapist acknowledged a group member's additional difficulty but without signposting a direction from which appropriate help might come, e.g. an individual session, or tried unsuccessfully to address the additional difficulty but showed a lack of competence in this area
4	Therapist managed group members' expressions of additional concerns and was mostly able to offer succinct advice and reassure that these difficulties could be addressed
6	Therapist managed to address all group members' expressions of additional problems and suggest appropriate options for their resolution without losing focus on the main teaching for the session

6. MAGNIFYING SUPPORT AND MINIMISING CRITICISM

0	Therapist did not acknowledge the power of other group members to influence each other for both good and ill
2	Therapist paid minimal attention to expressions of emotional and tangible support from group members to each other
4	Therapist encouraged group members to come up with solutions to members' problems based on what had been taught in the sessions, underlying support proffered and ensuring that criticism was reframed in terms of different behaviours rather than an attack on the person
6	Therapist magnified group support for a member and short-circuited personal attacks, utilising the period during which the group was assembling and departing to enhance alliances between members and pick up on members' concerns

7. UTILISING GROUP MEMBERS AS ROLE MODELS

0	Therapist focused entirely on himself/herself as the source of persuasion
2	Therapist made fleeting reference to the positive behaviour of a group member but without making it explicit to what other member that behaviour might be particularly relevant
4	Therapist, to large extent, tuned into the cultural/religious background, friendships in the group to build alliances that would reinforce the learning and application of material taught
6	Therapist adeptly tuned into the assumptive world of each group member and was able to draw on it to reinforce alliances between members and ensure application of material taught outside the session

8. THERAPIST PRESENTATION SKILLS

0	Therapist/s gave a didactic presentation with no written summary of material covered. If more than one therapist, there was no synchrony between therapists, they were not reinforcing what each said or coming to each other's aid at difficult moments
2	Therapist/s did provide written summary of material covered but it consisted largely of printed words and at a reading age above some of the group. When diagrams were provided they were overly complex. Role plays were not used or if used did not follow a format of therapist modelling, group member practice and therapist feedback. If more than one therapist, whilst they shared the burden of presentation, there was little humour or support between them and some defensiveness
4	Therapist/s provided written summaries, diagrams of materials covered at a level accessible to all group members. Role plays were used and appeared to have enhanced group members' understanding. If more than one therapist, the therapists synchronised with humour and encouragement, helping create an appropriate climate
6	Therapist/s provided written summaries, diagrams at a level accessible to all but also highlighted other resources, books, computer-assisted therapy that some members might derive additional benefit from. Role plays were used and followed a format of therapist modelling, group member practice and therapist feedback that accentuated the positives and problem solved the negatives. If more than one therapist, the therapists seemed to 'dance' very well, presenting material effortlessly with humour and without defensiveness

9. ADDRESSING GROUP ISSUES

0	Therapist did not address any group issues that arose, such as timing of the group, number of sessions, difficulties in scheduling individual sessions, conflicts between group members, confidentiality, ambivalence about attendance, dropouts, ending of group and relapse
2	Therapist did address some group issues but was unnecessarily defensive
4	Therapist addressed most difficulties expressed by group members in a spirit of openness
6	Therapist addressed all group issues in a collaborative way with group members, engaging them in a problem solving process

Intake questionnaire

Questionnaire – *please answer each question as best you can*

Name: Date:

Address:

d.o.b.

Telephone no:

Are you working?

What kind of work do you do?

What kind of work (if any) did you do in the past?

How do you spend your day?

How were things at school?

Did you have any particular problems at school? If you did what were they?

Do you have any qualifications? If so what are they?

What (if any) are the major problems you are having at the moment?

1.

2.

3.

Please indicate when the problems listed above began and also if there was a time when they got much worse.

1.

2.

3.

Have any very scary things happened to you or did you see such things happening to others? If so write them down below and put when they happened (include any abuse in childhood).

1.

2.

3.

Have you had any professional (doctor or counsellor) help for any of your difficulties? If you did please indicate when, for how long and from whom.

1.

2.

3.

Have your parents or brothers or sisters suffered with their nerves? If yes please indicate who and if you can what they suffered or are suffering from.

What has your mood been like?

How much have you been drinking alcohol in the past month?

Have you been taking any drugs? Please indicate any prescribed drugs as well as any other drugs that you may be taking.

1.

2.

Was there a time in the past when you took drugs that were not prescribed by your doctor? YES/NO

If yes to the above please indicate what drug/s you took, when and for how long.

1.

2.

Have you been in trouble with the law? YES/NO

Monitoring progress of group members

Disorder											
Group member's name											
Session 1											
Session 2											
Session 3											
Session 4											
Session 5											
Session 6											
Session 7											
Session 8											
Session 9											
Session 10											
Session 11											

Standardised Assessment of Personality – Abbreviated Scale

Only circle Y (yes) or N (no), in the case of question 3, if the client thinks that the description applies *most of the time* and *in most situations*.

1. In general, do you have difficulty making and keeping friends?... Y/N

   (yes = 1, no = 0)

2. Would you normally describe yourself as a loner? .... Y/N

   (yes = 1, no = 0)

3. In general, do you trust other people?........................ Y/N

   (yes = 1, no = 0)

4. Do you normally lose your temper easily? .... Y/N

   (yes = 1, no = 0)

5. Are you normally an impulsive sort of person?................ Y/N

   (yes = 1, no = 0)

6. Are you normally a worrier?................................. Y/N

   (yes = 1, no = 0)

7. In general, do you depend on others a lot? .... Y/N

   (yes = 1, no = 0)

8. In general, are you a perfectionist? .... Y/N

   (yes = 1, no = 0)

Depression Survival Manual

1. How depression develops and keeps going

Depression usually involves loss of a valued role, for example in a relationship or job. But by itself that is not sufficient; the person also has to become inactive, giving up on what they used to do and making sure they take a picture of most things from the worst angle (negative spin).

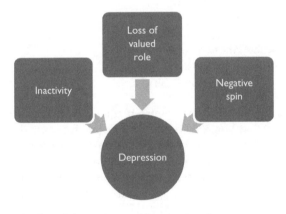

Figure 1 Lighting the fire of depression and keeping it going.

What have you stopped doing that you used to enjoy?

What is it that puts you off doing some of what you used to enjoy?

Is there something in particular making you go on strike for better pay and conditions?

Depression is kept going by a negative view of self, personal world, the future and depression about depression (Figure 2).

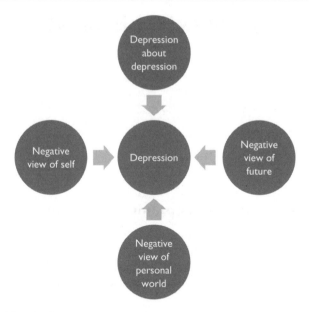

Figure 2 Fuel for the fire.

How do you feel about yourself?
How do you feel about others?
How do you feel about the future?
How do others feel about you?
Does the way you feel about yourself square with how others see you?
Are you sure that you are wholly responsible for your depression?
Are you responsible for working on a solution to your depression?
What sort of things could you timetable yourself to do?
Would you be more able to do them if you did them in small doses, e.g. phone call to friend rather than spend an evening with them?

2. No investments, no return

In depression it is as if the person stops investing in what might give them a sense of achievement or pleasure. The dice feel loaded against you, like a boxer knocked to the canvas thinking 'what is the point in getting up, I will only get knocked down!' If not investing is combined with putting a negative spin on your previous investments, e.g. 'that just showed how stupid I am!', then the result may well be depression, (Figure 3); the negative spin often involves seeing hassles as catastrophes.

Figure 3 Putting your money under the carpet and seeing hassles as catastrophes.

But if you don't invest there can be no return. It is rather like having some money, putting it under your carpet and then complaining because it has lost value with inflation. You might well think these days that the banks are not to be trusted! But you would probably advise a friend with some money to make lots of small, low risk investments in very different places or maybe just deposit accounts in different banks. Many people with depression have had all their investments in just one place, a relationship or a job. They may have been encouraged to keep investing in the one place because the returns were good. But it is just a question of time before any one investment runs out of steam, for example the person might lose a job or their partner dies. You can choose not to invest but it is a choice.

What investments are you making at the moment?

Is there a balance between things that might give you a sense of achievement and those that might give you a sense of pleasure (Figure 4)?

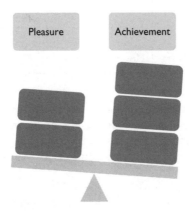

Figure 4 Investing in achievement and pleasure.

Sometimes the investments that you think will be good don't come off and sometimes ones that you don't expect to deliver do. Could you see yourself making a wider range of investments?

Is there a pattern to your mood, is it worse at certain times in the week?

Is there anything you could plan to do at the particular times you tend to feel low that might lift your mood a little?

If your major investment didn't work what do you take that to mean about you?

Use the ruler below:

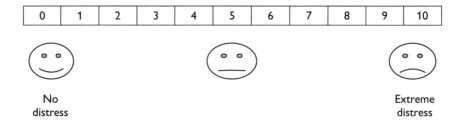

| 0 | 1 | 2 | 3 | 4 | 5 | 6 | 7 | 8 | 9 | 10 |

No
distress

Extreme
distress

to indicate how distressed you have been each day, morning, afternoon and evening and what, if anything, you were doing at the time.

Table 1 Activity and mood

	Monday	Tuesday	Wednesday	Thursday	Friday	Saturday	Sunday
Morning 0–10 Activity							
Afternoon 0–10 Activity							
Evening 0–10 Activity							

Looking at your activities and mood in Table 1, is there a pattern, e.g. worse in the morning, or when you are not doing things?

Could you come up with a better way of arranging your activities, e.g. get up with the alarm and go for the morning paper before you have a cup of tea rather than lie in bed?

Keep a record of any positive experiences in great detail, e.g. not just that 'it was great to bump into an old school friend' but 'it was great for John to remind me that when we were making a noise and the librarian said "this table out", we picked it up and began walking with it'.

3. On second thoughts

The first thoughts of those who are depressed are usually more negative than they need to be. Cognitive behaviour therapy is not only about becoming gradually more active but also about standing back and pausing at your first automatic thought and checking to see if there is a better second thought.

When you got up this morning what were your first thoughts about coming to the group?

Were these first thoughts more negative than they needed to be?

Did you or could you come up with better second thoughts?

Do you often think 'I think too much'?

Is it thinking that you do, or agonising?

Once you have reasonable second thoughts don't pick at them, decide what to do and do it. Become an Actor not a Ruminator. The more objective second thoughts might feel uncomfortable and take a lot of acting upon before they become second nature; don't get distracted by agonising, refuse to play the Ruminator.

To help you manage your moods pass them through the MOOD chart shown in Table 2. The first letter of MOOD, 'M', stands for monitor your mood, the second letter, 'O', stands for observe your thinking, what it sounds as if you have said to yourself, the third letter, 'O', is for objective thinking, more realistic second thoughts, and the final letter, 'D', is for deciding what to do and do it.

Table 2 MOOD chart

Monitor mood	Observe thinking	Objective thinking	Decide what to do and do it
1. Mood dipped standing drinking coffee looking out of the window.	Life is passing me by like the cars.	It is passing everyone by, it depends on what I do with it.	I could do some painting and decorating or maybe visit my sister. I'll do the painting/decorating today and visit sister tomorrow.
2. Mood dipped when I received a letter that I am not getting any unemployment benefit.	It's going to be awful.	It is going to be difficult, I will not be able to pay child maintenance but I do have a really good relationship with my daughter, ex will not be happy though. I will not be able to afford car insurance but Mum will not mind loaning it to me.	I will appeal against the decision with the help of my solicitor and ring Mum and ex.

In the first example of the use of the MOOD chart, the person is day-dreaming, gazing out of the window when they notice that their mood has dipped. Daydreams can be like a poisonous gas without a smell in that because nothing has actually happened, such as an argument, it can be difficult to pinpoint exactly what the person has said to themselves to feel the way they do.

To identify the 'toxic' negative thought the individual has to do a slow motion action replay of the situation they were in when the upset occurred to get something of a clue to their reflex/automatic thought. Their observed thinking (column 2) may be nothing more than an informed guess as to 'what it sounds as if they have said to themselves to feel the way they do'. It should be noted that in the first example, in column 3 the objective thinking, the person acknowledges that there is, as is often the case, a grain of truth in the observed thinking, i.e. it has some validity. But in column 3 the person is challenging the utility of thinking 'life is passing me by'. Finally in column 4 the person comes up with some investments: painting/decorating and visiting his sister.

In the second example the person encounters a hassle, the stopping of his benefit, but typically in depression any hassle is immediately viewed as a catastrophe, 'it is going to be awful'. A catastrophe can be shrunk back to a hassle by the client asking themselves 'what specifically is so bad about what has just happened?' and the person identified two issues, an inability to pay child maintainance or for car insurance. Because these concerns were made very specific they were then open to reappraisal and the person was able to reflect that at least his relationship with his daughter would not be harmed and there was possible financial help from his mother.

You can cross-examine your automatic negative thought in three different ways, you can ask:

How true is this?
How useful is this way of thinking?
Who says I should look at this in this way?

4. Just make a start

If you are depressed, waiting until you feel like doing something is like waiting for a big Lottery win! Depression is like dragging a ball and chain, to do anything is a major achievement (Figure 5).

You have to give yourself permission to break any task, e.g. cleaning the house, into small chunks: vacuum the living room, then have a break, e.g. cup of tea, and then do the next small task, e.g. empty and fill the dishwasher.

When you are doing the tasks, either those intended to give you a sense of achievement, e.g. cleaning the house, or pleasure, e.g. going for a walk,

Figure 5 Depression and the ball and chain.

you will probably feel you are going through the motions. But if you continue to invest, the taste of life is likely to come back but you can't say exactly when. It's a bit like beginning to exercise in the gym, all you get to begin with is aches and pains with little to show and it takes some weeks to notice a difference.

What thoughts have put you off doing things?

Have you been expecting yourself just to do things as you did before you became depressed and then because this all seems too much not doing anything?

If you put the thoughts that have sabotaged your activity through the filter of the MOOD chart, what more objective second thoughts (column 3) could you come up with?

5. Expectation versus experience and recalling the positive

In advance of an activity, the depressed person usually predicts that they are not going to enjoy the activity but they usually feel a bit better from doing the activity than if they don't (Figure 6).

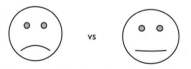

Figure 6 Expectation versus experience.

On a scale 0–10, where 10 is the best you have ever felt and 0 is the worst, how did you feel getting ready to come to the group today?

On a scale 0–10, how do you feel right now?

If you felt, say, 3/10 before coming out today and, say, 6/10 now, you could use the numbers 3 and 6 as a reminder, that there is a gap between 'expectation' and 'experience' and that you can trick yourself into inactivity by relying on your 'expectation' rather than your 'experience'.

But there is another problem in depression, to do with how you remember your experience. Tonight if your partner or a friend asked you how you got on in the group today what would you likely say?

Probably most would say one word, 'OK', a bit like asking your children what they did in school today, the reply is invariably 'nothing', but you know they must have done something! 'Nothing' is shorthand for 'I can't be bothered plugging in my brain, switching on and coming up with an answer', but if then a friend rings they go into graphic detail about something good that happened. If you are suffering from depression you tend to recall the good things in a vague way, e.g. 'OK, my team drew', you do not go into detail, e.g. 'it was superb when Liverpool equalised in the last minute of extra time'. So tonight if you talk of the group session don't just say 'OK or even some expletive!', try and recall in detail some good moment, e.g. a chat with a group member over coffee as the group was assembling. Then follow this up with keeping a detailed record of the positives in your week.

6. Negative spin or how to make yourself depressed without really trying

Imagine that you wanted to make someone depressed by what you say, so that for example if a child tells you enthusiastically that they got a 'B' in their maths exam, what could you say to make them depressed?

Possibilities are 'you should have got an A', i.e. you home in on the negative and discount the positive, getting a 'B'; this is called using a 'mental filter'. Other possibilities are 'you didn't try hard enough'; this is called 'jumping to conclusions' as without being inside the child's head you can't know how hard they tried. To make the child depressed you just focus your camera in such a way that the lens, setting and filter give a negative spin. You might feel like smashing the camera of an adult who makes a child depressed in this way! But if you are depressed you are probably using a camera with these odd settings to make yourself depressed! The first step in taking an objective picture is to become aware of the ten settings of the camera that cause problems, then to step around them (Table 3).

There are no water-tight distinctions between the information processing biases, and many people who are depressed customarily use a number of them.

Do any of these ring bells for you?

Which ones do you think you need to make a note of, to make yourself aware of what you might be doing when you are getting upset?

Table 3 Information processing biases

1.	Dichotomous (black and white) thinking, e.g. 'I'm either a total success or a failure'.
2.	Mental filter, focusing on the negative to the exclusion of the positive, e.g. 'how can you say it was a lovely meal, how long did we have to wait for the dessert to be served?'
3.	Personalisation, assuming just because something has gone wrong it must be your fault, e.g. 'John did not let on to me coming into work this morning, must have been something I said'.
4.	Emotional reasoning, assuming guilt simply because of the presence of guilt feelings, e.g. 'I can't provide for the kids the way I did, I've let them down, what sort of parent am I?'
5.	Jumping to conclusions, e.g. assuming that being asked to have a word with your line manager means that you are in trouble.
6.	Overgeneralisation, making negative predictions on the basis of one bad experience, e.g. 'I've had it with men after Charlie, you cannot trust any of them'.
7.	Magnification and minimisation, magnifying faults or difficulties, minimising strengths or positives, e.g. 'I am terrible at report writing and I am lucky to have got good appraisals for the last couple of years'.
8.	Disqualifying the positives, e.g. brushing aside compliments and dwelling on criticism.
9.	'Should' statements, overuse of moral imperatives, e.g. 'I must do . . . I should . . . I have to . . .'.
10.	Labelling and mislabelling, e.g. 'if I make a mistake I am a failure as a person'.

You might want to get hold of David Burns' book Feeling Good: The New Mood Therapy *from the library or buy it online to read more about these 10 biases in Chapter Three. It has also got lots of other useful information on depression.*

7. An attitude problem?

A person's attitude to life can be fine for many circumstances but run into problems if certain types of events (key events) occur; there are some examples in Table 4.

Do you see yourself as being as being addicted to approval (sociotrope)?

Do you see yourself as addicted to success (autonomous)?

Most things that people are addicted to are fine in themselves, but are a problem when they dominate their life. If you are a true sociotrope or autonomous you might want to consider weaning yourself off, there will be withdrawal symptoms and you may always find them tempting. There might be the odd slip but you can prevent it becoming a full-blown relapse by using the MOOD chart and spotting whether the upset is really to do with an attitude from the past. Today's upsets and past attitudes overlap to some extent (Figure 7).

What has upset you today might be a key event in that it opens the door to a particular attitude (e.g. a key event for a sociotrope might be not being praised by her boss for a piece of work today) and upset. Using the MOOD

Table 4 Attitudes and problems

Attitudes	Problems (key events)
'I must be liked all the time and in all circumstances' (a sociotrope – addicted to approval)	A relationship breaks up
'If I am not the top I am a flop' (the highly autonomous person may be addicted to achievement)	Fails to get promotion or an exam or is made redundant
'Everything has to be done just so' – the perfectionist	No longer given the time to get everything perfectly right
'To be happy you have got to have . . .' excessively rigid	When you cannot achieve what you judged necessary for happiness

Figure 7 Today's upset, past attitudes and key events.

chart the sociotrope might come up with a more useful attitude (objective thinking), e.g. 'approval is nice but no one can rely on it, it is not like oxygen', and then stop depressive rumination using the 'D' of the MOOD chart and get on and do something, invest.

Your attitudes might be about perfectionism or extreme rigidity about how things should be and there is nothing wrong with these attitudes in the right place but if certain key events occur it can be your undoing.

Use the MOOD chart for monitoring your mood, but try and be alert for any key event that has called onstream an 'attitude problem' and come up with/use your antidote to this 'gremlin', in the objective thinking column; don't stew on your upset once you have sorted it, get on to the 'D' of MOOD and '<u>D</u>o'.

If you are weighed down by a low opinion of yourself (Figure 8), you might play the sociotrope, autonomous or perfectionist to lift it for you, but long term it's too heavy. Alternatively you might numb the pain of low self-esteem by being very rigid, e.g. 'if I can continue this job or this relationship then just maybe I can think of myself as OK', but the anaesthetic (an overvalued role) eventually wears off, exposing the 'nerve'.

Total approval of others or total achievement or perfection in everything or very rigid

Poor opinion of self

Figure 8 Strategies unequal to the task of lifting low self-esteem.

By realising where your low self-esteem comes from you can begin to tackle it.

8. My attitude to self, others and the future

Your attitude to yourself, others and the future can play a major role in maintaining depression. The depressed person usually has a negative view of themselves. For some people low self-esteem is very long-standing but became much worse after the loss of a valued role, e.g. children leaving the nest or the loss of a job. For others the negative view of self is of more recent origin (Figure 9).

How has your view of yourself changed?

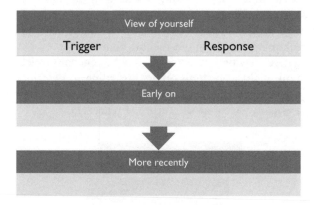

Figure 9 What makes me think about myself the way I do?

If your low self-esteem goes way back, what do you wish had been said to you that might have made a difference?

Do you think you would have been as bothered by recent upsets if your self-esteem was already intact?

Do you equate your worth as a person with an achievement or perhaps with the approval of someone important to you?

Is it possible to be worthwhile without this achievement or approval?

Do you think a jury would return a 'not guilty', 'guilty' or the Scottish 'not proven' verdict on you?

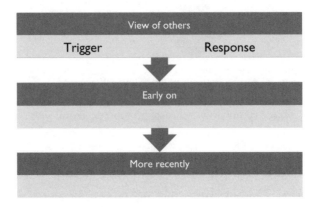

Figure 10 What makes me think of others the way I do?

What is the story you carry round with you of how other people are (Figure 10)?

Do you need to update the story, say in the light of your experiences in the group?

Do you use dichotomous thinking about yourself and others, e.g. they are either 'saints or sinners'?

Do you dwell on the mistakes of yourself or others, leaving the positives out of the reckoning, employing a mental filter?

With a negative view of yourself, you may be reluctant to let others get to know you. You might also think others are going to be critical of you, so better stay in your shell. The negative view of yourself and others conspires to produce a negative view of the future (Figure 11).

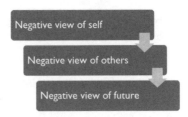

Figure 11 Negative view of the future.

The negative view of the future leads to inactivity, a failure to invest and thereby depression.

Can you be certain that the future is going to be negative?

Have there been good times in the past?

Can you be certain good times cannot come again?

Can you commit to constructing a future, despite life being a bit of a bomb-site at the moment?

9. Be critical of your reflex first thoughts, not how you feel

In depression the person tends to criticise themselves for what they have been feeling and yet have an uncritical acceptance of their automatic negative thoughts. To overcome depression the person has to climb a number of stepping stones, accepting without criticism what they are feeling, identifying negative automatic thoughts, distilling objective thoughts, then investing in life (Figure 12).

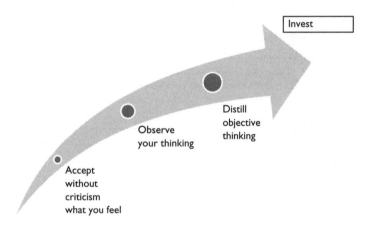

Invest

Distill
objective
thinking

Observe
your thinking

Accept
without
criticism
what you feel

Figure 12 Stepping stones out of depression.

Do you often think 'I shouldn't be feeling . . .'?

How useful has it been to blame yourself for what you have been feeling?

Who, other than yourself, says you should be blaming yourself for what you feel?

Sometimes people are so afraid of what they feel, that they try to distract themselves by feverish activity that ends in exhaustion, at which point the feelings return. This emotional avoidance is self-defeating and needs to be replaced by an acceptance of experienced emotion. However, within cognitive behaviour therapy the emotion experienced does not necessarily have the last word. To climb out of depression a first step is to acknowledge what you feel without apology, avoiding depression about depression. Depression is challenge enough without double depression.

10. Preventing relapse

The more episodes of depression you have had, the more likely you are to have another one. However, with the skills learnt in this programme you may well be able to stop a slip becoming a full-blown relapse. When you are feeling better, you may want to forget about the skills you learnt in the group because they remind you of the bad times in your life. But depression tends to create a fault line, and you could again crack along the fault line if you came across a similar set of circumstances. But if you have your own Survival Manual and take active steps to use your skills at the first signs of depression, you can nip it in the bud. So that you are prepared, it is useful to have 'fire drills' even when there is no 'fire' – reading your Survival Manual at good times.

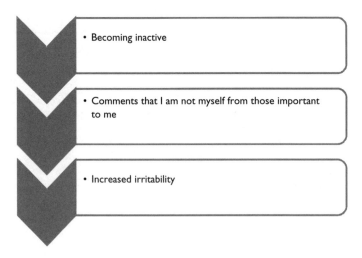

* Becoming inactive

* Comments that I am not myself from those important to me

* Increased irritability

Figure 13 Early warning signs.

Some common early warning signs are shown in Figure 13.

Are there any other signals you get when you are beginning to slide?

The temptation is to deny that you are beginning to slip (this is called cognitive avoidance) because the memory of last time is so painful. But if you acknowledge you are beginning to slip and use the tools from the programme, you can stop the depression gathering momentum. Depression is like a rock running downhill, stopping it near the top as it begins its descent is relatively easy.

What situations do you think might be most dangerous for you?

What would your gameplan be in the event of such triggers?

What changes to your week would you need to make?

What activities/contacts would you need to make?

What thoughts would be the best antidotes to the negative automatic thoughts that would come onstream?

How would you remind yourself to be patient with yourself while you give the tools a chance to make a difference?

How would you avoid blaming yourself, that you are experiencing signs of depression?

Which resources would you call upon: this Survival Manual, supportive friend, self-help book, therapist?

What thoughts might get in the way of accessing the help you need?

How would you answer the thoughts that might sabotage your seeking help?

Panic Disorder and Agoraphobia Survival Manual

If you are not a little anxious crossing a busy road there could be serious consequences. A little anxiety helps us perform properly. So that anxiety itself is not a problem, it makes you prepared for action, without it you would be a danger to yourself. However, some people have anxiety sensitivity, they fear the symptoms of fear or anxiety. They have come to believe that experiencing certain symptoms is harmful. A person may develop a 'fear of fear' by hearing others express fear of certain sensations, e.g. feeling faint in public, or hearing wrong information about the harmfulness of certain sensations, e.g. breathlessness/palpitations means there is something wrong with your heart, or witnessing a catastrophic event such as the fatal heart attack of a loved one.

If you experience negative events such as the death of a family member or someone close to you, poor close relationships, loss of a role or conflicts about your role, they may lead to bodily sensations that are not in themselves harmful but may result in the development and maintenance of panic attacks if you already have high anxiety sensitivity.

A panic attack is a sudden wave of anxiety that reaches a peak within a few minutes, and may include palpitations, light-headedness, breathlessness and fear of losing control. If at least some of the panic attacks occur for no reason, e.g. when you are asleep or somewhere with no danger, and occur repeatedly, this is classified as panic disorder. Many people with panic disorder worry about the next panic attack and avoid situations they think might trigger them, e.g. a busy shop; this avoidance is called agoraphobia. Those suffering from panic disorder and agoraphobia not only fear their bodily sensations but also have fears of the situations that they are avoiding, e.g. 'if I go there I will be stranded if I have a panic attack'. Sometimes it is not just places that are avoided because of a fear of a panic attack but certain activities, e.g. physical exertion, sexual relations, taking a hot shower or bath, drinking coffee, watching an exciting or scary film.

1. Putting a 'danger' label on bodily sensations and using 'safety' procedures guarantees panic

Imagine that you are at a railway station with a friend happily awaiting your train. The friend points out an unattended bag and says 'I wonder whose that is?' and you might look around for the owner. But when your friend says 'could be a terrorist bomb?' your heart might miss a beat and you probably look around more earnestly. It is as if the 'label' you put on the 'bag' makes a big difference to your body's reaction. In a similar way if you put a catastrophic label on everyday bodily sensations, e.g. your heart racing, and tell yourself 'my heart racing means I'm having a heart attack', this makes your bodily sensations, e.g. heart racing, even stronger. In panic disorder the sufferer is constantly scanning their body for unusual bodily sensations and once detected they are catastrophised, i.e. a danger label is attached, resulting in more bodily symptoms; the person becomes even more alarmed and a vicious circle (Figure 1) is set up.

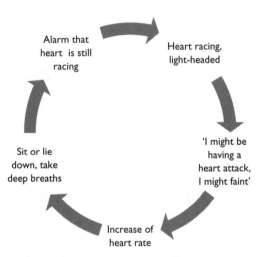

Figure 1 The vicious circle of panic.

Starting in the one o'clock position in Figure 1, you might wake up noticing that your heart is racing and feel light-headed. Going clockwise around Figure 1, you might think that you are having a heart attack and are going to faint; this catastrophic interpretation causes an increase in heart rate, the six o'clock position in Figure 1. You might then take some 'safety precautions', the eight o'clock position, perhaps breathing deeply, opening a window or sitting down. But then you find that these 'safety' procedures are not making much if any difference, you become 'alarmed', the eleven o'clock position, which continues to fuel the palpitations and light-headedness, coming full circle to the one o'clock position. Because the sufferer from panic disorder keeps literally going round in circles with their symptoms, they often end up at the local A&E Department to be told usually that there is nothing wrong with their heart. Overcoming panic disorder involves breaking the circle in Figure 1 by challenging the reflex automatic catastrophic thoughts about unusual bodily sensations, four and eleven o'clock positions, and avoiding the 'safety' procedures, the eight o'clock position.

2. If you can think yourself into panic can it be that dangerous?

Just read over the following pairs of words:

Breathless	Suffocate
Dizzy	Faint
Chest tight	Heart attack
Unreality	Seizure or going insane
Numbness	Stroke
Palpitations	Dying
Lightheadedness	Losing control
Nausea	Vomiting uncontrollably

As you read through the above words, you may have noticed the beginning of symptoms of panic. If you can bring on such symptoms can they really be that serious? Can you bring on a stroke in the next few minutes just by thinking about it?

3. Being on 'sentry duty' for bodily sensations triggers an alarm

Generally we only notice what we are looking for, e.g. when looking for a parking space we might not take in a partner's questions about what present to buy for whom but might take in the patrolling traffic warden. Focus just now on whether there are any pins and needles, numbness, warmth in your right big toe, now switch your attention to your left big toe and notice what sensations you have: warmth, numbness, pins and needles. When focusing on your left big toe you probably didn't notice what was happening to your right big toe. Leaving your camera on bodily sensations sets the scene for becoming alarmed about them. If a friend is holding a glass of wine you might say to them 'are you OK, only I noticed your hand shaking slightly there?', they might react somewhat abruptly with a denial that there is any shaking but then focus attention on their hand, hold the glass more tightly so as not to 'shake' and end up putting the glass down because it is uncomfortable. (You might need to explain that you were just winding them up!) In order to manage panic attacks it is necessary to learn to focus externally rather than internally.

4. If you can bring on a panic attack can it be that serious?

Try breathing quickly and deeply (hyperventilate) for just a minute. Did you notice any physical sensations when you stopped? If you experienced some sensations, were they anything like those of a panic attack. If hyperventilation did not produce any sensations try holding your breath for 30 seconds. What did you notice? Anything like your panic symptoms? If holding your breath did not produce any sensations, try running on the spot for a minute. What did you notice? Anything like your panic symptoms? Most sufferers from panic disorder can find some exercise that if they do for long enough produces symptoms that are like their panic attacks. Can such symptoms really be that serious if you can bring them on? No matter how long you tried to bring a stroke or a heart attack on you could not do it but you can bring on a panic attack.

5. Slow motion action replay of your most recent bad panic attack and monitoring your attacks

Some panic attacks are much worse than others. When was your last bad panic attack? Jot down in the panic diary shown in Table 1 when it was and where you were (the first column in the diary).

Table 1 Panic diary

Time and place of panic attack – situation	On a scale 0–10, where 10 is the worst possible, how bad was this attack?	During this attack what thoughts went through your mind?	Did you do anything special to manage this attack?	What would have been a better way of thinking and behaving in this situation?

In the second column put a number, 1–10, that indicates how severe the attack was, say 8. Now take yourself back to this attack and try and remember what went through your mind and put this in the third column, e.g. 'thought I was going to faint and make a show of myself'. Then in the fourth column write what you did, e.g. 'rushed home'. Then in the final column write down how you might have played it differently, e.g. 'stayed where I was, stayed standing, told myself you can't faint in a panic attack if your heart is racing because if your heart is racing your blood pressure is going up, you can only faint when blood pressure goes down'. If you keep the diary and practise playing the attacks differently, gradually you will see that the panic attacks happen less often and that they are not as severe when they do happen, eventually petering out.

6. Monitoring your avoidance

Many people with panic disorder avoid certain situations. On a scale 0–8, where 8 is always avoid it and 0 is would not avoid it, indicate below with a number how much you avoid the following situations:

Travelling alone or by bus	
Walking alone in busy streets	
Going into crowded shops	
Going alone far from home	
Large open spaces	

As you gradually dare yourself to tackle these avoided situations, to begin with you may get more panic attacks. But if you keep practising, these attacks gradually become less severe and less frequent, your scores come down and you reclaim your life. Have a think about what dares you could attempt this week. It is important that you do not try too much, overcoming the agoraphobia is like, as a child, gradually daring yourself in a swimming pool to try things in order to swim, if you try too much too soon it is like throwing yourself in at the deep end, it will just put you off. It doesn't matter how small your steps are, you will get to where you want if you keep training.

7. Beginning to dare

To reclaim your life you have to begin with 'baby steps' to approach what you avoid. Think of it as climbing a ladder back to what you did before your first panic attacks (Figure 2). Week by week try and climb a rung of

	Example	
Week 10	Travel to city centre alone and shop as I used to before the panic attacks	
Week 9	Travel by bus alone to city centre and shop briefly at a quiet time, do old routine in the gym	
Week 8	Travel by bus alone to city centre and meet friend, shop together	
Week 7	Three times in the week get the bus to supermarket by self and shop briefly at a time when it is not busy, go to the gym at a time when it is not busy and do some light exercise	
Week 6	Daily travel by bus unaccompanied three stops but met by relative, continue going to local shops, go accompanied to supermarket but stand in queue by self	
Week 5	Daily go to local shop when it is busy, go to supermarket when accompanied but shop by myself for a few minutes meeting up with relative in café, travel by bus accompanied	
Week 4	Daily walk to local shop by myself when it is not busy, go to supermarket accompanied, stay at home alone all day	
Week 3	Daily walk around the block by myself, stay at home alone for a half day	
Week 2	Drink just a couple of cups of coffee a day, daily walk to the end of the road and back by myself, stay at home alone for 60 minutes	
Week 1	Take a hot shower daily, walk to the end of the road by myself and meet relative there, stay at home alone for 30 minutes	

Figure 2 Ladder to life.

the ladder. An example training schedule is shown in the second column of Figure 2. In the third column put in what might be the rungs of the ladder for you. It is always a bit of a guess as to what the next rung of the ladder should be and if you try a rung and can't manage it, you just have to make a smaller step. For example, in Figure 2, if the person struggled with their week 6 assignment and felt overwhelmed by trying to travel three bus stops alone, they might try just one bus stop and get used to this before trying three bus stops again. In this way if at any step you feel overwhelmed you can always introduce an intermediate step. The idea is to make the steps difficult but manageable, not overwhelming.

As you climb the ladder you learn to tolerate panic symptoms, losing your 'fear of fear'. Overcoming 'fear of fear' is the passport to life.

8. Saboteurs of the 'dares'

Sometimes clients get stuck at a particular rung of the ladder; for example, they may have become able to shop accompanied but cannot do so by themselves and the reason may not be very apparent. Using the downward arrow technique (Figure 3) can unearth the bottom line, which can be targeted.

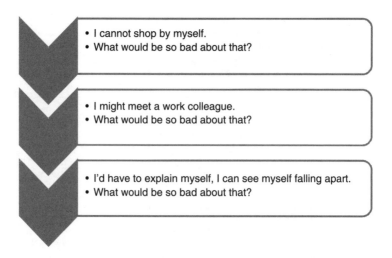

Figure 3 Downward arrow technique – example.

In the example in Figure 3 the bottom line is that the person has an image of themselves 'falling apart' and this could then be targeted by asking whether all images are necessarily true; I might have an image of being the most handsome/pretty person in this universe but would doubt this makes it true!

There are two ways of tackling feared consequences. The first is to ask how likely the worst outcome would be. If I were a betting person would I bet on this worst outcome? If I would not place a bet, do I really believe that the worst outcome is likely? So the person above with the fear of shopping alone might ask themselves 'would I bet my partner £50 that if I met a former colleague whilst shopping alone, I would fall apart? Money has a way of concentrating your mind so that you become realistic! The image of 'falling apart' can then be reconstructed with a more realistic scenario of, say, imagining asking the former colleague whether they had any planned holidays and then excusing yourself because you are in a hurry. The second strategy is to ask how awful the feared consequence might be. So that in the above example the person might respond 'if I fell apart in front of a former work colleague, they would likely think I was physically unwell, because that is likely to be more their experience'.

9. Seeing 'dares' as experiments – 'don't avoid realistic experiments'

A dare is a two-sided coin. On one side a dare is about gradually doing what you have been avoiding; on the other side, it is about performing a realistic experiment. For example, you might fear having a panic attack in a lift, fearing that you will have to get out quickly to get some air. You could test out whether you really have to make a dash for air, by deliberately holding your breath in the lift, seemingly making less air available and discover that there is in fact always enough air available. Or you might experience palpitations when you are alone in a busy city centre, you could test out whether your heart racing really is dangerous by walking very quickly for a few minutes, making your heart race even more and discovering that an increased heart rate signifies nothing at all. If your fear is of going crazy in front of others, you could test whether this is really possible by planning to go deliberately crazy in front of others at a particular time and discovering what actually happens at the appointed time.

10. Relapse prevention

Panic attacks do tend to recur at times of stress or loss, the secret is to not take them seriously. The temptation will be to withdraw from the situations in which the panic attack occurred, so the task is not to be bullied into changing your behaviour. If you have begun to engage in avoidance behaviour, construct a ladder to reclaim your life. In Table 2, there are examples of common catastrophic thoughts and their antidotes. Try adding your own common catastrophic thoughts and their antidotes.

Table 2 Catastrophic thoughts and their antidotes

I'll be trapped on the aeroplane, I'll make a show of myself.	I can go to the toilet or just close my eyes until the panic passes.
These pins and needles mean there is something wrong with my circulation, probably a blood clot on the way.	I can get pins and needles from everyday things such as leaning on my arm for a time, if I imagine a blood clot I will also imagine it dissolving.
It's ridiculous to feel unreal as if everything is far away when I'm in a queue. Others will see that I'm weird.	Feeling as if you are distant from your surroundings is a very common stress reaction. How can others measure how distant I feel?
I can't get close to anyone because of this sweating, they will notice, maybe even smell, that something is up.	Nobody has ever commented on my sweating, maybe I'm just 'on sentry duty' for this symptom, so I notice the slightest perspiration.
The light-headedness probably means a brain tumour, my dad had one.	Brain tumours aren't hereditary, you can feel light-headed for thousands of trivial reasons such as getting up quickly from a chair.

Review Table 2 on a regular basis so that in the event of a panic attack the antidotes can be easily recalled.

Post-traumatic Stress Disorder Survival Manual

Serious road traffic accidents, assaults, explosions are the type of events that can give rise to post-traumatic stress disorder. Such events can act like a 'pebble in water' (Figure 1) spreading out in their effects.

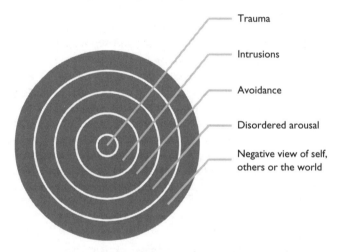

Trauma

Intrusions

Avoidance

Disordered arousal

Negative view of self, others or the world

Figure 1 'Pebble in the water' effect of trauma.

After an extreme trauma you might experience pictures of the incident coming into your mind, sometimes for no reason. At other times the memories are brought on by reminders. The memories are like unwelcome guests (intrusions in Figure 1) and may be joined by other intruders – nightmares of what did or could have happened. The intrusions are horrible and you most likely try to make sure that they are not triggered, by for example avoiding conversations about the incident or by staying away from the scene of the incident. Thus avoidance (see Figure 1) is the second major ripple effect of the trauma. If you are preoccupied by memories of the incident and are avoiding anything connected with it, this is likely to mean a major disruption of your life, resulting in disordered arousal (Table 1).

Table 1 Disordered arousal

- Disturbed sleep
- Increased irritability
- Poor concentration
- Hypervigilance (on 'sentry duty')
- Easily startled

The collective name for the symptoms in Table 1 is disordered arousal, which is the third ripple in Figure 1. As the wave of PTSD spreads out through intrusions, avoidance and disordered arousal it extends as far as a fourth and final ripple (Figure 1), a negative view of yourself, others or the world (e.g. 'I am bad', 'no one can be trusted', 'my whole nervous system is permanently ruined', the 'world is completely dangerous'). There is a common sense connection between an extreme trauma and flashbacks/ nightmares and avoidance but few victims anticipate how negative they have become about almost everything.

You are not alone with these reactions. You might find reading this brief Survival Manual a stepping stone to reading the self-help book Moving On After Trauma *(available online or from your bookshop) in which you can read about the steps taken by someone just like yourself to recover from PTSD. The book is also a guide for relatives and friends, who often feel that they are 'walking on egg shells' with the trauma victim – if they leave the victim alone the latter is inactive and accuses those close of abandoning them; alternatively if they encourage the victim to be more active they are accused of nagging. Many trauma victims try to cope with their sleep problems and fearfulness by increasing alcohol consumption or taking drugs; the latter can become problems in their own right, distracting attention from tackling the underlying PTSD.*

1.Normal reaction to an abnormal situation

Intrusions, avoidance, disordered arousal and disturbed relationships are a normal reaction to an abnormal situation. The good news is that the majority of people recover from PTSD and, for those who do not, 7 out of 10 recover by the end of cognitive behaviour therapy.

The trouble is that your reactions may not feel at all normal, you can feel a sense of danger/threat even though you know there is no danger. You can say all the sensible things to yourself but as soon as you are in a situation remotely like what happened to you the logic seems to go out of the window. Well, you are not going crazy, it just feels like it! The key problem is a 'dodgy alarm' (Figure 2). The brain has its own alarm called the amygdala; it is as if ordinarily the alarm is over to the left in the ten o'clock position, should something 'alarming' happen, e.g. a person approaches you with a weapon, the alarm rings and you pump oxygen to your muscles ready to take flight or maybe even fight. However, for some people when the alarm rings it becomes stuck in a 'war zone' position, the two o'clock position to the right.

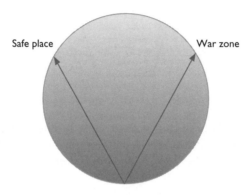

Figure 2 Dodgy alarm – amygdala.

In this position there is a sense of threat even though objectively there is little or no danger. The amygdala is also the seat of emotional memory, and it works on matching rather than logic, so that whenever you come across anything even vaguely like the incident it goes off. When it goes off you may feel a surge that appears to go from the top of your stomach into your chest.

It is as if you are in a war zone but others are in a safe place. This leads to a sense that you are in your own world (Figure 3) disconnected from those around you.

Figure 3 The PTSD bubble.

This sense of isolation, can lead to feelings of numbness/emptiness, feeling flat (Figure 4), as if somebody has left a fizzy drink standing around for a long time.

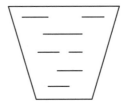

Figure 4 Emotional flatness.

Such emotional flatness can lead to guilt feelings such as not feeling warm towards your partner and a deterioration of relationships, e.g. no enthusiasm for returning a phone call to a friend.

Recovery involves:

- resetting the alarm (Figure 2), moving it gradually anticlockwise from the war zone position, to the vertical, twelve o'clock position (an area of less conflict) and finally back to the ten o'clock position, a safe place;
- stretching the bubble (Figure 3), gradually reconnecting with people;
- getting the 'fizz' back (Figure 4), by beginning to invest again in life;
- learning not to take the alarm's ringing seriously, by putting its activation into context.

2. Resetting the alarm

Overreacting in every possible way is one of the hallmarks of PTSD. Knowing that you overreact will lead you to avoid situations that might trigger these extreme responses. Without fully realising it, you have spotted that you have developed an oversensitive alarm and you have dedicated your life to not tripping it. Unfortunately just as exercise is usually necessary for back trouble despite an increase in discomfort, so too it is necessary to trip the alarm in order to reset it. Although you may know with your head, in your better moments, that certain situations are not really dangerous, your 'guts' do not. The 'gut' reactions change most powerfully when a person dares themselves to do what they have been avoiding and discover that nothing bad happens. The alarm can be coaxed back to a safe place by gradual dares.

The situation is rather like teaching a toddler to swim: the first dare might be to have them jump in and you catch them, then when they are comfortable doing that they might jump in next to you without your catching them, etc. Thus, for example, a person with PTSD following a road traffic accident might week by week take the steps in Figure 5.

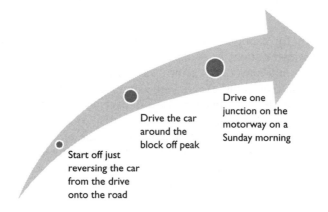

Drive one junction on the motorway on a Sunday morning

Drive the car around the block off peak

Start off just reversing the car from the drive onto the road

Figure 5 Resetting the alarm by daring small steps.

Each dare or step trips the alarm. It will feel awful at the time but afterwards the alarm moves anticlockwise a notch. What dares could you have a go at? Just jot them down below:

1. ....

2. ....

3. ....

Start off with the easiest of the dares, in this way gradually building your confidence. The idea is not to become a 'dare devil' but to gradually, simply dare to do what you would have done before the trauma. The more you can get back to doing what you did before, the better you are likely to feel.

Unfortunately learning anything is never smooth. It is often the case that after making significant progress the person comes across an all too vivid reminder of their trauma. It is very tempting at this point to abandon the training programme. But whilst the alarm may have moved slightly clockwise, continued dares soon repair the situation and the alarm is reset in a safe place. It is necessary to budget that training will be a matter of two step forwards and one back and not become demoralised.

Dares can show that what you feared is not as dangerous as you thought. In fact dares can be thought of as experiments to test out whether your gut reactions have much to do with everyday reality now. The letters of the word dare also stand for:

- **D**on't
- **A**void a
- **R**ealistic
- **E**xperiment

You might, for example, have a fear of a busy shopping centre, so a realistic experiment might be to dare yourself to go into such a centre for just one item and test out whether anything unbearable does actually happen. If you repeat the experiment a number of times you will have collected a great deal of evidence of no danger and you will become less fearful. A dare is a two-sided coin, on one side it is about changing your thinking by doing a realistic experiment and on the other side it is about changing your behaviour by daring to do something you have been avoiding. Dares are a gesture of defiance proclaiming that no horror has the last word.

3. Better ways of handling the traumatic memory

You have probably tried to blank the memory, distracting yourself by doing something or talking to someone. Trouble is that that works only briefly. Here is why: supposing if I said:

'Do not think about the orangutan'

As you continue to read you are still thinking of orangutans (perhaps you think he looks like somebody you know!). The more you try to deliberately not think of something the more you think about it.

Sufferers from PTSD fear that if they don't try to block the memory it will dominate and spoil their life. But if you try to block the memory you are guaranteed that it is constantly on your mental TV. Realistically, though, you cannot help but think about the incident sometimes as it has had such a big impact on your life. The secret of handling the traumatic memory is attention control, at times letting the memory just float in and out of your mind without getting involved/rising to the bait, whilst having a special time when you address your concerns about the incident and its effects. It is rather like children pestering you to do something whilst you are busy doing a task; if you just say 'go away, I'm busy' two minutes later they are back but if you say 'I'm busy right now but I'll fix your bike at about 11.0 a.m.', provided you do turn up at 11.0 a.m. they may leave you alone. There are a number of ways of dealing with the memory at the special time (Table 2).

Table 2 Better ways of handling the memory

- Write a page a day about the incident and its effects
- Dictate the story of the trauma and ask someone to write it down
- Dictate the incident into a recording device, e.g. mobile phone

Your first reaction to the alternative ways of handling the memory may well be 'no way', perhaps a feeling that you will be 'overwhelmed by the memory or that it will become uncontrollable'. But if you approach dares, a little step at a time, though it is uncomfortable it is manageable. Perhaps when you first begin to write/dictate you might leave out the most painful part or you can only write a few lines. That's fine, day by day you just gradually dare yourself to do a bit more. Usually after about two or three weeks of this you just become bored with what you are writing/dictating. When you are bored by something you no longer have nightmares about it, nor are you distressed in the day by the memory of it. The goal is to become as 'bored' as the orangutan looks; this usually takes about 20 minutes a day of writing/re-reading, dictating/reading/listening for about two to three weeks.

4. Safety first?

Since your trauma you probably do many things for safety that you didn't do before; just take a moment and jot a few down:

1. ....

2. ....

3. ....

Your safety behaviours might include repeatedly checking the front door is locked, or checking that the children are still breathing when they are asleep or perhaps insisting that you are in the front passenger seat not the rear or only driving to places you know.

To what extent do you try to persuade others close to you, to do what you now do?

. . . .

If not doing what you do now is really dangerous, what stops you making more efforts to persuade others to behave just like you?

. . . .

If there is a clear and present danger to those close to you, from their not behaving just like you, would you not insist and check on them even when they are out of sight and might laugh at you if you rang or left a text message?

. . . .

Is it that you do these 'safety behaviours' as a way of trying to avoid discomfort, rather than believing that not doing them is dangerous?

. . . .

Is it just embarrassment that stops you trying to persuade people in your local area via say local radio, to behave exactly as you do? Surely with your care of people you would do more?

. . . .

Am I truly putting safety first or are these new behaviours simply a way of trying to calm the stormy seas that I feel I'm sailing through?

. . . .

One possibility is that the new 'safety behaviours' are more about wanting to feel in control because you may have felt so out of control in the incident. Young children often engage in magical thinking, e.g. not stepping on the cracks on the pavement as they go to school so that teacher does not shout at them; can you be sure that your new 'safety behaviours' are not magical thinking? Consider dropping the new 'safety behaviours' by engaging in gradual dares.

5. Photographing the trauma and its consequences from different angles

The mind is rather like a camera and how you take a photograph of the trauma makes a big difference. For example, you might be leaving your camera on what could have happened and regularly watch a horror video of family members at your funeral. Not surprisingly, using the camera in this way is upsetting. You could instead focus on the reality, for example a nasty accident with some injuries; although unpleasant the reality video is much less upsetting than the horror video. Are you addicted to watching horror videos of what happened? If you are, what about practising switching your attention from the horror video to the reality video?

Reminders of your trauma can mean that you do not simply remember what happened but you re-experience it again, almost as if you are back again at the scene of the accident. When this happens the difference between 'then' and 'now' becomes blurred. Common reminders are smells, sounds or seeing your trauma on TV. These reminders have become 'transporters' taking you back in time. Unfortunately reminders are always about, but you can learn how not to board the 'transporter' by letting yourself experience what that particular smell, sound or sight means today. For example, if the smell of petrol takes you back to re-experiencing your accident you might deliberately let yourself smell petrol, reminding yourself that you are safe, just smelling it in the garage. Possibly it is the sight of a particular car, a knife or a loud bang. Just looking and listening to these now either in real life or on the internet can teach you that they do not always have awful consequences. In this way you recognise some similarity between the reminder and your trauma but at the same time spell out very important differences. When you come across any reminder play 'spot the differences'; like the childhood game, the more differences that you come up with the better you have done.

Guilt is often associated with PTSD; for example, you might be a bus driver who knocks down and kills an elderly person, when the latter without warning steps from the pavement into your path. In such circumstances it is easy to feel very guilty perhaps haunted by the expression of the person as the bus went towards them. But you can take a different angle using a responsibility pie (Figure 6).

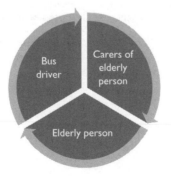

Figure 6 Responsibility pie.

Going clockwise around the pie you might decide the carers of the elderly person bear some responsibilty for letting them out unsupervised and it may that the elderly person deserves a slice of the pie because of their stubbornness, leaving only a small slice for the driver. Indeed the driver's slice may be even smaller if the bus was poorly maintained. Using the pie people often conclude that they are much less blameworthy than they first thought.

6. PTSD and negativity

Guilt may relate to the incident or to the consequences of the incident. For example you might think 'I should have warned the driver when I saw the oncoming car' or 'I should be over this by now' or 'I should be working/ providing'. Alternatively the negativity can be focused on blaming others e.g. 'the emergency service vehicle should have been better maintained and shouldn't have been speeding'. Such negative automatic first thoughts can have the sting taken out of them by coming up with more realistic second thoughts. One way of doing this is to use the MOOD chart (Table 3). The first letter of MOOD, 'M', stands for monitor your mood, the second letter, 'O', stands for observe your thinking, what it sounds as if you have said to yourself, the third letter, 'O', is for objective thinking, more realistic second thoughts, and the final letter, 'D', is for deciding what to do and doing it.

Table 3 MOOD chart

Monitor Mood	Observe thinking	Objective thinking	Decide what to do and do it
1. Mood dipped standing drinking coffee looking out of the window.	I should be over this by now	Who said I should, it is not my fault if I have not had the right tools to get over PTSD	I could dare myself to go swimming
2. Mood dipped when I saw my neighbour going to work	I am weak I can't face going back to where it happened	I can't be that weak I have started some dares, I'll get back to work gradually, I just have to pace it	I will ring some colleagues and meet up with them socially first

Whenever your mood dips you will have greater access to the memory of the incident, it will seem more vivid and real. It is therefore important to take the sting out of your reflex negative thought as quickly as possible; the longer you pick at or ruminate about the automatic thought, the more difficult it is to take a photograph from a different angle. In theory you can come up with better second thoughts without writing things down using the MOOD chart, but it is a bit like learning maths for the first time and trying to do the sums in your head.

It is as if the negative view of self, others and the world, the fourth ripple in Figure 1, gets washed up on the 'shore line', solidifies and becomes a magnifying glass through which anything negative is 'read', e.g. the unexpected visit of a relative is viewed, not as a slight hassle, but as a catastrophe. Operating with the 'magnifying glass' becomes so familiar to PTSD sufferers that they often do not realise they are using it. But the habitual use of the magnifying glass results in feelings of detachment and estrangement from others. The first step in weaning yourself off use of the magnifying glass is becoming aware of the differences in your 'reading' with and without this apparent 'aid'.

Spend a few minutes completing Table 4 and the questions that follow.

Table 4 My views before and now

	Myself	Others	The world	The future
View now				
View before				

What do you think others close to you think of you now?. . . . .
. . . .
. . . .

Do they agree with you about the amount of danger you are in?. . . . . . .
. . . .
. . . .

If they don't agree about the level of danger, why might that be?. . . . . . .
. . . .
. . . .

Do they agree with how you look at what happened in the incident?. . . .
. . . .
. . . .

Looking back at your answers above they are probably very different depending on when you took the photograph (before or now) and whether it is your view or others'. The social support provided by others or indeed the lack of it can also influence your observed thinking. If your observed thinking is exaggeratedly negative this will influence your behaviour, which is likely to be avoidant.

7. Restoring relationships

PTSD puts a great strain on relationships. Often the sufferer is irritable over the most minor of events, no longer shows affection and cuts themselves off from relatives and friends. Many sufferers feel guilty that they no longer have feelings of warmth to their partner. The apparent demands of others exceed their resources and they feel 'on a short fuse' (Figure 7).

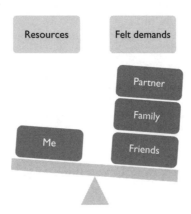

Figure 7 Disturbed relationships.

High levels of stress are experienced when the felt demands exceed the resources and the see-saw tips up. The imbalance is expressed via irritability, straining relationships. Yet those who view themselves as supported are more likely to recover.

One way of helping to restore relationships is to question what you take to be the demands of others. For example, how true is it that your partner and children insist you provide financially in the way you did before the incident? How true is it that friends see you as a lesser person for not being able to do what you did before? Who is setting unrealistic standards, yourself or those around you?

Sufferers from PTSD tend to go into their own world, the 'bubble' in Figure 3, and stop investing in relations and friends. But because there is no investment there can be no return. Recovery from PTSD depends on gradually beginning to invest in those close to you again. You might start off with going for a walk with your partner, asking your partner about their day, giving a hug or perhaps telephoning a friend for a few minutes. To begin with you may well feel that you are going through the motions but eventually some enthusiasm will come back.

In order to moderate your outbursts you might imagine a set of traffic lights on red as soon as you notice the first signs of irritability. Then when the lights go to amber ask yourself is what has just happened really the end of the world? Did they really do it deliberately to wind me up? Then when the lights go to green go into another room to calm down. To begin with, many people go through the lights on red and it may take a few weeks' practice to learn to obey them. It may be that if you trust your partner or family member enough you can ask them to remind you to use the traffic lights when you are getting irate.

Many PTSD sufferers stop communicating with family members after their trauma and the latter are left bewildered as to how to cope. Initially rather than try to explain yourself ask those around you to read this Manual; this may act as a stepping stone to their understanding the trauma self-help book *Moving On After Trauma*.

8. Writing the gameplan for the next chapter of your autobiography

Because the trauma has had such a big influence on your life, it can become the only lens through which you look at life. Though you might recall pleasures and achievements from before the incident you will probably only do so briefly and just long enough to dwell on what you have lost as a consequence of the trauma.

The first step forward is to recognise that you are using a trauma lens, then to stand back and instead see the bigger picture. To do this, spend some time collecting photographs, memorabilia and writing in graphic detail about your pleasures and achievements before the trauma. You could regard this as a first chapter of your autobiography. The second chapter you have already written or dictated is about the trauma. The following chapters are all about the life you are going to construct and your gameplan for dealing with likely difficulties. In writing the third and later chapters you could summarise in your own words those strategies you have found most useful in stopping domination by the trauma. In this way these chapters become your own personalised Survival Manual that you can make ready reference to at the first sign of difficulties.

Social Phobia Survival Manual

Talking about your social phobia is likely to be the most difficult thing in the world because it means the spotlight will be on you. This is why comparatively few people with social phobia attend for treatment. But without treatment few get better. One study of people with social phobia showed 63% of them still suffering social phobia 12 years after it began.

Social anxiety (which includes social phobia and shyness) has two main ingredients, fear and avoidance. If you greatly fear small groups you might be put off going to group therapy and if you avoid social gatherings like Christmas works parties, you don't learn that they are not that dangerous and you are really anxious when forced to attend a social gathering, e.g. a meal after a wedding. Both fear and avoidance are necessary to the running of the engine of social anxiety (Figure 1).

Figure 1 The engine of social anxiety.

Which social situations would you like to conquer? Common concerns of people with social phobia include: being introduced, meeting people in authority, using the telephone, having visitors come to the house, being watched doing something, being teased, eating at home with an acquaintance, eating with the family, talking to someone you are physically attracted to, writing in front of others and public speaking. Underline those that are an issue for you and put a number 0–10 next to the items you have underlined to indicate how much you fear this situation. Perhaps also write down below if there is any other social situation that is an issue for you and how much you fear it:

. . . .

. . . .

Starting with the less fearful situations (the lower scores) gradually dare yourself to enter those situations. The more often you enter the feared situation the more your fear reduces, if you avoid the situation that turns the wheel of fear in Figure 1.

As you are driving the 'social phobic's car' you assume others are out to get you. But instead of checking out whether they really are dangerous (are some worse than others?), you turn inwards on yourself, focusing on your bodily sensations, e.g. turning stomach, feeling shaky, and explain this discomfort as a response to the high expectations of others.

It is if other people are hypercritical teachers surrounding you (Figure 2).

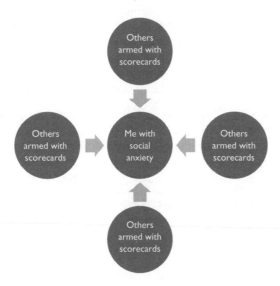

Figure 2 The social anxiety story.

In social phobia the individual regards themselves as such an 'oddity' that they believe others must be looking at them and negatively evaluating them.

But the story that non-social phobics carry around is shown in Figure 3.

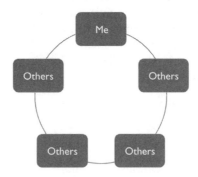

Figure 3 The normal story.

In Figure 3 others might notice you in passing but no more so than others. Further, they are unlikely to bother making a judgement of you unless you do something either very kind or harmful.

1. Beliefs that maintain social anxiety

If you have started daring yourself to encounter some of the situations that you fear, as recommended above, this will likely trigger some socially anxious thoughts/beliefs. Make a note below of any such thoughts coming onstream as you let yourself be the focus of attention:

. . . .

. . . .

The following seven beliefs are usually held firmly by people suffering from social phobia and are the reflex thoughts often experienced in social situations. But how true are they for you? Are these ideas useful? How did you come by these ideas?

1. *'Others zoom in on my negatives'*

People suffering with social phobia believe others focus on their peculiarities, e.g. sweating, whereas non-sufferers believe that others react to them as a whole person. To test out whether others really do focus on 'oddities' try an experiment: in conversation with people you know do something unusual a couple of times, e.g. pull your ear lobe or rub your nose, then see if there is any sign of them having noticed. The person with social phobia has a story about themselves based around their perceived deficit, e.g. blushing, whereas the story others (the viewers) are using sees them as a whole person – warmth, smiles, interest – and the perceived deficits are at worst only a minor part of the whole picture.

2. 'They have put me under the microscope and found me wanting'

Why would others bother putting you under the microscope? What would they be seeking to discover? How do you know that they feel negatively about you? What is the evidence that they all feel negatively about you? Do some feel more negative about you than others? Can you be sure what others think of you, if they are a bit shy?

3. 'Others have high expectations of how you should be socially'

It is as if the person with social phobia believes that there are Commandments about how they should be socially, e.g. 'I must have something interesting to say', as opposed to a guideline, e.g. 'it might be an idea to ask them how their moving house went, just show some interest'. Social life flows more easily with the equivalent of a Highway Code rather than Commandments; sometimes you need to drive on the right, e.g. when overtaking a parked vehicle; if there was a Commandment 'Thou shalt always drive on the left' traffic would soon come to a standstill.

4. 'I should worry when I'm going to have to meet people'

What is the advantage of worrying before you meet people?

What is the disadvantage of worrying before you meet people?

Would you conduct the following experiment: resolve not to worry before your next meeting with someone and see whether it goes any better or worse than your last meeting?

5. 'After talking to people, I should put my performance under the microscope and agonise about it'

What is the advantage of this?

Has it helped you improve the quality of your contact with people?

6. 'Don't tell anything about yourself, certainly not how you feel'

Can you be sure that this idea is not contributing to your difficulties? In Figure 4 follow the arrows round clockwise from the one o'clock position.

Figure 4 The price of not letting others get to know you.

7. 'I should remember previous humiliations in detail, they should guide how I operate with people'

When really bad things happen to people such as being in a very serious car crash it can then become very vivid in their mind – the sights, sounds and smells. Because it remains so vivid it might put the person off driving or being a passenger in a car. Most get around this by reminding themselves that in all their years of travel by car they had never experienced anything like it and it was really a one-off and they gradually dare themselves to get back into the car. In a similar way for people with social phobia there can be vivid recall of some humiliation, e.g. being teased over a long period at school or being heavily criticised by parents when you expressed any disagreement with their views. These memories can be so strong that you don't just remember them but you feel again all the bodily symptoms that you felt at the time of your humiliation. Whilst you cannot just forget such memories, you can begin to make sure that they do not have the last word, by stepping around them and acknowledging that the 'humiliators' are probably not like most adults. You can give adults a chance and see what the results are. You could keep a daily count of the number of non-humiliators.

2. Second thoughts

The person with social phobia feels that they are an 'oddity', they don't fit in, but they make the mistake of thinking it is abnormal if you think of yourself in such a way. Do a survey, ask people if they 'feel odd, don't fit in'; you could be surprised by the results! Most people think 'I am like them but they are not like me!', being inconsistent is actually normal, 'join the human race'.

Your thoughts about your thoughts (or feelings) are called metacognitions and it is these that are as much of a problem in social phobia as the thoughts/images/feelings that arise first. There is a special way of cross-examining your socially anxious thoughts and coming up with better second thoughts and behaviours (Table 1).

Table 1 On second thoughts

Social situation that made me anxious	Bumped into a neighbour on the train.
What I thought	I'm trapped, what will I say? He will notice me sweating.
What I did	Mopped my face with a tissue, made an excuse that it was very hot on the train.
What I did afterwards	Agonised that he must think I am an idiot.
What would be a better way of thinking and behaving that I could try out next time, in a similar situation?	Just take an interest in the other person as if they were guests on a chat show and let them know something of me, let go of my 'safety behaviour' mopping my face. Don't 'pick' at the memory.

In the example in Table 1 'What I did' refers to safety behaviour. These are behaviours the socially anxious person engages in to stop themselves 'falling apart'; in the example given the person repeatedly mopped their face. But there are a great range of safety behaviours, some observable such as avoiding eye contact, some more subtle such as washing the dishes/preparing the food rather than have conversations, and others are more covert plans such as not revealing any personal details. What safety behaviours do you use?

3. What do others really notice?

The socially anxious person feels that they are being scrutinised by others, particularly strangers. Try doing something that you normally do, in the way you usually do, e.g. go into a shop and buy a newspaper and make a careful note of the assistant's reactions and behaviour. Then the next day do the same again, but this time brush the bottom of your nose with your hand and make a note of the assistant's reaction. Perhaps the following day, as you are being given change pull your ear lobe and again note the reactions. On the following day try scratching under one of your armpits as you are given change and notice the reactions. Then ask yourself what do the results of these experiments mean?

4. Daring to drop safety behaviours

Your safety behaviours are designed to avoid catastrophe. But many safety behaviours exhaust people and probably make a disaster more likely to happen. For example, the car driver who drives very slowly leaving lots of space in front might encourage others to overtake and cut in front, perhaps creating the very circumstances they wish to avoid. In a similar way you might find that your safety behaviours are more trouble than they are worth. If you are at a social gathering use your usual safety behaviours with one person, then with the next person you meet try and put all your attention on them, 'forgetting' to use your safety behaviours, then compare which was the easiest. It is daring to drop your safety behaviours even for a brief period but the more that you do this the more your confidence increases.

5. Checking out whether other people do 'see' what you think they 'see'

There is often a gap between how a person sees themselves and how others see them. How we see ourselves often has more to do with our history. In the case of a person who is socially anxious their view of themselves may be more to do with a combination of factors: having been bullied or teased, parents who modelled social anxiety or passed on exacting standards about what was acceptable. This combination of factors may make a person feel both vulnerable and inadequate. Further, for the socially anxious person this felt inadequacy may be made 'obvious' to others in many different ways, e.g. blushing, stammering, boring conversation, trembling hands, quavering voice. But others may not notice such signs and if they do may not see them as catastrophic. The socially anxious person may see themselves as insignificant, others may beg to differ. The difficulty for the person with social anxiety is that they may refuse to believe any positive feedback from others, discounting it on some grounds or other, 'e.g. 'they are just a really nice person'.

One way of getting a reality check on what others see is to write down what you think others would see if you were in a brief conversation with others. Then have a brief conversation with a friend or family member and have it recorded on a digital camcorder or mobile phone then look at it when it is played back. In reviewing the playback ask yourself, is it as bad as you thought it was going to be? Did your face go as red as you expected? Did you stammer as much as you thought you would? Was the person you were talking to interested in you? Then play it back again and try to be objective about what you see, imagine you are someone who is reasonably well disposed to you, what do you make of what you see now? Did you notice that as you become the more objective other person you become less critical of what you are seeing?

Just as it is possible to distort a football match by having people watch only recorded highlights of the fouls, it is possible to distort what you think other people see without lying by using a mental filter. For example, you might focus on the fact that you stammer or blush but neglect that you smiled and the other person seemed interested – an example of applying a mental filter. The socially anxious person is over-alert for signs of danger, so they might pick up that the other person has a blank expression and interpret this negatively on the basis that 'if a person is not obviously for me then they are against me'; this is an example of all or nothing thinking and it leaves out of the equation that the person might be neutral. It is often as if the socially anxious person holds themselves wholly responsible for anything other than a wholly positive response from others and in addition they view absence of the latter as a catastrophe. Rather than escape from (or avoid) the social situation you might pause as if at traffic lights when you believe you encounter 'rejection', and *then* ask 'What alternative explanations are there for the other person's behaviour? What is the story with them? Are they perhaps shy? Is it that they are not interested in the particular subject matter of the conversation? Are they preoccupied with some personal concern?' Then when the lights go to green decide what to do, perhaps change the subject matter of the conversation and focus intensely on what you or they say, rather than your internal feelings. In summary when assessing your social performance check out whether you have used:

- personalisation
- mind-reading
- all or nothing thinking
- a mental filter.

If you have used one or more of the above, do a re-take.

6. Revisiting feared situations and what makes a person likeable

Make a list of feared social situations from least to worst, e.g. paying at the checkout in a supermarket, eating in a cafe by yourself, eating in a restaurant in company, asking your boss for information, chatting in a group at lunch time. Then write down your prediction of what will happen if you approach the feared situation, tackle each in turn but concentrate on the other person not yourself. In this way assess whether the anticipation is worse than the experience. Develop second thoughts about the situations you fear using Table 1.

Write down a list of people that you really like and put them in order from most liked to least liked. Then using the same list of people, put them in order of who would be most at ease meeting a group of strangers. Comparing the two lists are the most socially skilful the most likeable? If your liking of others seems not to do with their low social anxiety how do you know that others do not like you in spite of your social anxiety? In a group of social anxiety sufferers you will probably like some members more than others despite their social anxiety.

If you went for an interview, or to see your local councillor or MP and they knocked their cup of coffee over at the start would you feel less warm, more warm or neutral about them? Strangely you can get others to relax more with 'mistakes'. Perhaps one of the reasons for mistrust of senior managers and politicians is that they appear to perform socially so effortlessly. It may be that what you think of as a 'mistake' is to a degree at least an asset.

7. Haunted by the memory of humiliation – if I knew then what I know now

Sometimes the person with social phobia is haunted by the memory and feelings associated with a humiliation, e.g. being asked to take a turn reading in school, being unable to do so, then being teased by other children. Further, these same feelings may be resurrected again as an adult whenever you are put in the spotlight. Make a note of any such memories – where you were, what happened, how you felt. Then imagine you are revisiting the scene of the humiliation and you see the younger you upset. With the knowledge you have as an adult how would you comfort the younger you? Would you give the younger you a hug? Would you tell you as an adolescent/child that not everybody is the same as the 'teasers' or perhaps that the 'teasers' have their own problems and can only feel good by 'rubbishing' others? If you experience very strong negative emotion it may be that it is really this younger version of yourself that is getting upset and needs soothing before you can move on and make an adult response.

8. Worry before, during and after a social encounter

Worry is normal and is only a problem when it interferes with your daily activities. Some worry is necessary in order to plan how to handle a situation. So that trying to eliminate worry before a social encounter is striving for an unrealistic goal. For example, if you know a particular relative/friend is going to visit you, by way of preparation you might run through what they might like to eat. Are they vegetarian? What interests/ hobbies do they have? It is reasonable to try and sort out what the 'story' of the other person is so that you have some 'doors' through which you might enter their world. However, in social phobia the focus is much less on the other person but rather on the internal sensations that might be experienced at the time of the encounter and the 'inside' view of what the other person might see. If the 'story' of the other person is considered at all, the person with social phobia will assume that they are going to be very critical. Consequently the level of anticipatory worry is such that for the social phobic it may well take away enjoyment in the lead-up time to the encounter. Thus the goal prior to a social encounter is to engage in worry to the extent that it is preparatory, then to disengage from worry and switch attention to other matters, continuing to focus on the latter despite some feelings of anxiety.

For the social phobic, worry about the social encounter may take the form of a horror video about what is going to happen. The constant replay of this horror video before meeting someone serves to heighten anxiety. However, the horror video can be swapped for a reality video that acknowledges probable discomfort but graphically predicts good enough impression management. In analysing their performance afterwards, the person is likely to use some of the information processing biases detailed in Section 5 to put a negative slant on how they connected with the other person. Dwelling on this 'negative slant' makes the person with social phobia at best very fearful of the next social encounter and at worst such situations are avoided (see the introduction to this Manual).

Obsessive Compulsive Disorder Survival Manual

OCD can show itself in behaviours such as checking/cleaning, lining objects up and hoarding but sometimes the OCD is less visible and might consist simply of trying to block unwanted thoughts/images, pure obsessions; about 20–30% of OCD sufferers have pure obsessions. A journey through the minds of others can help the person suffering from OCD see that they are not quite as weird as they think, rather it is their response to their mental life that is the problem.

1. 'And I thought I was weird'

The OCD sufferer watches the same programmes on their mental TV (Figure 1) as the normal, non-OCD person, but the OCD sufferer is distressed by what they see. If you doubt that 'normal' people watch the same 'programmes', ask a group of friends 'would you all dare to be totally truthful about the thoughts and images that have gone through your mind in the last 30 minutes?' There is likely to be an embarrassed silence, followed by some laughter, but nobody prepared to declare all! Try doing a survey of friends/family: ask each of them individually whether they would be prepared to disclose all thoughts/images that have come to mind in the last 30 minutes.

Figure 1 OCD sufferers give programmes a poor reception.

The mind is rather like your local railway station, you can't control what 'trains' of thought come in, it may not be the train you want, your train may be delayed and you may be frustrated seeing all these other trains coming and going and people happily boarding them. But eventually a train you want arrives. In OCD it is as if the sufferer tries to stop the train/s they don't want by jumping onto the track. The noise from the train may be irritating, preventing conversation, but trying to stop the unwanted trains is not a good idea. The unwanted trains often have destinations that are in the opposite direction to what the OCD sufferer wants (Figure 2). A nurse might feel that being caring is very important to her (the arrow to the right in Figure 2), but the images/thoughts that go over in her mind are in the opposite direction, for example stabbing patients. Or a devoutly religious person may have images/thoughts of screaming obscenities in church.

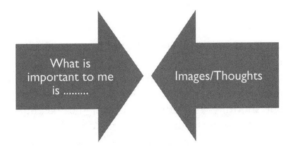

Figure 2 Obsessions – going against the grain.

2. OCD – a serious misinterpretation of mental life

Thoughts/images can be triggered by something, e.g. seeing someone very attractive, or can occur for no reason, e.g. bored, daydreaming and we have a thought/image of someone very attractive. There is no control of what pops into one's mind; at times it can be very inconvenient and other images/thoughts would be more conducive to the task at hand, but fighting them is rather like my protesting today about bad weather on a Bank Holiday Monday, when I would quite like to go for a walk. The mind is always untidy, but played skilfully you can still get a sense of fulfilment, achievement and pleasure, but in OCD the sufferer gets hooked by trying to get their mind 'tidy' *before* engaging with life. It is rather like a student studying for an exam constantly making lists of what they are going to revise but never getting round to actually revising. It is not that making a list in the first place is not a good idea but it becomes an end in itself rather than a means to an end. Figure 3 shows how OCD feeds on itself.

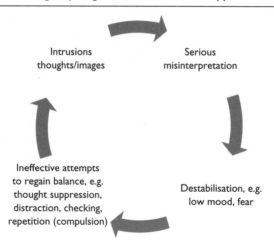

Figure 3 The maintenance of OCD.

The OCD cycle, in Figure 3, starts in the eleven o'clock position with a thought/image that may have been triggered by some event or combination of events, e.g. longer than expected period of illness and stress about work, or have no obvious trigger. For the sake of illustration the thought/image might be about shooting all family members; the likelihood is that such intrusions occur in an individual who is particularly caring/committed to their family. The problems set in when the person seriously misinterprets (the one o'clock position in Figure 3) these intrusions as meaning they are likely to shoot family members. The person has fused together the intrusion and the likelihood of a catastrophic event – thought action fusion (TAF). Not surprisingly this makes them feel off balance (the five o'clock position in Figure 3), fearful, low mood. The person may then seek to regain their balance by repeating the same behaviour (a compulsion), e.g. washing or cleaning and/or trying to block the thoughts or images. But the intrusions are in effect on an elastic band; the harder they are pushed away the more they spring back. (Try not to think of pink elephants for 30 seconds, start right now, time it . . . how many times did you actually think of pink elephants in the 30 seconds?). Performing a compulsion brings the sufferer relief from their anxiety but they feel driven to repeat the behaviour because of such relief. Just as a person who is an alcoholic might get temporary relief from their anxiety by having a drink so too the person with OCD might engage in a compulsive behaviour that brings relief, but for both of them their behaviour makes matters worse in the long run. When the coping strategies don't work (the seven o'clock position in Figure 3) this further fuels the intrusions and the OCD cycle continues. Cognitive behavioural treatment breaks the cycle by challenging the serious misinterpretation, ineffective coping strategies and low mood.

3. OCD – playing by different rules

OCD sufferers differ from non-OCD sufferers in attaching a different significance to their intrusive thoughts/images. It is as if the intrusive/ thoughts images are an unattended piece of luggage at a railway station – most people would hardly notice it, but the OCD sufferer notices, as they are very on guard for danger. Not only do they have a thought it could be a bomb but the image/thought and its consequences are so vivid that the thought/image event become one (thought event fusion; TEF). Actions are then taken to remove the 'threat'. However the actions of the OCD sufferer create more problems than they solve. The ways in which the rules and actions of the OCD sufferer are counterproductive can be illustrated by considering their actions with regard to the completion of a jigsaw. Imagine the following examples:

1. The person has to make sure they have the four corner pieces to start with. Not bad you think, probably many people do this. But then they want to count the number of pieces to check there are the same number as indicated on the box. Bit weird you may think. But then they are not quite sure they have correctly counted the number of pieces, so they count again. Whilst counting they get distracted and so have to start all over again. Getting weirder you may think. Then they count just one time more to be certain. What's going wrong here?

In this example the individual is pursuing feeling certain, they cannot tolerate being uncertain. But this side of the grave there is no certainty; can you be absolutely certain that a close relative has not just died as you are reading this? Faced with this uncertainty an OCD sufferer might abandon reading and go and ring the relative. They might feel relieved when the person answers the phone. But this only encourages them to ring when there is any uncertainty. One of the treatment targets in OCD is intolerance of uncertainty.

2. The person won't do the jigsaw because it shows a picture of harm coming to someone they love. What's going wrong here? What if they would do it but a bit reluctantly if someone was with them? What would this mean?

In this example the person is fusing together an image of harm and an action, harming them. It is a thought action fusion (TAF), but a special type, a moral TAF, in that thinking a thought is almost the same as doing it. If they would do the jigsaw if accompanied, this suggests that responsibility is a big issue; if others are involved responsibility is divided but that responsibility is too much (inflated responsibility) if they are solely involved in actions/consequences. Inflated responsibility is one of the treatment targets in OCD.

3. What if they wouldn't do the jigsaw if it showed some thoughts/images that go over and over in their mind that they are embarrassed or ashamed or disgusted about?

This is a further example of TAF. Just as in a restaurant a person has to consider all the options on the menu in order to choose what is 'good', so too it is impossible to choose a moral good without also considering the moral bad. Further, it is not what is being considered (the scrutinising of the menu) that itself leads to actions, but the planning that leads to action, e.g. after scrutinising the menu asking for a vegetarian menu. That is, morality is about planning and actions rather than intrusive thoughts/images.

4. What if they wouldn't do the jigsaw because its very old, a bit dirty? Or because someone horrible had done this jigsaw? What if they would do it but with gloves?

In this example there is a fear of contamination, but it is a form of magical thinking, imagining that just because someone horrible had done the jigsaw, the person could be contaminated by them – the thought and object have become fused (thought object fusion; TOF) and they need to take steps to prevent the harm by using gloves.

5. What if they have got to order all the pieces in a perfect straight line or a proper circle before starting? What if this order is broken?

The above example suggests a perfectionism at work, everything has to be 'just so' in order to proceed. This perfectionism is a very inefficient way of working; most things can be done to a 'good enough' standard, reserving 'perfectionism' for that which really requires it.

6. What if they keep hoarding such jigsaws in case they want to do them?

Just about anything could come in handy at some time. It seems likely that an intolerance of uncertainty underlies hoarding, wanting to be certain that everything is available. The contradiction is that in amassing so much material, that which is likely to be wanted is 'unavailable'. Hoarders usually have both a negative belief about their hoarding, e.g. everything is just a mess' and a positive belief, 'at least I won't be without', together with an implicit assumption that to be without is catastrophic.

7.   What if they put pieces together that don't belong?

In OCD sufferers are putting together pieces that do not belong together (Figure 4), vertically from the centre, thought action fusion (TAF), left downward diagonal, thought object fusion (TOF), right downward diagonal, thought event fusion (TEF). If these fusions are used habitually OCD may develop.

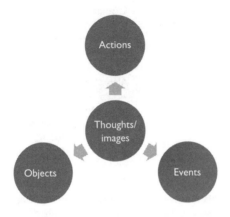

Figure 4 Problem fusions.

8.   What stops you completing the jigsaw? Can you identify any fusion?
9.   How would you persuade others to complete the jigsaw?
10. If your way is right, why wouldn't you persuade others to do it your way?

4. Developing a different story about your mental life

If you tell yourself a horror story about your intrusions (thoughts/images), e.g. 'they mean I am mad/bad/wicked', you will feel distressed, just as a young child would be distressed and have trouble sleeping if read a horror story before bed. With a child one puts their fears, e.g. about wolves, into a context, how many wolves did they count today?, how many wolves did their older brother/sister count today? etc., so too the fears of the OCD sufferer have to be placed in context. One way of doing this is to use the beat (b) OCD form (Table 1).

In the example given in Table 1, the OCD sufferer has identified her magical thinking about the need to do things three times and, by a consideration of how others act in the same situation, has identified her exaggerated sense of responsibility. Instead of obsessive rumination (column four of Table 1) about these concerns she has decided to test out (a behavioural experiment) the need for the magical behaviour and

Table 1 **bOCD**

*bOCD is a mnemonic for remembering how to shrink disturbing thoughts about images/ thoughts to size. In the first column, detail the thought/images that may have besieged you today and indicate, if you can, what may have triggered them. The **O** of OCD here stands for observe your thoughts about your thoughts/images and record these in the second column. The **C** of OCD here stands for consider alternative thoughts to your thoughts about your images/ thoughts and, if you can, record these in the third column. The **D** of OCD here stands for daring to begin to act as if the thoughts in the third column are true.*

I am **besieged** by these images/ thoughts	**Observe** your thinking about these, images/ thoughts:	**Consider** alternative thoughts, ones that others may have about these *same* images/ thoughts. Also **Consider** why you would not try to persuade others of the truth of your thoughts about the besieging army of images/ thoughts:	**Dare** to act, however briefly, as if the thoughts in column 3 (C) are true, and see what happens. Record the 'dare' and the consequences.
I don't remember switching the cooker off, the house could burn down, the kiddies next door could die in the fire.	This means there is danger, I should go home and check.	I'll probably be OK, even if I can't remember having switched the cooker off, it is unlikely to end in catastrophe. Just because I have thoughts about it doesn't mean it's going to happen – thought event fusion. There would be no point in trying to persuade my boss that I needed to go home from work just because I couldn't remember having switched the cooker off, he would look at me as if I was daft. I wouldn't try to persuade my mum to stop whatever she is doing and go home if she couldn't remember having switched the fire off, why is it OK for her and not me?	This time I will dare myself not to go home but I will ring my mum to go around and check, at least it is a start. Rang my mum who said 'do you think I've got nothing better to do', but she went round and later rang me to say everything was OK. I felt down that I had obviously inconvenienced her.

continues

Table 1 (continued)

Harm is going to come to my Gran, she is getting on, she had a fall at home last week, tripped on a footstool.	I must ring her throughout the day, if I just do things three times, switch the kettle on and off three times before making a drink, trace my eye around a picture exactly three times – if I'm interrupted I will have to start again.	I might make her trip even more because she keeps having to rush to the phone when I ring. I wouldn't try to persuade my mother to ring through the day because she would tell me she visits once a day and that's enough, she told Gran off for leaving the footstool around as she doesn't use it. Grandad used it before he died. I exaggerate my responsibility for what happens to Gran, she has to do her bit, Mum and sister do their bit and I'll do my bit.	Just ring Gran morning and evening. Dare to have a day off from doing things three times and see does anything terrible happen to Gran the next day.

adjust her behaviour to be more in line with an objective view of how much responsibility she does bear. 'Dares' are an experiment, testing out whether there really will be any harm from not engaging in the compulsive behaviour and whether the mind does really operate in the way the person with OCD believes, e.g. whether thinking harm is going to come to Gran makes harm happen to her. The letters of Dare can be thought of as standing for Don't Avoid a Realistic Experiment. If your thoughts about your thoughts/ images really bother you, test out that they would really stand up in 'Court' before you accept them.

The bOCD is for use whenever you feel plagued by the OCD. A common trigger for an intense wave of OCD is a deterioration in mood. For example, an OCD sufferer away on holiday might be little troubled that clothes were not washed instantly, but when they return home there is again a felt urgency to immediately wash clothes. It is therefore useful for OCD sufferers to tackle not only the army of besieging thought/images using bOCD but also more generally any dips in mood.

5. Managing your MOOD

To help you manage your moods pass them through the MOOD chart (Table 2). The first letter of MOOD, 'M', stands for monitor your mood, the second letter, 'O', stands for observe your thinking, what it sounds as if you have said to yourself, the third letter, 'O', is for objective thinking, more realistic second thoughts, and the final letter, 'D', is for deciding what to do and doing it.

Table 2 MOOD chart

Monitor mood	Observe thinking	Objective thinking	Decide what to do and do It
1. Mood dipped arriving back home from holiday.	I'll have to get the washing done, here I go again getting obsessed about the washing.	Everyone has to do washing when they come home from holiday, I used to do it even before my OCD.	Get on and do the washing, if I start to get plagued by it I will use the bOCD form.
2. Mood dipped hearing that I have got to reapply for my own job.	I am going to be unsuccessful with the time I have had off for the OCD.	The time off won't help, but they do know I am very conscientious, maybe too much of a perfectionist for my own good. Colleagues are in the same boat.	I will arrange some practice role plays with my boss.

6. Daring to postpone 'safety' behaviour

With OCD, sufferers feel out of control. But postponing a safety behaviour, like checking you have really locked the car on the drive, for just a minute, can give a sense of control. Gradually the time for which you postpone things can be gradually increased. The period for which you postpone the safety behaviour constitutes a mini-experiment in which you test out the belief that something terrible will happen if the behaviour is not performed. It is a useful short-term goal to become able to postpone the 'safety' behaviour for 15 minutes; this is a reasonable testing period for the observed thinking, rather like a test-drive with a possible new car. Long-term the goal would be to give up the 'safety' behaviour and return to your way of operating before the OCD. Keep a daily record of the duration of your postponements.

Sometimes it is not so much that the OCD sufferer engages in an observable behaviour, such as checking the car is locked, but they agonise about some image or thought, e.g. do they really love their partner? In such instances it is important not to suppress the thought, to do so has a rebound effect, but to cultivate a detached mindfulness about the thought. The first step in detached mindfulness is that thoughts/images/questions are just that, in and of themselves; they do not have a significance but a significance can be accorded to them, if and when a person decides to do so. They are best treated as the type of background noise one hears whilst in conversation with a person in a room full of people chattering. An odd background phrase or word might briefly capture your attention but you focus on the person you are talking to, whilst making a mental note to address the overheard snippet at another time, perhaps when you meet the other person. The 'special time' is the period when you address the concern using bOCD. Often the concern has evaporated by the time you have the opportunity to use bOCD; if it hasn't it is addressed systematically using the form.

7. Managing relationships

If an OCD sufferer is stressed by a relationship or conflict they are more likely to engage in OCD behaviour, so that effective management of rela-tionships can reduce OCD symptoms. One way of doing this is by checking that you are observing the communication guidelines in Table 3.

If you are very stressed out by some situation either at home or work you are more likely to engage in obsessive behaviours and/or thoughts. In order to de-stress you might have to communicate effectively with those around you. One way of ensuring this is to keep to the guidelines ('Highway Code') in Table 3. For example, you might be stressed out in work and you could just go and complain to the boss. But even though you may be correct in

Table 3 Communication guidelines

1. In stating a problem, always begin with something positive
2. Be specific
3. Express your feelings
4. Admit to your role in the problem
5. Be brief when defining problems
6. Discuss only one problem at a time
7. Summarise what the other person has said and check with them that you have correctly understood them before making your reply
8. Don't jump to conclusions, avoid mind-reading, talk only about what you can see
9. Be neutral rather than negative
10. Focus on solutions
11. Behavioural change should include give and take and compromise. Any changes agreed should be very specific

your complaint your boss might not listen because it is 'just a complaint'. However, if you say something positive first (first rule of the 'Highway Code'), such as 'I appreciate you're really busy at the moment but if we could make a time to discuss . . .' then the complaint is more likely to be taken seriously. If the complaint is expressed in a vague way, e.g. 'I just can't stand this job' or 'I don't like your attitude', it makes it difficult for the recipient of the complaint to deal with. However, if it is specific (second rule in Table 3), e.g. 'I don't like it that for the last week of every month I have to do two jobs instead of one', the other person has a chance of doing something about it. The complaint has to be expressed with feeling (rule 3 in Table 3) otherwise the other person will think it doesn't matter to you, but if expressed with too much emotion the other person may not look at the detail of your complaint, withdraw and dismiss you as having a personality problem. If you can admit to your role in the problem, e.g. 'I know I do stress myself out a bit by being a perfectionist but two jobs instead of one for a week every month is a bit much', it encourages the other person to listen, particularly if you have been very brief in stating what bothers you (rule 5 in Table 3). But people are often not brief, they break rule 6 by bringing up another problem, e.g. 'oh by the way I've got to have the school holidays off this year', and the conversation may then go off in a different direction with the original problem unresolved. Sometimes people don't check out what the other person is trying to say before going on the offensive; in this example an employer might respond with 'hmm it is going to be difficult to get extra help on a Friday because lots of people like to make a long weekend of it', to which the response might be 'so you don't care if I am in pieces at the end of the month'. Here the employee is breaking rule 8, jumping to conclusions/mindreading instead of seeking to clarify what her boss is saying 'are you saying that the last week in the month, there could be help Monday–Thursday but Friday would be difficult?' and the tone of the latter is neutral rather than negative (rule 9,

Table 3). Finally the communications should usually involve a compromise so that both parties feel they won (rule 11, Table 3). If one person obviously loses they are subsequently likely to take revenge in some way. The discussions should be solution focused (rule 10, Table 3) rather than blaming and involve give and take, e.g. 'I will do extra work the last week in the month, so that the accounts can be completed for the end of the month, if I get some help Monday to Thursday'.

The same communication guidelines can be used by OCD sufferers with family members/friends as they gradually try to engage in a more normal life. For example, an OCD sufferer with a fear of contamination might for the first time in a long time agree to go out for a meal with relatives but only if they agree in advance that they will not 'fuss' if the OCD sufferer just has bottled water.

8. The thought police – revision

It is as if the OCD sufferer employs a thought/image policeman with the following job description:

1. You will be responsible for law and order in the mind. Thought/image policemen are expected to operate with a belief that any misdemeanour must be severely punished, otherwise law and order will break down.
2. You must be alert for any signs of danger, investigate any signs, only stop when you are certain there is no danger.
3. If something bad happens the person employing you should be regarded as the biggest suspect no matter what they are capable of.
4. You must make it known to your employer that any misdemeanours, i.e. thoughts/images that come to mind that are the opposite of what they value or believe in, are 'hanging' offences.
5. You should keep your employer informed that if something could go wrong it most likely will go wrong and that therefore actions necessary to prevent catastrophe are to be given pride of place
6. A responsible thought/image policeman makes his employer aware that thoughts/images are indicative of what will happen in the real world so his task is to advise on the zapping of certain thoughts/images.
7. The thought/image policeman is responsible for summoning backup, the decontamination unit, when thoughts/images are disgusting or are about someone/something that is digusting.

How is your thought/image policeman operating? Which of 1–7, above is he particularly good at? How costly is it for you when you regard this thought/image policeman as credible? If you give this thought/image policeman a 15-minute coffee break does anything terrible happen? If you are unsure try it and see. What were the results? What about reducing costs by making him work part-time, perhaps a day on duty, then a day off, and see if you are any worse off on the days he is not on duty? What about seeing him as having no credibility and making him redundant? What about telling him to take a hike?

Generalised Anxiety Disorder Survival Manual

'If I am not worrying about one thing, I am worrying about another.'
'I even worry about not worrying.'
'I also worry about worrying.'
'I imagine the worst.'

If the above sounds familiar you may have always been a worrier, but it has possibly become worse, 'uncontrollable', after some disappointments. Persisting uncontrollable worry lies at the heart of generalised anxiety disorder (GAD). More than three out of five of those undergoing cognitive behaviour therapy for GAD fully recover by the end of treatment.

Uncontrollable worry is like a fire, there are lots of different materials you can put on it to keep it going, and different people with GAD tend to put on different combinations of materials. In Figure 1, the fire of uncontrollable worry is started by a belief that worry is uncontrollable and usually also by a belief that worry is dangerous:

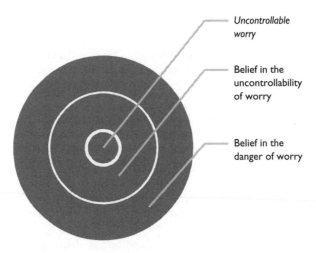

Figure 1 Starting the fire of uncontrollable worry.

Two questions for you:

1. How much do you believe that your worrying is uncontrollable? A 0 would be not believing it at all, a 100% would be totally believing it and 50% 'so so' . . . . . .
2. How much do you believe that your worrying is dangerous? A 0 would be not believing it at all, a 100% would be totally believing it and 50% . . . . . .

Once the fire is started you can keep it going by adding 'coals' (Figure 2).

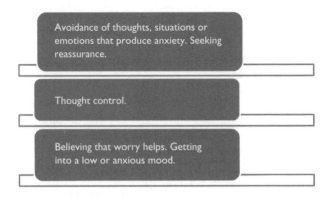

Figure 2 Keeping the fire of anxiety burning.

How do you think that you keep your anxiety going?

1. Worry is controllable

It may often feel like worry is uncontrollable but think what happens to your worrying when the phone goes; at least for the duration of the call you have let go of the worry. In the same way if you are vigorously exercising you find that you are not worrying.

Worries are a bit like a child pestering you, if you say 'go away' within minutes they are back. But if you say that you will attend to the child/worry at a particular time, there is a chance that they will leave you alone until the special time. It is a matter of putting worries in boxes to be sorted out at particular times, leaving you freer to get on with life. However, just like children, worries can have 'temper tantrums' when you tell them there is a time and a place for their concern to be addressed. The best way of handling child tantrums is a technique called planned ignoring where you refuse to make eye contact or get involved in any discussion with the child until they have calmed down. As a parent begins to implement this strategy the child's tantrums often get worse before they get more manageable, because the child feels they are losing control of the adult. So too as you practise planned ignoring of worries, initially they can feel even more pressing but calmly telling yourself that you will sort the content out properly at a special worry time, a 15–30 minute period at a particular time, you can gradually develop a sense that worry is controllable. Often what you were worrying about earlier has evaporated by the time your worry time comes around. For example, you may have woken in the night worrying about a particular concern and planned to note it and ignore it until your scheduled worry time at say 6.30 p.m. but by the time it comes around the issue has evaporated, it is no longer a source of concern. In this way you can learn that many worries just take care of themselves. The worry time strategy is a way of changing your beliefs about worry (what are called metacognitions) and these include the belief that worry is uncontrollable and that all worries deserve immediate attention. If a worry is still an issue at the worry time, writing about it for a couple of minutes or dictating it into a recorder, can help you come up with another way of looking at the particular concern. Using a worry time means that a continuing issue has been thought through about as far as you can take it. Outside the worry time you are not 'thinking' about the issue but 'agonising' about it, rather like 'picking at a sore'. The idea is not to 'pick at sores' but to sort them out as best you can at the worry time. For many GAD sufferers the 'inflammation' that comes from the 'picking' at the 'sore' is worse than the 'sore' itself.

2. Worry is not dangerous

Most sufferers from GAD believe that their worrying is dangerous. You might fear that your worry might mean that you will lose control or go insane. Perhaps you fear that your worrying will cause a heart attack or stroke. You can test out these beliefs in lots of different ways. One way is to take your pulse, then take your pulse again when you dare yourself to deliberately try and worry about something. You will find that you cannot even increase your pulse rate when you worry. If you fear that your worry might drive you insane, have a half hour when you dare yourself to worry as much as possible and then the next half hour just go about your business in your normal way. At the end of the hour ask yourself did you or others see any more signs of insanity in the first half hour as in the second half hour? Testing out your metacognitions (beliefs about worry) in this way is a matter of doing dares. The word 'dare', also stands for Don't Avoid a Realistic Experiment, so if you feared your worry could bring on a heart attack or a stroke, a realistic experiment might be to compare what symptoms of a heart attack/stroke you showed on a typical day with those you showed on a day when you worried as much as possible.

3. Giving up reassurance seeking and blocking of thoughts

Worry is the 'Beast' in the adult pantomime of 'Beauty and the Beast', you may worry that you are at the mercy of the 'Beast' and it is dangerous. Others can tell you that the 'Beast' is not dangerous or you can seek reassurance that there is no danger but in the end you have to tell yourself there is no danger by changing your metacognitive belief about 'worry' to, for example, 'it's just an actor wearing a frightening mask'. The temptation is to run away from the 'Beast' but it is part of the pantomime of life and you just exhaust yourself, it's like trying to run away from your shadow.

If you try to block a thought it becomes more powerful. Try just now not to think of a 'black polar bear'; what happened . . .? You find you can't stop thinking of black polar bears!

4. Worry doesn't work

GAD sufferers often worry because they believe that this will stop bad things happening or they will be more prepared. If you believe there are advantages in worrying, the worry is likely to continue even though you know there are also disadvantages to worry such as interfering with your sleep or making you irritable. But does worrying really stop bad things happening? This week worry about not winning the National Lottery on Saturday, then on Saturday night when the winning numbers are announced, see if all your worry stopped you missing out on the jackpot.

There is a comfort in worrying in that you feel you can prevent bad things happening but it is 'magical thinking', like a child not stepping on the cracks on the pavement on the way to school so that the teacher does not tell them off. The 'magical thinking' makes the child feel in control. It may be that on one particular day the teacher does not tell the child off, perhaps because they are distracted with naughtier children, and the child might conclude not stepping on the cracks works. In a similar way, if a catastrophe does not occur the GAD sufferer might think that their worrying works.

5. Stop yourself 'making mountains out of molehills

In deciding to postpone almost all your worries to the worry time, you are working on a new metacognitive belief that 'almost all worries turn out to be molehills'. Further, even if the worry is a mountain, e.g. having a very serious illness, you are operating on another new metacognitive belief: 'why should I spend time agonising about it, better live each day as best I can and make plans in the worry time'.

In your worry time you can put worries into perspective by assessing whether they are a molehill or a mountain. A 'molehill' is something trivial, such as it may be raining on your day's holiday, and a 'mountain' something like the death of a person you were very close to. In Figure 3 there is a 'road' from 'mountain to molehill'.

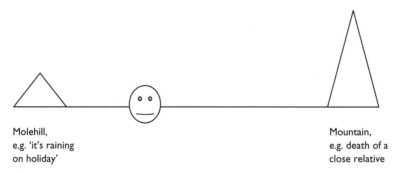

Molehill,
e.g. 'it's raining
on holiday'

Mountain,
e.g. death of a
close relative

Figure 3 The road from mountain to molehill.

If, for example, you were concerned that you might not find the right present for someone, looking at Figure 3 you might think it is not a catastrophe like a death, but a bit more serious than finding it raining on holiday, and locate it nearer the molehill, with an expression of slight concern.

6. Have realistic expectations, learn from mistakes

Both the 'worry time' and the 'mountain to molehill road' are part of a new gameplan for dealing with the cut and thrust of everyday life. They sound very easy, but usually they take a lot of practice, as old habits die hard. Some days you will be much better at applying them than others but gradually you can increase how often you apply them. Nevertheless it does tend to be two steps forward and one back. It is necessary to be very patient with yourself whilst you learn these new skills; beating yourself up at each slip makes it worse. If there is a slip in the application of these strategies, do a 'slow motion action replay' of how this came about so you can learn from it. For example, it may be that one morning you had a lie-in and you started thinking of all you had to do so that by the time you got up you were in the wrong frame of mind to apply either of the above strategies. In reviewing this 'off day' you might decide to look at the 'road from mountain to molehill' each time you sit down or have a drink and have an alarm clock go off at the worry time.

7. Accept hassles as inevitable, problem solve them as best you can

The frame of mind that you bring to bear on life's hassles has a big effect on how you handle them. If you think that because there are hassles in your life either you or others must be to blame then this distracts you from getting on and sorting out the hassle. Technically it means that you are not problem orientated or more exactly are problem disorientated, like a spinning top in a sea of problems! However you organise life there will be hassles. To sort out a hassle go through the steps show in Figure 4.

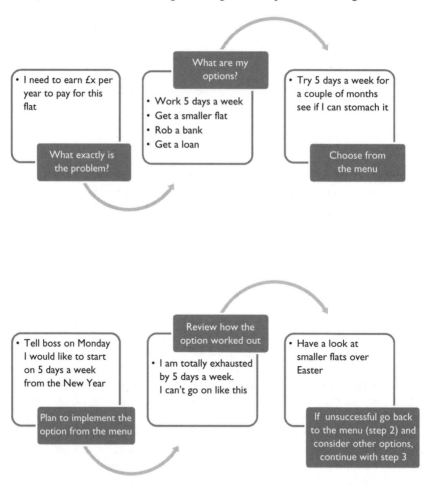

Figure 4 The steps of problem solving.

For clients with GAD the most difficult part of problem solving is not actually the steps shown in Figure 4, but the step before in which they suffer from problem disorientation, in which, continuing the example above, the person might spin around thinking 'I'm stupid I should know what I want to do by this stage in my life, I've moved house so many times it's ridiculous, if I hadn't given money to "y" I wouldn't be in this position but I know they needed it'. The first task is to stop spinning, then to focus on something very specific. Problem solving is like taking a photograph, the subject has to be in sharp focus for a decent picture. At the top left of Figure 4 problem solving involves very precisely defining what the problem is. Many problems are not solved because they are 'too fuzzy'; for example, 'I don't know how I am going to stay here' as opposed to 'I need to earn £x to stay in this flat'. Once the problem is tightly defined, solutions begin almost to suggest themselves.

There can be no certainty that a chosen solution will work out because you haven't got a crystal ball, but many people with GAD insist on waiting until they feel certain before taking action. As a consequence they go round in circles revisiting the same arguments and become frustrated with themselves. Tolerating some uncertainty in choosing from the menu of options is critical to moving on with the problem solving process. It is necessarily unknown whether the chosen option will work out and so it is important not to blame yourself if it does not work out. If the chosen solution does not work out return to the menu, choose and try something else until successful.

Problem solving may be sabotaged by 'a problem disorientator', called TIC, which stands for task interfering cognitions (cognitions are thoughts or images), e.g. 'You know you are not up to this, who are you trying to kid, you know you will cock it up again'. The TICs run in parallel alongside TOCs, task orientated cognitions, which are the problem solving thoughts such as: What exactly is the problem here? What are my options here? (Figure 4). The secret is to calmly keep switching from TIC to TOC, i.e. TIC/TOC. If you continue to refuse to take the TICs seriously rather like a toddler having tantrums the TICS lose their power.

8. Use a turnstile rather than have an open door

From time to time everyone feels overwhelmed, you have answered the phone, there's a knock at the front door and you are already running late. Dealing with everything at the same time is stressful. But sufferers from GAD have an almost constant sense of being overwhelmed, feeling that the demands on them exceed their resources. The stress can be reduced by making a list of all that needs to be done, then putting the items on the list in order of importance. The tasks are then placed outside a turnstile and the most important item is let through first. Do just a 'good enough' job on this task then have a break, say a cup of tea, to celebrate its completion. Then let the next task through, complete this task, have a break, then the next and continue in this way. Do not have an open door for tasks, doing a number at the same time. If you have an open door when you are doing one task you will be thinking you should be doing another (task interfering cognition), and at the end of the day you may feel that you have accomplished nothing with a lot of tasks half done. It may be that a real emergency (something for which there would be serious consequences if you didn't attend to it immediately) crops up and you have to put what you are doing back outside the turnstile to focus on the emergency, but this should be the exception and you would still be maintaining doing one thing at a time.

Perfectionism, an excessive sense of responsibility and automatically assuming that because you feel guilty you are guilty can all sabotage completing tasks. For most tasks others simply expect a 'good enough' not a perfect performance. It is important to distinguish between the usually very few tasks that need to be done perfectly and the many where 'good enough' will suffice. It can suit others very well to make you take on total responsibility for tasks, when in fact they and probably others are partly responsible. Sometimes the responsibility of others is indirect in that they do not give you the tools to do the job, e.g. one person left to do the work of three colleagues. As a consequence it is likely that some of the recipients of your work will be unhappy, e.g. keeping one of them waiting, and this might lead to guilt feelings on your part. But if you take all guilt feelings as evidence of personal failure then you will be very stressed. It is important therefore not to take on board responsibility for the queue of tasks but just for working your way through it systematically.

9. Make realistic predictions, don't get hooked by the worst case scenario

Sufferers from GAD expect the worst and therefore take excessive precautions, e.g. not letting their young children climb. If a situation is ambiguous, e.g. being told that their boss wants to see them, they will assume the worst, e.g. that they are going to be reprimanded. Even when it becomes apparent that what was most feared is not going to happen, it brings only momentary relief as they switch their attention to another worry. It is as if the GAD sufferer is hooked by worst case scenarios. Sometimes it is not just thinking that something bad will happen but there is an accompanying graphic image of what they fear, e.g. attending casualty with their young child.

Worst case scenarios are probably best regarded as being like fire drills at your place of work, worth doing very occasionally so that you have a gameplan for that eventuality. But such drills/scenarios are disruptive if done on a regular basis. It is therefore generally more useful to swap the horror video for a reality video, the statistically most likely sequence of events – that which you would bet money on happening.

10. Practise tolerating uncertainty and anxiety

Earlier it was mentioned that problem solving always means trying out some solutions that you cannot be certain will work and as such there is a need to tolerate some uncertainty whilst you see how the chosen solution works out. Tolerating uncertainty is often particularly difficult for GAD sufferers because of a dislike of any anxiety symptoms (anxiety sensitivity), which are seen as a threat and perhaps also as an abnormality. The goal of GAD sufferers is often to create a mill pond and they carefully monitor whether this is being achieved; if this goal state is not reached they become alarmed. A more reasonable goal state is a river, with constant waves, and exceptionally these waves are either very high or the river is like a mill pond. Thus though it is possible to become very relaxed after exercise or a relaxation exercise (these involve tensing and relaxing each muscle group in turn), to expect such a state routinely in the day is unrealistic. Nevertheless exercise, relaxation exercise and meditation are very good ways of changing gear, and that which seemed something of a mountain (see Figure 3) beforehand is often shifted in the molehill direction. Tolerating the symptoms of anxiety can be likened to tolerating the feelings of discomfort that arise during exercise. Further, the anxiety discomfort is no more significant than the physical discomfort in exercise.

11. Don't avoid thoughts, greet each thought!

GAD sufferers often find some thoughts alarming and try to distract themselves from them, but the more you try to distract yourself from a thought the more prominent it becomes. Right now don't think of a green polar bear . . . you are probably finding that you can't help but think of them. This is called the rebound effect: the more you push away a thought or image, the more it springs back. Stay with alarming thoughts long enough to sort them out, don't just see them as very negative and run. What do you fear might happen if you stayed a little longer with your disturbing thoughts, greeting such thoughts? Just jot down what you fear:

. . . .

. . . .

. . . .

Common answers are 'the pain would be unbearable', 'I would just get so low/angry'. Don't avoid experiencing the intense emotion. If you let yourself experience and name the emotion there are special ways of moving on using the MOOD chart, (Table 1), but if you block the emotion it goes underground and has a way of gnawing away at you.

To help you manage shifts in mood pass them through the MOOD chart. The first letter of MOOD, 'M', stands for monitor your mood; the second letter, 'O', stands for observe your thinking, what it sounds as if you have said to yourself; the third letter, 'O', is for objective thinking, more realistic second thoughts; and the final letter, 'D', is for deciding what to do and doing it.

Table 1 MOOD chart

Monitor mood	Observe thinking	Objective thinking	Decide what to do and do it
1. Mood dipped noticing the two children playing.	Anthea's head seems slightly smaller than her sister's. If I hadn't had a complicated delivery she wouldn't have mild learning difficulties.	I'd have given my left arm not to have had a complicated delivery, I can't blame myself. Anthea is perfectly happy.	Join in the game with my daughters.
2. Mood dipped thinking of Anthea's future.	How is she going to manage when she is older and I am not around?	I've probably got another fifty years and with the family there is always going to be someone there for her.	Must give a ring about her attending the Monday night club/disco.

In the second example on the MOOD chart Anthea's mum's first thoughts (first 'O') were of a horror video of her daughter's future, the second thoughts (second 'O') are a more objective reality video. It is important that the horror video is not replaced by a fantasy, e.g. 'I am sure everything will be all right', there is no advantage in positive thinking simply in describing matters as they are really likely to be. This does not mean that Anthea's mum might not have moments when she is upset by an image of her daughter much older and alone, but they are fleeting moments from which she can move on.

To help change 'observed thinking'(first thoughts) into 'objective thinking'(second thoughts) you can use the questions in Figure 5.

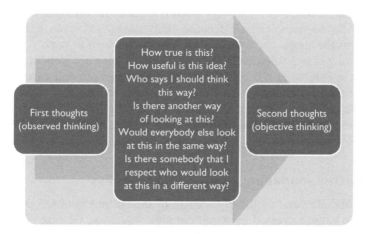

Figure 5 From first thoughts to second thoughts.

In practice you may often not have the opportunity to use the MOOD chart until your worry time.

12. Dare to live

Many GAD sufferers are committed to avoiding any risk but they are in a quandary because they are also committed to other goals such as encouraging their children to be independent. Living is impossible without taking calculated risks. Thus a parent might allow their 14-year-old and a friend to go to the local town centre but most would probably not allow a 10-year-old to do so. Just as a child's confidence is built up by the doing of gradual dares, so too adults are likely to get a sense of achievement and pleasure from calculated risk taking, Total avoidance of risk is likely to result in a sense of imprisonment. There is a need to dare to live.

Most GAD sufferers expect the worst but the actual experience is usually not as bad. If you think of a possible forthcoming challenge, e.g. meeting up with old school friends, make a note of how bad you think it will be on a scale 0–10, where a 10 is absolutely awful and 0 is wonderful. Then if you dare to meet up with them, score what the actual experience was like on the same scale 0–10. In anticipation you are probably quite anxious, your score might well be a 7/10 but usually the actual experience is better, say 4/10. If you keep scoring expectations and experiences you will probably find there is a gap, the situations are much worse in imagination than in the real world. Once you know that you have an expectation experience gap, you can stand back from yourself and almost laugh at yourself when you are getting very anxious.

Picking at worries has become a habit for GAD sufferers, with often a long chain of 'what ifs . . .?', e.g. 'what if I can't find the right present . . . what if he/she doesn't think I could be bothered . . . what if I am late getting to the shops . . . what if I can't find anywhere to park . . . what if what I want is too expensive?' The GAD sufferer may not stop long enough to answer one 'what if?' before rushing on to the next and experiences a sense of their mind racing away. The chain can be cut short by answering each 'what if?' as it arises; if there is no obvious answer then it can be postponed to be addressed systematically in the worry half hour. Don't 'pick' at your worries.

13. Better managing sleep and irritability

Sleep difficulties and irritability are two of the symptoms of GAD. Lack of sleep can cause increased irritability in almost anyone. Getting off to sleep can be a particular difficulty for GAD sufferers, who often complain that at this time their mind races from one worry to another. The sleep difficulties are increased further if you become irritated that you are not yet asleep; perhaps you begin thinking 'if I don't get to sleep soon I'll be exhausted tomorrow'. The more irritated you become, the more difficulty you have in catching sleep. Often sufferers try and cope by going to bed steadily later, some to such an extent that they end up sleeping more in the day than at night.

Sleep difficulties can be tackled by having a fixed routine involving going to bed at the same time whether tired or not. If worries intrude they can be dealt with using the worry time strategy (Section 1), but if you are not asleep within 20–30 minutes calmly get up, focusing attention elsewhere, for example by reading or having a warm milky drink, and only go back to bed when you are really tired. Again if not asleep within 30 minutes calmly get up and switch attention. In this way the bed stops becoming associated with a battle zone in which you fight to get to sleep. Sleep tends to happen when you are not trying.

Many GAD sufferers find that they are 'snappy' and this can lead to strained relationships. Close relationships can be eased by asking others to read this self-help manual to 'put them in the picture' and by practising a traffic light routine for anger. Imagine a set of traffic lights on red as soon as you notice the first signs of irritability. Then when the lights go to amber ask yourself is what has just happened really the end of the world? Did they really do it deliberately to wind me up? Then when the lights go to green go into another room to calm down. To begin with, many people go through the lights on red and it may take a few weeks of practice to learn to obey them. It may be that if you trust your partner or family member enough you can ask them to remind you to use the traffic lights when you are getting irate.

The Personal Significance Scale (PSS)

Name: _____ Date: _____

Please read the following statements carefully and circle the number that best corresponds to the extent to which you agree with each statement regarding your intrusive thoughts and images.

Specific thoughts, images: _____

_____

_____

Please use the following scale:

0 Not at all	1	2	3	4 Somewhat	5	6	7	8 Totally/ Definitely

1. Are these thoughts really personally significant for you?	0 1 2 3 4 5 6 7 8
2. Do these thoughts reveal something important about you?	0 1 2 3 4 5 6 7 8
3. Are these thoughts a sign that you are original?	0 1 2 3 4 5 6 7 8
4. Do these thoughts mean that you might lose control and do something awful?	0 1 2 3 4 5 6 7 8
5. Do these thoughts mean that you are an imaginative person?	0 1 2 3 4 5 6 7 8
6. Do these thoughts mean that you might go crazy someday?	0 1 2 3 4 5 6 7 8

7. Is it important for you to keep these thoughts secret from most or all the people you know?	0	1	2	3	4	5	6	7	8
8. Do these thoughts mean that you are a sensitive person?	0	1	2	3	4	5	6	7	8
9. Do these thoughts mean that you are a dangerous person?	0	1	2	3	4	5	6	7	8
10. Do these thoughts mean that you are untrustworthy?	0	1	2	3	4	5	6	7	8
11. Would other people condemn you if they knew about your thoughts?	0	1	2	3	4	5	6	7	8
12. Do these thoughts mean that you are really a hypocrite?	0	1	2	3	4	5	6	7	8
13. Do these thoughts mean that you have an artistic talent?	0	1	2	3	4	5	6	7	8
14. Would other people think you are crazy or mentally unstable if they knew about your thoughts?	0	1	2	3	4	5	6	7	8
15. Do these thoughts mean that one day you may actually carry out some actions related to the thoughts?	0	1	2	3	4	5	6	7	8
16. Do these thoughts mean that you enjoy the company of other people?	0	1	2	3	4	5	6	7	8
17. Do these thoughts mean that you are a bad, wicked person?	0	1	2	3	4	5	6	7	8
18. Do you feel responsible for these thoughts?	0	1	2	3	4	5	6	7	8
19. Is it important for you cancel out or block the thoughts?	0	1	2	3	4	5	6	7	8
20. Would other people think you are a bad, wicked person if they knew your thoughts?	0	1	2	3	4	5	6	7	8
21. Do you think that you should avoid certain people or places because of these thoughts?	0	1	2	3	4	5	6	7	8

22. Do these thoughts mean that you are weird?	0	1	2	3	4	5	6	7	8
23. Should you fight against and resist these thoughts?	0	1	2	3	4	5	6	7	8

24. Do these thoughts have any other significance for you? Details:

_____

_____

25. What caused your thoughts to occur when they started?

_____

_____

26. Why do these thoughts keep coming back?

_____

_____

Scoring of PSS

Items 3, 5, 8, 13 and 16 are buffer items and are not included in the scoring of the PSS. Thus for scoring purposes there are 18 items on the instrument and scores can therefore range from 0 to 144. However, Whittal *et al.* (2010) also excluded the first item 'Are these thoughts really personally significant for you?' from their study so that the scale they used comprised 17 items, with scores ranging from 0 to 136. Whittal *et al.* have explained (personal communication) that the focus of their study was clients with pure obsessions and as such clients would necessarily endorse this symptom, consequently it was excluded. In the Whittal *et al.* (2010) study, the mean pre-treatment PSS score was 86.0 (standard deviation 24.0) and the post-treatment mean 46.0.

References

Abramowitz, J.S., Taylor, S. and McKay, D. (2005) Potentials and limitations of cognitive treatments for obsessive-compulsive disorder. *Cognitive Behavior Therapy*, 34, 140–147.

Adult Psychiatric Morbidity in England, 2007: Results of a household survey (2009) Health and Social Care Information Centre, Social Care Statistics.

Alford, B.A. and Beck, A.T. (1997) *The Integrative Power of Cognitive Therapy*. New York: Guilford Press.

American Psychiatric Association (2000) *Diagnostic and Statistical Manual of Mental Disorders (DSM-IV-TR)*. Washington, DC: American Psychiatric Association.

Amies, P.L., Gelder, M.G. and Shaw, P.M. (1983) Social phobia: a comparative clinical study. *British Journal of Psychiatry*, 142, 174–179.

Andrews, G.M., Hobbs, M.J., Borkovec, T.D., *et al.* (2010) Generalized worry disorder: a review of DSM-IV generalised anxiety disorder and options for DSM-V. *Depression and Anxiety*, 27, 137–147.

Arntz, A. (2003) Cognitive therapy versus applied relaxation as a treatment for generalised anxiety disorder. *Behaviour Research and Therapy*, 41, 633–646.

Arroll, B., Goodyear-Smith, F., Kerse, N., Fishman, T. and Gunn, J. (2005) Effect of the addition of a 'help' question to two screening questions on specificity for diagnosis of depression in general practice: diagnostic validity study. *British Medical Journal*, 331, 884–886.

Atkins, D.C., Dimidjian, S., Bedics, J.D. and Christensen, A. (2009) Couple discord in couples during couple therapy and in depressed individuals during depression treatment. *Journal of Consulting and Clinical Psychology*, 77, 1089–1099.

Barlow, D.H. and Cerny, J.A. (1988) Psychological Treatment of Panic. New York: Guilford Press.

Beach, S.R.H. and O'Leary, K.D. (1986) The treatment of depression in the context of marital discord. *Behaviour Therapy*, 17, 43–49.

Beck, A.T. (1987) Cognitive models of depression. *Journal of Cognitive Psychotherapy: An International Quarterly*, 1, 5–37.

Beck, A.T. (2008) The evolution of the cognitive model of depression and its neurobiological correlates. *American Journal of Psychiatry*, 165, 969–977.

Beck, A.T. and Steer, R. (1993) *Manual for the Beck Anxiety Inventory*. San Antonio, TX: Psychological Corporation.

Beck, J.G. and Coffey, S.F. (2005) Group cognitive behavioural treatment of PTSD. Treatment of motor vehicle accident survivors. *Cognitive and Behavioral Practice*, 12, 267–277.

Beck, A.T., Ward, C.H., Mendelson, M., Mock, J.E. and Erbaugh, J.K. (1962) Reliability of psychiatrics diagnoses: a study of consistency of clinical judgements and ratings. *American Journal of Psychiatry*, 119, 351–357.

Beck, A.T., Rush, A.J., Shaw, B.F. and Emery, G. (1979) *Cognitive Therapy of Depression*. New York: Guilford Press.

Beck, J.G., Coffey, S.F., Foy, D.W., Keane, T.M. and Blanchard, E.B. (2009) Group cognitive behaviour therapy for chronic posttraumatic stress disorder: an initial randomized pilot study. *Behavior Therapy*, 40, 82–92.

Blanchard, E.B. and Hickling, E.J. (1997) *After the Crash: Assessment and Treatment of Motor Vehicle Accident Survivors*. Washington DC: American Psychological Association.

Blanco, C., Heimberg, R.G., Schneier, F.R. and Fresco, D.M. (2010) A placebo-controlled trial of phenelzine, cognitive-behavioral group therapy and their combination for social anxiety disorder. *Archives of General Psychiatry*, 67, 286–295.

Bockting, C.L.H., Scheme, A.H., Koeter, M.W.J., Wouters, L.F., Huyser, J., Kamphuis, J.H. and Spinhoven, P. (2005) Preventing relapse/recurrence in recurrent depression with cognitive therapy: a randomized control trial. *Journal of Consulting and Clinical Psychology*, 7, 647–657.

Brewin, C.R., Andrews, B. and Valentine, J.D. (2000) Meta-analysis of risk factors for post-traumatic stress disorder in trauma exposed adults. *Journal of Consulting and Clinical Psychology*, 68: 738–766.

Bright, J.I., Neimeyer, R.A. and Baker, K. (1999) Professional and paraprofessional group treatments for depression: a comparison of cognitive-behavioral and mutual support interventions. *Journal of Consulting and Clinical Psychology*, 67, 491–501.

Brown, G.K., Have, T.T., Henriques, G.R., Xie, S.X., Hollander, J.E. and Beck, A.T. (2005) Cognitive therapy for the prevention of suicide attempts: a randomized control trial. *Journal of the American Medical Association*, 294, 563–570.

Bruce, S.E., Yonkers, K.A., Otto, M.W., Eisen, J.L., Weisberg, R.B., Pagano, M., She, M.T. and Keller, M.B. (2005) Influence of psychiatric comorbidity on recovery in generalised anxiety disorder, social phobia and panic disorder: a 12 year prospective study. *American Journal of Psychiatry*, 162, 1179–1187.

Buckner, J.D., Cromer, K.R., Merrill, K.A., Mallott, M.A., Schmidt, N.B., Lopez, C., Holm-Denoma, J.M. and Joiner, T.E. (2009) Pretreatment intervention increases treatment outcomes for patients with anxiety disorders. *Cognitive Therapy and Research*, 33, 126–137.

Burke, B.L., Arkowitz, H. and Menchola, M. (2003) The efficacy of motivational interviewing: a meta-analysis of controlled trials. *Journal of Consulting and Clinical Psychology*, 71, 843–861.

Burns, D. (1999) *Feeling Good: The New Mood Therapy*. New York: Avon Books

Cabedo, E., Belloch, A., Carrió, C., Larsson, C., Fernández-Alvarez, H. and García, F. (2010) Group versus individual cognitive treatment for obsessive-compulsive disorder: changes in severity at post-treatment and one-year follow-up. *Behavioural and Cognitive Psychotherapy*, 38, 227–232.

Chambless, D.L., Caputo, G.S., Bright, P. and Gallagher, R. (1984) Assessment of fear of fear in agoraphobics, The Bodily Sensation Questionnaire and the Agoraphobic Cognitions Questionnaire. *Journal of Consulting and Clinical Psychology*, 52, 1090–1097.

Champion, L.A. and Power, M.J. (1995) Social and cognitive approaches to depression. Towards a new synthesis. *British Journal of Clinical Psychology*, 34, 485–503.

Clark, D.A. and Beck, A.T. (2010) *Cognitive Therapy of Anxiety Disorders*. New York: Guilford Press.

Clark, D.M. (1986) A cognitive model of panic. *Behaviour Research and Therapy*, 24, 461–470.

Clark, D.M. and Ehlers, A. (2004) Posttraumatic stress disorder: from cognitive theory to therapy in Leahy, R.L. (ed.), *Contemporary Cognitive Therapy: Theory, Research and Practice*. New York: Guilford Press.

Clark, D.M., Ehlers, A., McManus, F., Hackmann, A. and Fennell, M. (2003) Cognitive therapy versus fluoxetine in generalised social phobia: a randomised placebo-controlled trial. *Journal of Consulting and Clinical Psychology*, 71, 1058–1067.

Clark, D.M., Ehlers, A., Hackmann, A., McManus, F., Fennell, M., Grey, N., Waddington, L. and Wild, J. (2006) Cognitive therapy versus exposure and applied relaxation in social phobia: a randomized controlled trial. *Journal of Consulting and Clinical Psychology*, 74, 568–578.

Clark, D.M., Layard, R., Smithies, R., Richards, D.A, Suckling, R. and Wright, B. (2009) Improving access to psychological therapy: initial evaluation of two UK demonstration sites. *Behaviour Research and Therapy*, 47, 910–920.

Connor, K.M., Davidson, J.R.T., Churchill, L.E., Sherwood, A., Weisler, R.H. and Foa, E. (2000) Psychometric properties of the Social Phobia Inventory (SPIN). *British Journal of Psychiatry*, 176, 379–386.

Craske, M.G., Barlow, D.H. and Meadows, E.A. (2000) *Mastery of your Anxiety and Panic: Therapist Guide for Anxiety, Panics and Agoraphobia (MAP-3)*. San Antonio, TX: Graywind/Psychological Corporation.

Craske, M.G., Farchione, T.J., Allen, L.B., Barrios, V., Stoyanava, M. and Rose, R. (2007) Cognitive behavioural therapy for panic disorder and comorbidity: more of the same or less of more? *Behaviour Research and Therapy*, 45, 1095–1109.

Cuming, S. and Rapee, R.M. (2010) Social anxiety and self-protective communication style in close relationships. *Behaviour Research and Therapy*, 48, 87–96.

Department of Transport (2008) *Road Casualties in Great Britain: Main Results: 2006*.

Dugas, M., Ladoucer, R., Eliane, L., Freeston, M.H., Langlois, F., Provencher, M.D. and Boisvert, J. (2003) Group cognitive-behavioral therapy for generalised anxiety disorder: treatment outcome and long-term follow-up. *Journal of Consulting and Clinical Psychology*, 71, 821–825.

Dugas, M.J., Savard, P., Gaudet, A., Turcotte, J., Laugesen, N., Robichaud., M., Francis, K. and Koerner, N. (2007) Can the components of a cognitive model predict the severity of generalised anxiety disorder. *Behaviour Therapy and Research*, 38, 169–178.

Ehlers, A. and Clark, D.M. (2000) A cognitive model of posttraumatic stress disorder. *Behaviour Research and Therapy*, 38, 319–345.

Ehlers, A., Clark, D.M. and Hackman, A. (2003) A randomised controlled trial of cognitive therapy, self-help booklet and repeated assessments as early interventions for PTSD. *Archives of General Psychiatry*, 60, 1024–1032.

Ehlers, A., Bisson, J., Clark, D.M., Creamer, M., Pilling, S., Richards, D., Schurr, P.P., Turner, S. and Yule, W. (2010) Do all psychological treatments really work the same in posttraumatic stress disorder? *Clinical Psychology Review*, 30, 269–276.

Ewing, J.A. (1984) Detecting alcoholism: the CAGE Questionnaire. *JAMA*, 252, 1905–1907.

Feeley, M., DeRubeis, R.J. and Gelfand, L.A. (1999) The temporal relation of adherence and alliance to symptom change in cognitive therapy for depression. *Journal of Consulting and Clinical Psychology*, 67, 578–582.

Fineberg, N.A, O'Doherty, C. and Rajagopal, S. (2003) How common is obsessive compulsive disorder in a dermatology outpatient clinic? *Journal of Clinical Psychiatry*, 64, 152–155.

First, M.B., Spitzer, R.L., Gibbon, M. and Williams, J.B.W. (1997a) *Structured Clinical Interview for DSM IV Axis I Disorders – Clinician Version (SCID-CV)*. Washington, DC: American Psychiatric Press.

First, M.B., Spitzer, R.L., Gibbon, M. and Spitzer, R.L. (1997b) *Structured Clinical Interview for DSM IV Axis II Personality Disorders – (SCID-II)*. Washington, DC: American Psychiatric Press.

Foa, E.B. and Jaycox, L.H. (1999) Cognitive-behavioral theory and treatment of posttraumatic stress disorder. In Spiegel, I.D. (ed.), *Efficacy and Cost-effectiveness of Psychotherapy* (pp. 23–61). Washington, DC: American Psychiatric Association.

Foa, E.B., Ehlers, A., Clark, D.M., Tolin, D.F. and Orsillo, S.M. (1999) The Posttraumatic Cognitions Inventory (PTCI): development and validation. *Psychological Assessment*, 11, 303–314.

Foa, E.B., Huppert, J.D., Leiberg, S., Langner, R., Kichic, R., Hajcak, G. and Salkovskis, P.M. (2002) The Obsessive-Compulsive Inventory: development and validation of a short version. *Psychological Assessment*, 14, 485–496.

Free, M. (2007) *Cognitive Therapy in Groups, Guidelines and Resources for Practice*. New York: John Wiley & Sons.

Gaynes, B.N., DeVaugh-Geiss, J., Weir, S., Gu, H., MacPherson, C., Schulberg, H.C., Culpepper, L. and Rubinow, D.R. (2010) Feasibility and diagnostic validity of the M-3 Checklist: A brief, self-rated screen for depressive, bipolar, anxiety and post-traumatic stress disorders in primary care. *Annals of Family Medicine*, 8, 160–169.

Goodman, W., Price, L., Rasmussen, S. and Mazure, C. (1989) The Yale-Brown Obsessive Compulsive Scale. Development, use and reliability. *Archives of General Psychiatry*, 46, 1006–1011.

Gorman, J.M. and Coplan, J.D. (1996) Comorbidity of depression and panic disorder. *Journal of Clinical Psychiatry*, 57: 34–41.

Hackmann, A., Clark, D.M. and McManus, F. (2000) Recurrent images and early memories in social phobia. *Behaviour Research and Therapy*, 38, 601–610.

Hagen, R., Nordahl, H.M., Kristiansen, L. and Morken, G. (2005) A randomized trial of cognitive therapy vs. waiting list for patients with comorbid psychiatric disorders: The effects of cognitive group therapy after treatment and six and 12 months follow up. *Behavioural and Cognitive Psychotherapy*, 33, 33–44.

Herbert, C. (1996) *Understanding Your Reactions to Trauma: A Booklet for Survivors of Trauma and Their Families*. Witney, Oxon, England: Oxford Stress and Trauma Centre.

Hien, D.A., Jiang, H., Miele, G.M., Cohen, L.R., Brigham, G.S., Capstick, C., Kulaga, A., Robinson, J., Suarez-Morales, L. and Nunes, E.V. (2010) Do treatment improvements in PTSD severity affect substance abuse outcomes? A secondary analysis from a randomized clinical trial in NIDA's clinical trials network. *American Journal of Psychiatry*, 167, 95–101.

Hirshfeld-Becker, D., Micco, J.A., Simoes, N.A. and Henin, A. (2008) High risk studies and developmental antecedents of anxiety disorders. *American Journal of Medical Genetics*, 148, 99–117.

Hooley, J.M., Orley, J. and Teasdale, J.D. (1986) Levels of expressed emotion and relapse in depressed patients. *British Journal of Psychiatry*, 148, 642–647.

Hope, D.A., Heimberg, R.G. and Bruch, M.A. (1995) Dismantling cognitive-behavioral group therapy for social phobia. *Behaviour Research and Therapy*, 33, 637–650.

IAPT (2008) *National Guidelines for Regional Delivery – Improving Access to Psychological Therapies: Implementation Plan: Curriculum for High-intensity Workers*. Department of Health Mental Health Programme.

IAPT (2010a) *Data Handbook v 1.0*. Department of Health Mental Health Programme.

IAPT (2010b) *Data Handbook Appendices v 1.0*. Department of Health Mental Health Programme.

Jack, D.C. (1999) Silencing the self: inner dialogues and outer realities. In Joiner, E.T and Coyne, J.C (eds), *The Interactional Nature of Depression*. Washington DC: American Psychological Association.

Jaurrieta, N., Jiménez-Murcia, S., Alonso, P., Granero, R., Segalas, C., Labad, J. and Menchon, J.M. (2008) Individual versus group cognitive behavioural treatment for obsessive-compulsive disorder: follow up. *Psychiatry and Clinical Neurosciences*, 62, 697–704.

Johnson, J.E., Burlingame, G.M., Olsen, J., Davies, D.R. and Gleave, R.L. (2005) Group climate, cohesion, alliance, and empathy in group psychotherapy: multilevel structural equation models. *Journal of Counseling Psychology*, 52(3), 310–321.

Kelley, L.P., Weathers, F.W., McDevitt-Murphy, M.E., Eakin, D.E. and Flood, A.M. (2009) A comparison of PTSD symptom patterns in three types of civilian trauma. *Journal of Traumatic Stress*, 22, 227–235.

Kessler, R.C., Sonnega, A., Bromet, E., Hughes, M. and Nelson, C.B. (1995) Posttraumatic stress disorder in the National Comorbidity Survey. *Archives of General Psychiatry*, 52, 1048–1060.

Kessler, R.C., Chiu, W.T., Demler, O., Merikangas, K.R. and Walters, E.E. (2005) Prevalence, severity and comorbidity of 12-month DSM IV disorders in the

National Comorbidity Survey Replication. *Archives of General Psychiatry*, 62, 617–627.

Kroenke, K., Spitzer, R.L. and Williams, J.B. (2001) The PHQ-9: validity of a brief depression measure. *Journal of General Internal Medicine*, 16, 606–613.

Kroenke, K., Spitzer, R.L. and Williams, J.B. (2007) Anxiety disorders in primary care: prevalence, impairment, comorbidity and detection. *Annals of Internal Medicine*, 146: 317–325.

Lamb, S.E., Hansen, Z., Lall, R., Castelnuovo, E., Withers, E.J., Nichols, V., Potter, R. and Underwood, M.R. (2010) Group cognitive behavioural treatment for low-back pain in primary care: a randomised controlled trial and cost-effectiveness analysis. *Lancet*, 375, 916–923.

Laposa, J.M. and Rector, N.A. (2009) Cognitive bias to symptom and obsessive belief threat cues in obsessive-compulsive disorder. *Journal of Nervous and Mental Disease*, 197, 599–605.

Lazarus, R.S. (1999) *Stress and Emotion: A New Synthesis*. London: Free Association Books.

LeDoux, J.E. (1998) *The Emotional Brain: The Mysterious Underpinnings of Emotional Life*. London: Weidenfeld and Nicolson.

MacKenzie, K.R. (1983). The clinical application of a group climate measure. In Dies, R.R. and MacKenzie, K.R. (eds), *Advances in Group Psychotherapy: Integrating Research and Practice* (pp. 159–170). New York: International Universities Press.

Marks, I.M. and Mathews, A.M. (1979) Brief standard self-rating for phobic patients. *Behaviour Research and Therapy*, 17, 263–267.

Marom, S., Gilboa-Schectman E., Aderka, I.M., Weizman, A. and Hermesh, H. (2009) Impact on treatment effectiveness and gains maintenance in social phobia: a group naturalistic study of cognitive behaviour group therapy. *Depression and Anxiety*, 26, 289–300.

Martin, D.J., Garske, J.P. and Davis, M.K. (2000) Relation of the therapeutic alliance with outcome and other variables: a meta-analytic review. *Journal of Consulting and Clinical Psychology*, 68, 438–450.

McLean, P.D., Whittal, M.L., Thordarson, D.S., Taylor, S., Sochting, I., Koch, W.J., Paterson, R. and Anderson, K.W. (2001) Cognitive versus behaviour therapy in the group treatment of obsessive-compulsive disorder. *Journal of Consulting and Clinical Psychology*, 69, 205–214.

McMillan, D., Gilbody, S., Beresford, E. and Neilly, L. (2007) Can we predict suicide and non-fatal self-harm with the Beck Hopelessness Scale? A meta-analysis. *Psychological Medicine*, 37, 769–778.

Meichenbaum, D. (1985) *Stress Inoculation Training*. London: Pergamon Press.

Meyer, E., Souza, F., Heldt, E., Knapp, P., Cordioli, A., Shavitt, R.G. and Leukefeld, C. (2010) A randomized clinical trial to examine enhancing cognitive-behavioral group therapy for obsessive-compulsive disorder with motivational interviewing and thought mapping. *Behavioural and Cognitive Psychotherapy*, 38, 319–336.

Miller, W.R. and Rollnick, S. (2002) *Motivational Interviewing: Preparing People for Change*. New York: Guilford Press.

Moore, S.A. (2009) Cognitive abnormalities in posttraumatic stress disorder. *Current Opinion in Psychiatry*, 22, 19–24.

Moran, P., Leese, M., Lee, T., Walters, P., Thornicroft, G. and Mann, A. (2003) Standardised assessment of personality abbreviated scale (SAPAS): preliminary validation of a brief screen for personality disorder. *British Journal of Psychiatry*, 183, 228–232.

Murphy, R.T., Rosen, C.S., Cameron, R.P. and Thompson, K.E. (2002) Development of a group treatment for enhancing motivation to change PTSD symptoms. *Cognitive and Behavioral Practice*, 9, 308–316.

Murphy, R.T., Thompson, K.E., Murray, M., Rainey, Q. and Uddo, M.M. (2009) Effect of a motivation enhancement intervention on veterans engagement in PTSD treatment. *Psychological Services*, 6, 264–278.

Najavits, L.M. (2002) *Seeking Safety: A Treatment Manual for PTSD and Substance Abuse*. New York: Guilford.

National Institute for Health and Clinical Excellence NICE (2004) Depression: management of depression in primary and secondary care. London: NICE.

National Institute for Health and Clinical Excellence (2006) Obsessive-compulsive disorder: core interventions in the treatment of obsessive-compulsive disorder and body dysmorphic disorder. London: NICE.

National Institute for Health and Clinical Excellence NICE (2009) Depression in adults: NICE updated guideline (October 2009). London: NICE.

Neimeyer, R.A. and Feixas, G. (1990) The role of homework and skill acquisition in the outcome of group cognitive therapy for depression. *Behavior Therapy*, 17, 433–446.

Nezu, A.M. and Nezu, C.M. (1989) *Problem-solving Therapy for Depression: Theory Research and Clinical Guidelines*. New York: John Wiley & Sons.

Norton, P.J, Hayes, S.A. and Springer, J.R. (2008) Transdiagnostic cognitive-behavioral therapy for anxiety: outcome and process. *International Journal of Cognitive Therapy*, 1, 266–279.

Obsessive Compulsive Cognitions Working Group (2005) Psychometric validation of the Obsessive Belief Questionnaire. *Behaviour Research and Therapy*, 43, 1527–1542.

O'Connor, K., Freeston, M.H., Gareau, D., Careau, Y., Dufour, M.J., Aardema, F. and Todorov, C. (2005) Group versus individual treatment in obsessions without compulsions. *Clinical Psychology and Psychotherapy*, 12, 87–96.

Oei, T.P.S. and Browne, A. (2006) Components of group processes: have they contributed to the outcome of mood and anxiety disorder patients in a group cognitive-behaviour therapy program? *American Journal of Psychotherapy*, 60, 53–70.

Oei, T.P.S. and Green, A.L. (2008) The Satisfaction With Therapy and Therapist Scale – Revised for group psychotherapy: psychometric properties and confirmatory factor analysis. *Professional Psychology, Research and Practise*, 39, 435–442.

Oei, T.P.S. and Boschen, M.J. (2009) Clinical effectiveness of a cognitive behavioural group treatment program for anxiety disorders: a benchmark study. *Journal of Anxiety Disorders*, 23, 950–957.

Ost, L.G. (1987) Applied relaxation: description of a coping technique and review of controlled studies. *Behaviour Research and Therapy*, 25, 397–409.

Prins, A., Ouimette, P. and Kimerling, R. (2004) The primary care PTSD screen

(PC-PTSD): development and operating characteristics. *Primary Care Psychiatry*, 9, 9–14.

Prochaska, J.O., DiClemente, C.C. and Norcross, J.C. (1992) In search of how people change: application to addictive behaviours. *American Psychologist*, 47, 1102–1114.

Rachman, S. (2003) *The Treatment of Obsessions*. New York: Oxford University Press.

Rapee, R.M. and Heimberg, R.G. (1997) A cognitive-behavioral model of social anxiety in social phobia. *Behaviour Research and Therapy*, 35, 741–756.

Rees, C.S. and van Koesveld, K.E. (2008) An open trial of group metacognitive therapy for obsessive-compulsive disorder. *Journal of Behavior Therapy and Experimental Psychiatry*, 39, 451–458.

Reiss, S. and McNally, R.J. (1985) The Expectancy Model of Fear. In Reiss, S. and Bootzin, R.R (eds), *Theoretical Issues in Behavior Therapy* (pp. 107–121). New York: Academic Press.

Resick, P.A, Galovski, T.A., O'Brien Uhlmansiek, M., Scher, C.D., Clum, G.A. and Young-Xu, Y. (2008) A randomized clinical trial to dismantle components of cognitive processing therapy for posttraumatic stress disorder in female victims of interpersonal violence. *Journal of Consulting and Clinical Psychology*, 76, 243–258.

Roberge, P., Marchand, A., Reinharz, D. and Savard, P. (2008) Cognitive-behavioral treatment for panic disorder with agoraphobia: a randomized controlled trial and cost-effectiveness analysis. *Behavior Modification*, 32, 333–351.

Ryum, T., Hagen, R., Nordahl, H.H., Vogel, P.A. and Stiles, T.C. (2009) Perceived group climate as a predictor of long-term outcome in a randomized controlled trial of cognitive-behavioural group therapy for patients with comorbid psychiatric disorders. *Behavioural and Cognitive Psychotherapy*, 37, 497–510.

Salaberria, K. and Echeburua, E. (1998) Long term outcome of cognitive therapy's contribution to self-exposure in vivo to the treatment of generalised social phobia. *Behavior Modification*, 22, 262–284.

Salkovskis, P.M. and Harrison, J. (1984) Abnormal and normal obsessions: a replication. *Behaviour Research and Therapy*, 22, 549–552.

Salkovskis, P.M., Clark, D.M. and Gelder, M.G. (1996) Cognition-behaviour links in the persistence of panic. *Behaviour Research and Therapy*, 34, 453–458.

Salkovskis, P.M., Wroe, A.L., Gledhill, A., Morrison, N., Forrester, E. and Richards, C. (2000) Responsibility attitudes and interpretations are characteristic of obsessive compulsive disorder. *Behaviour Research and Therapy*, 38, 347–372.

Schmidt, N.B., Woolaway-Bickel, K. and Trakowski, J. (2000) Dismantling cognitive-behavioral treatment for panic disorder: questioning the utility of breathing retraining. *Journal of Consulting and Clinical Psychology*, 68, 417–424.

Schmidt, N.B., Richey, J.A., Buckner, J.D. and Timpano, K.R. (2009) Attention training for generalized social anxiety disorder. *Journal of Abnormal Psychology*, 118, 5–14.

Schneier, F.R., Foose, T.E., Hasin, D.S., Heimberg, R.G., Liu, S.M., Grant, B.F. and Blanco, C. (2010) Social anxiety disorder and alcohol use disorder co-morbidity in the National Epidemiologic Survey on alcohol and related conditions. *Psychological Medicine*, 40, 977–988.

Scocco, P., Barbierri, I. and Frank, E. (2007) Interpersonal problem areas and onset of panic disorder. *Psychopathology*, 40, 8–13.

Scogin, F., Jamison, C. and Gochneaut, K. (1989) The comparative efficacy of cognitive and behavioural bibliotherapy for mildly and moderately depressed older adults. *Journal of Consulting and Clinical Psychology*, 57, 403–407.

Scott, M.J. (2008) *Moving On After Trauma: A Guide for Survivors, Family and Friends*. London: Routledge.

Scott, M.J. (2009) *Simply Effective Cognitive Behaviour Therapy: A Practitioner's Guide*. London: Routledge.

Scott, M.J. and Stradling, S.G. (1990) Group cognitive therapy for depression produces clinically significant reliable change in community-based settings. *Behavioural Psychotherapy*, 18, 1–19.

Scott, M.J. and Stradling, S.G. (1998) *Brief Group Counselling: Integrating Individual and Group Cognitive-Behavioural Approaches*. Chichester: John Wiley and Sons.

Scott, M.J., Stradling, S.G. and Greenfield, T.A. (1995) The efficacy of brief group cognitive therapy programmes for anxiety and depression and the relevance of a personality disorder diagnosis. World Congress of Behavioural and Cognitive Therapies, Copenhagen, Denmark, 11–15 July.

Shafran, R. (1997) The manipulation of responsibility in obsessive compulsive disorder. *British Journal of Clinical Psychology*, 36, 397–407.

Sharp, D.M., Power, K.G. and Swanson, V. (2004) A comparison of the efficacy and acceptability of group versus individual cognitive behaviour therapy in the treatment of panic disorder and agoraphobia in primary care. *Clinical Psychology and Psychotherapy*, 11, 73–82.

Shaw, B.F. and Hollon, S.D. (1979) Group cognitive therapy for depressed patients. In Beck, A.T., Rush, A.J. and Emery, G. (eds), *Cognitive Therapy of Depression*. New York: Guilford Press.

Shaw, B.F., Elkin, I., Yamagughi, J., Olmsted, M., Vallis, T.M., Dobson, K.S., Lowery, A., Sotsky, S.M., Watkins, J.T. and Imber, S.D. (1999) Therapist competence ratings in relation to clinical outcome in cognitive therapy of depression. *Journal of Consulting and Clinical Psychology*, 67, 837–846.

Shear, K.M., Brown, T.A. and Barlow, D.H. (1997) Multicenter Collaborative Panic Disorder Severity Scale. *American Journal of Psychiatry*, 154, 1571–1575.

Simons, M., Schneider, S. and Herpertz-Dahlman, B. (2006) Metacognitive therapy versus exposure and response prevention with pediatric obsessive-compulsive disorder: a case series with randomized allocation. *Psychotherapy and Psychosomatics*, 75, 257–264.

Smits, J.A.J. and Hofmann, S.G. (2009) A meta-analytic review of the effects of psychotherapy control conditions in anxiety disorders. *Psychological Medicine*, 39, 229–239.

Spitzer, R.L., Kroenke, K., Williams, J.B.W. and Lowe, B. (2006) A brief measure for assessing generalized anxiety disorder. *Archives of Internal Medicine*, 166, 1092–1097.

Stangier, U., Heidenreich, T., Peitz, M., Lauterbach, W. and Clark, D.M. (2003) Cognitive therapy for social phobia: individual versus group treatment. *Behaviour Research and Therapy*, 41, 991–1007.

Stein, M.B. and Stein, D.J. (2008) Social anxiety disorder. *Lancet*, 371, 1115–1125.

Stein, M., Forde, D., Anderson, G. and Walker, J. (1997) Obsessive compulsive disorder in the community: an epidemiological survey with clinical reappraisal. *American Journal of Psychiatry*, 154, 1120–1126.

Stemberger, R.T., Turner, S.M., Beidel, D.C. and Calhoun, K.S. (1995) Social phobia: an analysis of possible developmental factors. *Journal of Abnormal Psychology*, 104, 526–531.

Stewart, R.E. and Chambless, D.L. (2009) Cognitive behavioural therapy for adult anxiety disorders. *Journal of Consulting and Clinical Psychology*, 77, 595–606.

Taylor, S., Federoff, I., Koch, W., Thordarson, D., Fectau, G. and Nicki, R. (2001) Posttraumatic stress disorder arising after road traffic collisions: patterns of responses to cognitive-behavior therapy. *Journal of Consulting and Clinical Psychology*, 69, 541–551.

Teng, E.J., Bailey, S.D., Chaison, A.D., Petersen, N.K., Hamilton, J.D. and Dunn, N.J. (2008) Treating comorbid panic disorder in veterans with posttraumatic stress disorder. *Journal of Consulting and Clinical Psychology*, 76, 704–710.

Thompson, A.R., Wilde, E. and Boon, K. (2009) The development of group CBT for the treatment of road-traffic-accident-related post-traumatic stress disorder. *The Cognitive Behaviour Therapist*, 2, 32–42.

Thrasher, S., Power, M., Morant, N., Marks, I. and Dalgleish, T. (2010) Social support moderates outcome in a randomized controlled trial of exposure therapy and (or) cognitive restructuring for chronic posttraumatic stress disorder. *Canadian Journal of Psychiatry*, 55, 187–190.

Tolin, D.F. and Maltby, N. (2008) Motivating treatment-refusing patients with obsessive-compulsive disorder in motivational interviewing. In Arkowitz, H., Westra, H.A., Miller, W.R. and Rollnick, S. (eds), *The Treatment of Psychological Problems*. New York: Guilford Press.

Torres, A.R., Prince, M.J., Bebbington, P.E., Bhugra, D., Brugha, T.S., Farrell, M., Jenkins, R., Lewis, G., Meltzer, H. and Singleton, N. (2006) Obsessive-compulsive disorder: prevalence, comorbidity, impact and help-seeking in the British National Psychiatric Morbidity Survey 2000. *American Journal of Psychiatry*, 163, 1978–1985.

Tucker, M. and Oei, T.P.S. (2007) Is group more cost effective than individual cognitive behaviour therapy? The evidence is not solid yet. *Behavioural and Cognitive Psychotherapy*, 35, 77–91.

Tversky, A. and Kahneman, D. (1974) Judgement under uncertainty. Heuristics and biases. *Science*, 185. 1124–1131.

Van Balkom, A.J.M., van Boijen, C.A., Boeke, A.J.P. van Oppen, P., Kempe, P.T. and van Dyck, R. (2008) Comorbid depression, but not comorbid anxiety disorders, predicts poor outcome in anxiety disorders, *Depression and Anxiety*, 25, 408–415.

Weathers, F.W., Litz, B.T., Herman, D.S., Huska, J.A. and Keane, T.M. (1993) The PTSD Checklist (PCL): reliability, validity and diagnostic utility. Paper presented at the Annual Meeting of International Society for Traumatic Stress Studies, San Antonio, TX, October 1993.

Weerasekera, P. (1996) *Multiperspective Case Formulation: A Step Towards Treatment Integration*. Malabar, FL: Krieger Publishing.

Wegner, D.M., Schneider, D.J., Carter, S.R. and White, T.L. (1987) Paradoxical effects of thought suppression. *Journal of Personality and Social Psychology*, 53: 5–13.

Weiss, D.S. and Marmar, C.R. (1997) The Impact of Event Scale-Revised. In Wilson, J.P. and Keane, T.M. (eds), *Assessing Psychological Trauma and PTSD* (pp. 399–411). New York: Guilford Press.

Weissman, M.M., Bland, M.B. and Canino, G.J. (1997) The cross-national epidemiology of panic disorder. *Archives of General Psychiatry*, 54, 305–309.

Weissman, A. and Beck, A.T. (1978) Development and validation of the Dysfunctional Attitude Scale. Paper presented at the Annual Convention of the Association for the Advancement of Behavior Therapy, Chicago.

Wells, A. (1994) A multidimensional measure of worry: development and preliminary validation of the Anxious Thoughts Inventory. *Anxiety, Stress and Coping*, 6, 289–299.

Wells, A. (1997) *Cognitive Therapy of Anxiety Disorders: A Practice Manual and Conceptual Guide*. Chichester: Wiley.

Wells, A. (2000) *Emotional Disorders and Metacognition*. Chichester: Wiley.

Wells, A. (2004) Metacognitive therapy: elements of mental control in understanding and treating generalized anxiety disorder and posttraumatic stress disorder. In Leahy, R.L. (ed.), *Contemporary Cognitive Therapy: Theory, Research and Practice*. New York: Guilford Press.

Wells, A. (2008) *Metacognitive Therapy for Anxiety and Depression*. New York: Guilford Press.

Wells, A. (2010) A pilot randomized trial of metacognitive therapy vs applied relaxation in the treatment of adults with generalized anxiety disorder. *Behaviour Research and Therapy*, 48, 429–434.

Wells, A. and Sembi, S. (2004) Metacognitive therapy for PTSD: a core treatment manual. *Cognitive and Behavioral Practice*, 11, 365–377.

Wells, A., Stopa, L. and Clark, D.M. (1993) The Social Cognitions Questionnaire. Unpublished. The psychometric properties of the SCQ are in Wells (1997), p. 29.

Westbrook, D. and Kirk, J. (2005) The clinical effectiveness of cognitive behaviour therapy: outcome for a large sample of adults treated in routine practice. *Behaviour Research and Therapy*, 43, 1243–1261.

Westra, H.A. and Dozois, D.J.A. (2006) Preparing clients for cognitive behavioral therapy: A randomized pilot study of motivational interviewing for anxiety. *Cognitive Therapy and Research*, 30, 481–498.

Westra, H.A., Arkowitz, H. and Dozois, D.J.A. (2009) Adding a motivational interviewing pre-treatment to cognitive behavioural therapy for generalised anxiety disorder: a preliminary randomised controlled trial. *Journal of Anxiety Disorder*, 23, 1106–1117.

White, J., Keenan, M. and Brooks, N. (1992) Stress control: a controlled comparative investigation of large group therapy for generalised anxiety disorder. *Behavioural Psychotherapy*, 20, 97–114.

Whittal, M.L., Thordarson, D.S. and McLean, P.D. (2005) Treatment of obsessive-compulsive disorder: cognitive behaviour therapy vs. exposure and response prevention. *Behaviour Research and Therapy*, 43, 1559–1576.

Whittal, M.L., Robichaud, M., Thordarson, D.S. and McLean, P.D. (2008) Group and individual treatment of obsessive-compulsive disorder using cognitive therapy and exposure plus response prevention: a 2-year follow-up of two randomized trials. *Journal of Consulting and Clinical Psychology*, 76, 1003–1014.

Whittal, M.L., Woody, S.R., McLean, P.D., Rachman, S.J. and Robichaud, M. (2010) Treatment of obsessions: a randomized control trial. *Behavior Research and Therapy*, 48, 295–303.

World Health Organization (1992) *The ICD-10 Classification of Mental and Behavioural Disorders*. Geneva: World Health Organization.

Zettle, R.D. and Herring, E.L. (1995) Treatment utility of the sociotropy/autonomy distinction: implications for cognitive therapy. *Journal of Clinical Psychology*, 51, 280–289.

Zimmerman, M. and Mattia, J.I. (2000) Principal and additional DSM-IV disorders for which outpatients seek treatment. *Psychiatric Services*, 51, 1299–1304.

Zimmerman, M., McGlinchey, J.B., Chelminski, I. and Young, D. (2008) Diagnostic co-morbidity in 2300 psychiatric out-patients presenting for treatment evaluated with a semi-structured diagnostic interview. *Psychological Medicine*, 38, 199–210.

Index

Page numbers in *italic* indicate figures and tables.